ALLEN COUNTY PUBLIC LIBRARY
3 1833 01541 1413

D1572431

Homer E. Capehart

Homer E. Capehart

A Senator's Life, 1897-1979

WILLIAM B. PICKETT

Indiana Historical Society
Indianapolis 1990

Printed in the United States of America

The paper in this publication meets the minimum requirements of American National Standard for Information Sciences—Permanence of Paper for Printed Library Materials, ANSI Z39.48-1984. ∞

Library of Congress Cataloging-in-Publication Data

Pickett, William B. (William Beatty), 1940-
Homer E. Capehart : a senator's life, 1897-1979 / William B. Pickett.
p. cm.
Includes bibliographical references (p.) and index.
ISBN 0-87195-054-5 (alk. paper) : $27.95
1. Capehart, H. E. (Homer Earl), 1897-1979. 2. Legislators—United States—Biography. 3. United States. Congress. Senate—Biography. 4. Indiana—Politics and government. 5. United States—Politics and government—1933-1945. 6. United States—Politics and government—1945- I. Title.
E748.C218P53 1990
328.73'092—dc20
[B]

90-5056
CIP

For Janet

Contents

Preface

To most Americans of his era Sen. Homer E. Capehart was the archetypical midwestern Republican. Together with his conservative colleague from Indiana, Sen. William E. Jenner, he tended to believe the worst about Democratic presidents. He distrusted not only their domestic politics but also their views on foreign relations. He desired to slow social legislation; he hesitated to see the United States become the leader of the free world. Foreign policy especially concerned him. In 1945 he was sure that President Franklin D. Roosevelt had "sold out" to the Soviet Union during the Yalta Conference. A few years later he was certain that Roosevelt's successor, President Harry S Truman, had similarly sold out, even allowing Communists to infiltrate departments of the federal government.

Still, in many ways this man who died a decade ago was an extraordinarily able figure in American politics. He was good at what he understood, perhaps even brilliant. His natural tendency was to reach out and explain, and to believe that he understood even when he did not.

His life was a remarkable success story. The son of a southern Indiana farmer, he had risen from very modest origins. His early years were starkly poor. His formal education did not extend beyond high school. After service in World War I he determined to prove himself, and soon was on his way. He became a master salesman, first of farm equipment, then electric popcorn machines, then phonographs. Next he became an executive. Bankers and manufacturers discovered they could profit by investing in what he recommended. An awareness of markets, a network of salesmen, and abundant drive made him a veritable phonograph entrepreneur. He lost control of his company at the beginning of the Great Depression, but managed to persuade the Rudolph Wurlitzer Company to produce coin-operated phonographs, so-called jukeboxes. By the mid-1930s he was a millionaire. Restless, worried about the expanding power of the federal government, and looking for a new challenge, he turned to politics. In 1944, at the age of forty-seven, he was elected to the United States Senate.

He became a power in the Republican party in Indiana. When he entered politics he encountered a party that in many ways was little different from what it had been in the nineteenth century. The politics of the Hoosier state, Republican or Democratic, were decentralized, even local, and leadership was rural, white, male, and Protestant. Party workers were interested in state jobs for themselves and their friends. Both the GOP (Grand Old Party) and its rival, the Hoosier Democracy, centered attention on the governor's office, for its occupant controlled patronage. During the New Deal, the Democrats had enjoyed a large popular support, as jobs and tax dollars flowed from Washington in an apparently unending stream. The Republicans needed energy, which Capehart provided. He became their catalyst for victory. A hulking man, he was constantly in motion, with a round face and flattened nose, a cigar jammed into the corner of his mouth, and large hands that gripped. He was hard not to notice. He possessed a contagious enthusiasm, a capacity to bring people together.

Only recently have students begun to see the politics of the 1940s and 1950s in full dimension. Early accounts of conservative opposition to Presidents Roosevelt, Truman, and even Dwight D. Eisenhower stressed national and international issues and observed the increasing worry of large government—of bureaucracy—and what critics said was the New Deal's resemblance to alien philosophies. In foreign relations, according to these estimates, the heartland did not see the international dangers. After World War II, midwesterners simply looked back to an earlier time. Recently, however, has come more careful examination of local and regional opposition to the New Deal and the Fair Deal, by which the federal government moved into virtually all aspects of life. Interpretation of Indiana politics has changed accordingly. Commentators once considered Hoosier politicians as intense patriots, believers in private property and free enterprise, operating from instinct. Investigation of the lives and careers of such figures as Capehart now shows that opposition to the New Deal resulted not only from traditional political reactions to large economic events and war but also from new ideas about the nation's problems and novel approaches in solving them. Like many Republicans of his time, whatever their statements, Capehart by 1938 had accepted the need for government intervention. He questioned neither humanitarian aid during economic depression nor federal coordination of a wartime economy. But he worried about a growing dependence on government. He feared the effect of the New Deal on the work ethic, the tradition of individualism. In foreign relations, international intervention produced entanglements with other nations and more federal spending. Neither was needed, he believed, considering America's overwhelming power in the postwar world.

Unlike some of the senators with whom he associated, Capehart was pragmatic and flexible in his conservatism, holding to principle but seeking to accomplish what was possible. During his years as a senator, he sometimes became confused, and he aroused erstwhile supporters and critics alike with unwarranted attacks on Democratic domestic and foreign policies. But even when he erred, the error was in the path he took rather than in his choice of destinations. Most of the time his capacity for sound judgment rallied Hoosier veterans, farmers, and businessmen and brought accomplishment in the direction of what was best for the Republic.

Unfortunately for his political career, the early 1960s marked the beginning of still another era in national politics. Although a core of conservative voters remained, the ages, occupations, and interests of many Hoosiers changed, moving in a liberal direction. To them Capehart's political identity was lackluster, part of the past. The senior senator from Indiana tried to respond to this new era. But he could not easily do it. The tactics he had used as a newcomer to politics twenty-four years earlier no longer sufficed. Having wielded influence in the national political arenas of Washington and New York, now older with an established image and view of the national interest, he also had lost some of his flexibility. In 1962 the youthful and quick-witted speaker of the Indiana House of Representatives, Birch E. Bayh, Jr., in a close election sent him into retirement.

Acknowledgments

CONTEMPORARY biography is a treacherous undertaking. Although the telephone and electronic media have removed many of the historian's traditional sources, the techniques of oral history make available through taped interviews the testimony of persons who participated in the events of the recent past. But the task is not an easy one. The investigator first must perform research in the books, periodicals, and manuscript collections. Then, having located and contacted the interviewee, with recorder and blank cassettes ready, he or she must travel to the appointed location and conduct the interview. This is followed by transcription, initial typing, editing, obtaining the interviewee's release, and final typing, duplication, binding, indexing, and cataloging of the transcript. At its best the effort is worth the trouble, yielding humorous and candid material that enlivens and clarifies. Sometimes the interviewee talks at length, giving in colorful detail what previously was little known. Still, the pitfalls are numerous. The researcher must attempt simultaneously to probe and to encourage and, afterwards, must make sense of uncertain, sometimes contradictory statements based on fleeting memory. Needless to say, such an enterprise is impossible without assistance.

The subject, the late Homer Earl Capehart, cooperated fully and without hesitation, providing unrestricted access to his papers and, even when it hurt, complete freedom in their use and interpretation. His wife, Irma, their daughter, Patricia Pearson, both now deceased, and their son, H. Earl Capehart, Jr., also provided interviews and helped locate additional sources.

Faculty of the Indiana University department of history gave essential support. John E. Wilz, James T. Patterson, Donald F. Carmony, and the late Oscar O. Winther provided inspiration and guidance. Martin Ridge and Richard S. Kirkendall, as directors of the Indiana University Oral History Program, also assisted. The one person most responsible for the initiation and completion of this undertaking, however, was Robert H. Ferrell, Distinguished Professor of History at Indiana University. He was there with a nod of "yes," words of encouragement, and expert assistance.

The following people also helped with research or writing: Birch E. Bayh, Jr., Minnie B. Cooksey, Dwight Dively, Ralph D. Gray, Hazel Hopper, Charles Hyneman, William E. Jenner, John Krivine, Louis Lambert, Betty L. Moore, Frances McDonald, James H. Madison, Thomas W. Mason, John Newman, Richard O. Ristine, Patricia G. Smith, Darlene Norman, Rebecca Shoemaker, Candace Schulenburg, Robert A. Taft, Jr., John Taylor, and John Unruh. The assisting institutions were *Billboard* magazine; Columbia University Oral History Research Office; Cornell University—Olin Library; Daviess County Courthouse; Dwight D. Eisenhower Library; Franklin D. Roosevelt Library; Harry S Truman Library; John F. Kennedy Library; Herbert C. Hoover Library; Indiana Commission on Public Records, State Archives Division; Indiana University at Bloomington—Business Library, Lilly Library, Main Library, Oral History Project, and Political Science Lab; Indiana State Library—Indiana, reference, and genealogy divisions and oral history program; Indiana State University—Cunningham Memorial Library; Indianapolis Public Library; *Indianapolis*

Star-News Library; Library of Congress; National Archives; New York Public Library; Ogle County (Ill.) Courthouse; Ohio Historical Society; Pike County (Ind.) Courthouse; Rose-Hulman Institute of Technology—John A. Logan Library; Syracuse University—George Arents Library; Washington (Ind.) Public Library; Wayne State University Library; and the Wurlitzer Company public relations office.

Indiana University, Rose-Hulman Institute of Technology, Rose-Hulman Division of Humanities, Social and Life Sciences, and Rose-Hulman Center for Technology and Policy Studies provided funds for travel, typing, photocopying, and computer programming.

Kathryn E. Pickett, retired women's editor of the *Indianapolis Star*, and my aunt, shared her understanding along with her experiences as a reporter and editor during overnight stays at her house in Speedway, Indiana. My friends, Douglas and Susie Woods, provided a place to stay in Washington, D.C., and Gordon and Ida Hollingsworth provided both physical and spiritual sustenance and shelter during summers of writing at White Bear Lake, Minnesota.

Most important, finally, were my father, Walter Nathan, and mother, the late Amy Beatty Pickett, who sought truth; my wife Janet, who never knew how many revisions she would type and how long it would take; and our sons, Robert and Jeffrey, with their irrepressible exuberance.

A special thanks for their early encouragement and editorial advice must go to Robert G. Barrows and Shirley S. McCord, editors at the Indiana Historical Bureau, and to Pamela J. Bennett, its director.

The persons responsible for seeing this book at last to publication were Peter T. Harstad, executive director of the Indiana Historical Society, Thomas A. Mason, director of publications, Paula Corpuz, project editor, and Kathleen Breen and Megan McKee, editorial assistants.

I

Early Years

WHEN Homer Earl Capehart was born a year before the Spanish-American War, not much had changed in southern Indiana since the time of the Civil War. Most of the inhabitants of the counties that stretched south of Indianapolis down to the Ohio River were still farmers. On the farms the soil was not always hospitable. The ground was clay and rocky. Often it was hilly, and machinery did not work well. Horses or mules were the main reliance, with work done in tedious twenty-minute stints, the length of time the animals could go before having to rest. On seventy-one acres in the community of Highbanks, near Iva in Jefferson Township, Pike County, in a small wooden house with a lean-to kitchen, the second child of Alvin T. and Susanna A. Kelso Capehart was born on 6 June 1897. Homer E. Capehart was to be a millionaire by the time he was forty-one, United States senator at forty-seven.[1]

The Capeharts were successful farmers. Great-grandfather Thomas C. Capehart, apparently of Swiss-German extraction, had raised three sons, and the eldest was George, Alvin's father. Homer Capehart was born in a makeshift family settlement of three frame houses perched on bluffs that overlooked the east fork of the White River. There Homer's sister,

Bessie Ann, had been born in 1891, and after Homer came William Paul in 1899 and Ivan Elwood in 1905.[2]

Homer's father was dark-haired, quiet, of medium height and build, and a believer in honesty, frugality, and Christian morality. Born in Highbanks in 1866, Alvin Capehart had left school after the fourth grade. After learning to farm, he became restless and went to Colorado to be a cowboy. Returning from his Western adventure, where he had saved a little money, he purchased land at the family settlement. He was a strict father; when his sons got into fights, they recalled, he whipped them all.[3]

Alvin's eldest son inherited his father's diligence, but his physical and emotional characteristics came from his mother. A large, strong-willed, energetic person, Susanna Capehart had named her son for her brother Andrew Homer Kelso, a Presbyterian minister. Under her supervision the family said prayers each morning and attended Sunday school and church.

With these forebears and in these surroundings, the red-haired, lanky boy with round face and protruding ears did chores, explored bluffs and ravines, and hiked with friends along the river. In the sunny days of spring when classes were over at the two-room Iva school he played catcher on the school yard baseball team. Only once in a while was life on the farm perilous. Awakening one night to a crackling sound, Homer went to the back door, looked out, and saw flames coming from the barn. He roused the family, then rushed to the barn and led the horses to safety. The barn burned to the ground.[4]

Homer's father in 1910 moved the family twenty-six miles north to Daviess County where he became a tenant on the sixteen hundred-acre Graham farm, and for thirteen-year-old Homer the change brought new experiences. Homer won a white Chester boar as first prize at the county corn contest. He now lived five miles from the town of Washington, a

H. Earl Capehart, Jr.

Homer E. Capehart, age 14, Daviess County corn champion

railroad center. By the time he entered high school in 1912, one of his friends was a town boy, Marion C. Borders, whose father was an engineer on the Baltimore and Ohio Railroad. On one occasion, Borders recalled, the boys were inspecting a Baltimore and Ohio locomotive at the Washington shop. Climbing into the engineer's compartment, they discovered the machine had fire in its boiler. Unaware that it faced a slight decline, they opened the throttle a crack. Pistons started, wheels turned, and the behemoth began rolling down toward the main track. Fortunately a nearby workman threw a chock in front of the wheels.[5]

Capehart's classmates liked him, and sometimes he joined in their fun. One night he, Borders, their friend Robert Hyatt, and several other boys locked Patrick O'Donnell in a chicken coop. A policeman apprehended the group on advice from O'Donnell's father and put them in jail for a few hours.[6]

During his years in high school Homer did well enough, but he did not shine. Placed in the back row of the junior class of some sixty-five students when a photographer took the class picture, he did not stand out from his classmates. Only in retrospect did he appear notable, with thick red hair parted on the left, forehead pale from wearing his farm cap, prominent ears, heavy eyelids, a squint that appeared as a scowl, in dark coat and tie, and white collar turned up.[7] Capehart's record was certainly undistinguished if compared to that of the class president, John S. Hastings. Homer had enrolled in the same college preparatory curriculum: algebra, geometry, English literature, Latin, ancient and American history, civics, botany, physiology, chemistry, music, and mathematics, as well as bookkeeping, mechanical drawing, and typing. He received a 74 in freshman algebra and solid geometry. Higher marks in bookkeeping and mechanical drawing brought his average to the low 80s, the top half of his class. Hastings was a much better student. "It should be the ideal of every high school graduate," Hastings remarked in his yearbook statement as class president, "to attend college during some period of their life, if at all possible." The son of a lawyer, he could go to college.[8]

Capehart was not to graduate from Washington High, but from a school in Illinois. In December 1915, during Homer's senior year, Alvin Capehart sold the equipment and livestock and took the family to Polo, Illinois, 250 miles to the north and west, where he worked for daily wages on a dairy farm.[9]

After graduation from Polo High School in 1916, the youth tried a few odd jobs, in one instance filing edges off castings at the J. I. Case Plow Works Company in Racine, Wisconsin.[10] His parents returned to Daviess County where by year's end he rejoined them. He answered a newspaper advertisement for a job selling door-to-door for the Rumford Baking Powder Company. Knowing that one brand of baking powder was little different from another, he concentrated on the "special" that Rumford offered with every pound can: a choice of cookbook, mixing spoon, or biscuit cutter. He decided to emphasize the kitchen items, telling housewives that "you're going to buy somebody's baking powder, if you do any baking at all. Why don't you buy a can from me and get one of these handy kitchen tools, too?" He sold 120 cans in two days, a company record.[11]

Then came an embarrassing venture in Indianapolis. Attracted by the city, he and a fellow Rumford salesman took a room at a run-down hotel and found work as yard boys at the Van Camp estate on North Meridian Street (in later years he would purchase the property and build the Stouffer Inn). After two weeks he awoke one morning to find himself alone. His partner had vanished, taking most of Capehart's clothes, along with his suitcase and money. Walking to the freight yard of the Vandalia Railroad, the farm boy climbed into an empty coal car and did not get home until four in the morning, cold, tired, and black with coal dust.[12]

Not long afterward, in April 1917, he entered the army. He had decided that he "might as well be shot by the Germans" as to follow mules "for the rest of my life." He hoped

H. Earl Capehart, Jr.

Homer E. Capehart, army private, 1917

the army would teach him to repair airplanes and listed his occupation as "mechanic." He found himself in the infantry.[13]

The army, it turned out, freed the young man from the confines of rural Indiana. After drilling at Jefferson Barracks, Missouri, he went to Arizona with Company F of the 12th Infantry. The regiment removed to San Francisco, and Capehart received promotion to private first class. As a mounted orderly at headquarters he ran errands and exercised horses. Reassigned to the Quartermaster Corps at Camp Lewis, Washington, he was promoted to sergeant, with the task of procuring feed for twelve thousand cavalry mounts. He was discharged in 1919. As for so many individuals of Capehart's generation, service in the army had brought a sense of the possibilities of life. It built confidence and a willingness to determine his own destiny.[14]

In the next few years Capehart rose rapidly in the world of business. For a while he was a sort of traveling mechanic. After a short time in Rockford, Illinois, as a night cook in a restaurant, the youth saw an advertisement in the *Chicago Tribune* by the Burton-Paige Manufacturing Company, which desired to engage someone who would show farmers how to use electric milking machines.[15] The job with Burton-Paige did not last, but it had its moments. One night after Capehart demonstrated a machine near Strawberry Point, Iowa, a young woman invited him to attend a social event. Women of rural Iowa frequently raised money for good causes by auctioning box lunches to admirers. Capehart's hostess was the organizer of the affair, and when the auctioneer failed to appear she asked Capehart to fill in. It occurred to him that he had nothing to lose. He picked up one of the boxes and began to talk. Soon he was enjoying himself; it was almost like selling baking powder. He encouraged the highest possible prices and made the affair a great success.[16]

Soon he found a job as a salesman, this time in the Nebraska tractor division of J. I. Case. For many years the company had manufactured a line of plows, colters, cultivators, harrows, planters, and stalk cutters. The company was introducing a tractor named the Wallis, the most efficient tractor for pulling three-furrow plows and, a brochure said, the first to "develop a draw-bar pull greater than its own weight." With its light chassis and high-speed engine, the tractor boosted Case's sales from over $3.5 million in the second half of 1919 to over $9 million the following year.[17]

Capehart became Case's star salesman. During one ten-day period he organized plowing competitions and tractor demonstrations in five Nebraska counties. He ran full-page ads in newspapers that challenged other dealers to contests in which the tractor that plowed its tract first would win. If no other tractors appeared, he would drive a Wallis himself to show that he had no competition. Within six months his sales reached $102,000. At the age of twenty-two he became a figure around the Case office.[18]

A national agricultural depression occurred in 1921-22. Farmers could no longer afford tractors. Case let Capehart go. But after a period of travel he met a recruiter for the Holcomb and Hoke Manufacturing Company of Indianapolis. This company was to give Capehart his opportunity. James I. Holcomb and Jacob F. Hoke, Jr., had formed a partnership a quarter century before to make and sell brushes, brooms, and artificial palm trees. The partners had manufactured portable bowling alleys called "boxballs." Hoke was the manager. Holcomb was the salesman, used installment credit, and set up his own sales school.[19] After the First World War the two men formed the Holcomb and Hoke Manufacturing Company to make and sell a glass-enclosed machine that cooked and sold popcorn and peanuts. The brightly lettered name "Butter-Kist" decorated the machine, which poured unpopped corn into a hopper and onto a hot plate, stirred it, and let it burst and fall into a pan to be buttered. The aroma of buttered popcorn and peanuts enticed customers. Although the machine cost $1,200, a huge price in those days, it soon appeared in candy stores, theaters, and amusement parks.[20]

Salesmanship was the essence of Holcomb and Hoke, for Butter-Kist needed salesmanship. Fortunately, a master salesman was behind it. Holcomb wrote everything down in his textbook, *Salesology of the Butter-Kist Popcorn and Peanut Machines*. Salesology was more than selling, he said, it was entrepreneurship. The Butter-Kist machine both produced and sold goods, allowing its owner to "get all the profit." The company advertised in national magazines and taught its customers economics. "A manufacturer who does not borrow some money is not supposed to have much of a business," announced the author of *Salesology.* Economic downturns were no obstacle. "When men are out of work, they loaf . . . while loafing they eat peanuts, popcorn." Holcomb pointed to increased sales of "roll your own" tobacco during the Panic of 1907. During slumps a popcorn factory could assist the return to prosperity. He talked about "capitalizing your resistance" and remarked that "if you are handed a lemon, start a lemonade stand."[21]

Stimulated by these ideas, some of which he had used at Rumford and J. I. Case, Capehart enlisted with Holcomb and Hoke. Starting in Green Bay, Wisconsin, he made one of his first sales to a twelve-year-old who had sent in a magazine coupon. He convinced the lad's parents that Butter-Kist could bring in enough to pay for itself and perhaps a college education. He convinced a local banker to lend the boy's parents the $250 down payment.[22]

Soon afterward he met Irma Mueller of Wrightstown, Wisconsin, a willowy, dark-haired young woman, the daughter of a banker. After teaching at a country school she had become a legal secretary. In 1922 they were married, and during the next years two boys, H. Earl, Jr., and Thomas Charles were born.

The work as a salesman with Holcomb and Hoke took Capehart beyond selling into entrepreneurship. For a short while he struck out on his own, becoming a partner in an advertising business in Green Bay. The partnership failed, and he worked as an agent for a hardware manufacturer. Then Holcomb and Hoke invited him to return as regional sales manager in Minneapolis, and soon thereafter Capehart became general sales manager in charge of a sales force of 325. The firm increased its capitalization from $150,000 to $750,000 and during the 1920s sold $20 million worth of popcorn machines.[23]

A decade after American entrance into World War I, Capehart had made a name for himself as a man who could sell almost anything. It was an extraordinary rise in the fortunes of a thirty-year-old businessman who had grown up in near poverty, graduated without distinction from a small rural high school, and set out in the world with few resources other than belief in himself.

2

Phonograph Entrepreneur

In 1927 Homer Capehart turned from popcorn machines to another sales possibility, so-called jukeboxes. By that time he was the picture of success. He carried 190 pounds on his 5′11″ frame, displayed a double chin, and puffed a fat cigar. His deep, booming voice made him sound like a baseball umpire.[1] Like James I. Holcomb he had become an author, setting forth his sales principles in a handbook entitled *Creative Selling.* Like Holcomb he offered a simple message: "Every man has access to wealth of power and energy, which, if properly applied would be more than sufficient to take him to any position to which he might aspire." With rhapsodic logic he asserted that profits were "earnings—and earnings represent money—and money is the object of all of life's work." A salesman should memorize "facts about the prospect's business, show an appreciation and knowledge of that prospect's business problems—and gain respect and confidence, so necessary and vital in today's life." Knowledge was power, and winning over a listener brought self-confidence. Selling took the same preparation needed to become successful in law or medicine. Salesmen needed to be diplomatic, conscientious, enthusiastic, and honest.[2]

The occasion for his new enterprise happened almost by chance. After touring Holcomb and Hoke sales regions in the East, he had decided to visit the office in Cleveland. There he noticed a newspaper article about a typesetter named Thomas W. Small who had developed an electrical mechanism with the appearance of a giant mousetrap. It was a changer for a stack of phonograph records. Automatically and without stopping, it played the records and then turned over the stack and played the other sides.[3]

That a lover of music might listen to both sides of a phonograph record without getting up was a fascinating idea. Thomas A. Edison had invented the first cylindrical tinfoil record player in 1877, and twelve years later the first coin-operated phonograph was playing in the Palais Royal Saloon in San Francisco. Large-horned, windup acoustic players gained popularity and reached two high points in sales—in 1904 when Enrico Caruso began recording for the Victor Talking Machine Company, and in 1917 with recordings of the Original Dixieland Jazz Band. During the World War and afterward, phonograph sales increased from $27 million to $158 million. But the public began to tire of the inadequacies of cylinders. Radio music, introduced in 1920, was far superior: less tinny, scratchy, and muffled. Bell Laboratories in 1924 then discovered how to record music with an electric microphone and amplification, and Brunswick Phonograph Company placed on sale the first electrical record player, the Panatrope. Victor introduced the Orthophonic Victrola. All that remained to be done toward the creation of a fully automated phonograph was accomplished by Small's invention.[4]

The automatic record changer created an opportunity, and the Holcomb and Hoke company was in a position to seize it. The firm already had entered the coin-operated phonograph business, competing with the Automatic Music Instrument Company of Grand Rapids, producer of the first

H. Earl Capehart, Jr.

Homer E. Capehart during phonograph years

all-electric jukebox. Holcomb and Hoke had called its 1926 machine, with drop-type changer, the Electramuse, and began to sell it nationally. By inserting a nickel in the slot, patrons of roadside eating places could listen to a recorded song, perhaps one they had heard on the radio. Having pondered the drawbacks of radio and the gravity-operated record changer, Capehart now decided that an automatic changer might enable Holcomb and Hoke to corner the market. Capehart brought to his company the new invention. He found Thomas Small's house in Cleveland, introduced himself, and the two men sat down to listen to records. The following morning he purchased the rights to the invention for $500 plus royalties.[5]

Capehart soon discovered that innovation, normally admirable in a salesman, could have drawbacks. In buying Small's changer he had not taken into account that the company had invested heavily to manufacture and sell the Electramuse. Holcomb and Hoke had made some good decisions; however, they also had fallen into some errors because of Holcomb's impulsiveness. These bad decisions had included a mechanical corn pollenizer, a badly priced aluminum cooker, and a coin-operated buttermilk dispenser that attracted flies.[6] The two owners thought they were vigilant in protecting their interests. Capehart invited Holcomb to an Indianapolis hotel to meet Small and see the new changer. Holcomb asked Small what he proposed to do with it. Small replied, "Ask Mr. Capehart. I sold it to him." Holcomb turned, muttered that the thirty-year-old Capehart was "just a kid" and "works for us," and stomped out. Next day he fired Capehart.[7]

Unlike in 1916 when he had awakened in another of the city's hotels to find his money, clothes, and roommate gone, Capehart this time possessed eight years of sales experience and had managed a national sales force. Instead of one set of clothes to wear home in a railroad coal car, he owned a closetful and had acquired rights to a valuable invention. Most important, he had loyal friends among the Holcomb and Hoke employees, including regional sales managers and Holcomb and Hoke's chief engineer, Edward E. Collison. Capehart decided to go into business for himself. He convinced three Marmon Motorcar officers—G. M. Williams, Hal L. Purdy, and Arthur R. Heiskell—to put up $2,500 each to develop the record changer. Their contract allowed the young entrepreneur, who contributed no money, a 25 percent interest in the enterprise and a salary; Small would get salary plus royalties.[8]

Entrepreneurship always involved risk, even during the boom of the late 1920s, and a patent attorney found that Small's changer infringed an existing patent. Possibly worried by Capehart's youthfulness, Williams, Purdy, and Heiskell lost confidence. Undaunted, Capehart purchased their interests for a $5,000, six-month promissory note and began a search for new investors.[9]

Everything then worked out. The star salesman of Holcomb and Hoke, now dismissed, found two adventurers in Huntington, Indiana, furniture makers John W. Caswell and Winfred Runyan, secretary-treasurer and president, respectively, of the Caswell-Runyan Company, who agreed to purchase not $10,000 but $50,000 worth of stock and produce cabinets for the new machine. The result was the Capehart Automatic Phonograph Corporation, incorporated on 4 February 1928. Its assets consisted of four automatic talking machines together with blueprints, drawings, patterns, and parts. Caswell became president and Runyan secretary-treasurer; Capehart was chief executive with the title of vice president. Caswell and Runyan controlled half the stock, Capehart the remainder. The new offices were in a five-room bungalow next to the Huntington furniture plant. Homer, Irma, and the two boys at once moved there (a few months later their third child, Patricia, was born). Within a short time Collison, by slightly altering the design of the changer, elim-

The Capehart Orchestrope, H. Earl Capehart, Jr.

Sketch of the Capehart Automatic Phonograph Corporation in Fort Wayne

The Capehart Orchestrope, H. Earl Capehart, Jr.

Orchestrope record changer

inated the patent infringement. Capehart paid off Williams, Purdy, and Heiskell. In the spring of 1928 the new company began manufacturing the Orchestrope: the first phonograph that could play, without stopping, both sides of twenty-eight records. Enclosed in a finished wood cabinet and outfitted with a coin slot, it became a jukebox.[10]

The Orchestrope appeared at an opportune time, when the phonograph industry was undergoing the stresses of reorganization. That year the Radio Corporation of America bought the Victor Talking Machine Company. Capehart introduced his new instrument ("the musical marvel of the age," he described it) in April 1928 at the Detroit Aviation Show and then at the National Music Industries Chamber of Commerce in New York City, where it obtained recognition as the outstanding musical development of the year. In its first public demonstration at the Chicago Radio Show it rivaled the acclaim given television. An Orchestrope furnished music for the Chicago Automobile Show.[11]

The Orchestrope was not unlike the Butter-Kist machine. High school students purchasing sodas after school, young people consuming bootleg liquor at speakeasies, and billiard players waiting for the next shot enjoyed music and were willing to spend for it. Many drugstores and cafés already had player pianos, but such instruments required constant attention. Jukeboxes, plugged in and turned on, made money by themselves. Capehart's brochures asked, "Would your customers pay five cents a selection to hear Paul Whiteman's Orchestra; do you think they would come in greater numbers, stay longer, and spend more if you offered entertainment by the most popular soloists and musical entertainers in America?" Purchasers answered, "Yes!" People listened to the latest recordings of Al Jolson, Rudy Vallee, Ted Lewis, Guy Lombardo, Fred Waring, and Ted Weems. By July 1928 Capehart had sold 685 Orchestropes at $785.80 apiece, only one-fourth of which was manufacturing cost.[12]

Like the Butter-Kist salesmen, the phonograph representatives left nothing to chance. Orchestropes would not sell themselves, although Capehart always said they did. They required salesmen who believed in the appeal of music and of profits per square foot, salesmen who were educators after the fashion of J. I. Holcomb. Fortunately many of the Butter-Kist salesmen were Capehart loyalists. They included Kenneth F. Valentine, an articulate young sales manager from Indianapolis; James E. Broyles, who had hired and taught salesmen for Holcomb; William E. Simmons, West Coast regional manager; Gerald C. Crary who had succeeded Capehart as general sales manager; and William R. Deaton, southeastern regional manager. Within months Capehart had even hired the Holcomb and Hoke treasurer, L. D. Thomas.[13]

Everyone in the sales organization benefited. District and regional sales managers sold the machine for $685 to three hundred dealers across the nation and received straight commissions of 10 percent of wholesale, $68. Dealers, in turn, sold to drugstore owners near local schools or to restaurant operators in factory areas for the $785.80 retail price. Holcomb had allowed storekeepers a profit of sixty cents on every dollar of popcorn. Capehart offered eighty cents on every dollar of coin-box receipts. Bouncing and bursting popcorn helped sell the Butter-Kist. Spinning records had the same effect for the Orchestrope. The glass front, Capehart said, allowed the customer to see the record "playing, changing, and turning." And even better than the aroma of popped corn, music increased the storekeeper's sales and produced profit of $5 a day.[14] Some restaurant owners would not believe that a machine could increase trade and take in enough money to make payments on its cost. Sales manager Valentine remembered that Capehart adopted an especially effective Holcomb technique. Since the Butter-Kist machine, about the size of an Orchestrope, had earned a profit of a dollar a day and brought in five cents per square foot of floor space and would have to earn a $55,000 annual profit to do as well,

Valentine had drawn many floor diagrams to allow storekeepers to see the $55,000 figure and compare it with yearly income from remaining floor space. Valentine had his salesmen employ the same logic for the Orchestrope. He used a two-week free demonstration in likely looking drugstores or confectioneries. Capehart servicemen changed records and, of course, emptied coin boxes. It took a stubborn proprietor to resist such a demonstration.[15]

The sales program hence was well conceived. A few operators installed Orchestropes in brothels, but Capehart, like Holcomb, sought dignified surroundings. He advertised in national magazines and trade journals, appealing to the desire for prestige and dependability.[16]

Everything went well until July 1928, when owners and dealers began to return Orchestropes. Summer heat had caused the records to sag on their stacking screws. If the listener did not mind the wavy tone of the song, the warping would have been tolerable. Unfortunately, when the warped record reached the bottom of the stack the weight of records above it caused it to break. The Capehart record player had become the Capehart record eater.

The Capehart Automatic Phonograph Corporation was in danger of bankruptcy. Capehart sent telegrams to every dealer, explaining that he would replace every Orchestrope without cost. Small and Collison held an emergency meeting and decided that the records had to lie flat but needed a mechanism that did not violate a patent held by the Phonograph Corporation of America. Capehart went to Pittsburgh and for $25,000 and a percentage of Orchestrope sales bought the patent for a new record holder. The crisis ended when the Huntington plant manufactured 685 new Orchestropes with lie-flat record magazines and sent them to replace the defective models.[17]

Caswell and Runyan, however, had enough, and after receiving letters from the Victor Talking Machine Company charging that the modified Orchestrope infringed Victor pat-

H. Earl Capehart, Jr.

Homer E. Capehart with new Cadillac, Fort Wayne, ca. 1929

ents, they asked Capehart to release them from their agreement.

Facing the alternatives of liquidation or another search for investors, the entrepreneur chose the latter. "Good will," he later would declare, "is the greatest asset in the world. You can't buy it. You've got to earn it." He obtained a new backer, Charles M. Niezer, director of the Tri-State Loan and Trust Company of Fort Wayne and president of the First National Bank. The Tri-State Company on 27 May 1929 bought $200,000 of preferred stock in the Capehart Automatic Phonograph Corporation. Niezer became chairman of the board of a newly named "Capehart Corporation," which then moved to Fort Wayne. Corporate assets had been $278,000. The new arrangement increased authorized capital from $50,000 to $650,000. Niezer agreed that the Tri-State Company would provide another $101,000 as a long-term loan when construction of the $101,000 Fort Wayne factory was finished. Capehart did not completely control the corporation, but then few young promoters ever do.[18]

The Capehart Corporation's gala opening occurred on 13 June 1929. A three-day open house and sales convention followed. The *Fort Wayne Journal-Gazette* reported that the corporation would employ three hundred workers and produce twenty-five instruments a day. Visitors walking through the plush lobby and into the twenty-six-thousand-square-foot main floor could see an Orchestrope on the assembly line, gaze at the new Cooper-Hewitt vapor lights, or go upstairs to visit the workers' clubroom and cafeteria. Fort Wayne residents drove out East Pontiac Street, parked their cars, and listened to musical programs from Orchestrope speakers in the Capehart "singing tower" above the plant's main entrance. Music in work areas, Capehart believed, stimulated workers.

The rising businessman, now a resident of Fort Wayne, was interested in every department of the factory and enjoyed walking the assembly line. He learned names, listened to complaints, and instituted one of the first group medical, casualty, and life insurance plans in the state.[19]

The money poured in, despite an increase in the Orchestrope's price from $785.80 to $1,250. A Des Moines dealer wrote that one of his buyers, a local sweetshop proprietor, had receipts of no less than $28 per week from a single Orchestrope. At an additional cost of $200, wall coin boxes, he said, enhanced profits by 15 percent. By autumn of 1929 the Capehart Corporation, grossing $4 million annually, was planning to double or triple volume. At the end of November the corporation began work to double its floor space, purchasing twenty acres of adjoining land. Capehart announced his intention to expand his work force to six hundred persons and to produce $12 million worth of phonographs.[20]

Meanwhile, the corporation had begun to produce different models. The Orchestrope with mirror slanted behind and

The Capehart Orchestrope, H. Earl Capehart, Jr.

Orchestrope, commercial model

The Capehart Orchestrope, H. Earl Capehart, Jr.

Orchestrope, aristocrat model

above the record-changing mechanism to allow patrons to watch the records move was now one of four commercial models. The club model, without a coin box, was for country clubs and hotel lounges. The auditorium model boasted a large speaker on top. The park model possessed amplifying equipment, mounted in a portable steel cabinet to protect it from weather. The home model was called the Aristocrat and featured a cabinet of walnut. Capehart had decided to sell not only profits but also prestige.[21] The home market especially attracted him. Profit from stock dividends and from interest on bonds had enabled many Americans to purchase automobiles, pianos, and, of course, as Capehart knew, home phonographs. If Americans would pay lump sums for automobiles, he thought they would pay for expensive home phonographs.[22]

In retrospect, the decision to concentrate on home sales was a cardinal error, for the New York stock market already had begun its collapse. Few people understood what had happened, and certainly not Capehart, who assumed that falling stock prices marked only another of the ordinary downturns in the business cycle. He moved forward with his plans. A well-known inventor from Columbia Phonograph, Ralph Erbe, had produced a record changer that was less bulky and more efficient. It played ten fewer records but could play ten- and twelve-inch records stacked together, on both sides. Capehart purchased this device and began producing the Capehart 400.

The entrepreneur hence had strayed from Holcomb's dictum that during a depression people spent coins, not folding money, and this fact became clear when he stopped production of coin-operated phonographs and turned to home models. By the end of 1930 there were eleven home models of Capehart phonographs and phonograph-radio consoles, each a variation of three designs: the Capehart Orchestrope for the Home ($1,250); the Amperion, a combination phonograph and radio in walnut, ranged from $975 to $1,175; and an Amperion in hardwood chest, for as little as $655. A national advertising campaign in the *Saturday Evening Post* and *House & Garden* brought home music to the attention of fashionable people otherwise befuddled by electric amplification. Circulars pointed to the record mechanism and thirteen-tube "superheterodyne" radio. Capehart exhorted his salesmen that "enthusiasm will sell the Capehart 400." At conventions he mingled with salesmen, dealers, and coin operators and shook their hands and remembered names.[23] He instructed regional and district managers to make lists of potential customers, individuals whose net worth was $50,000 or more. Depending on optional equipment, the Capehart 400 could sell for $1,095, with $310 profit to the dealer. Because the machine rarely cost more than $250 and sold to the dealer for $785, the corporation could gross $535. The Capehart factory finance department extended credit to dealers to cover shipments of phonographs. The approach worked. Vincent Astor, John J. Raskob, Henry Ford, and dozens of other well-known Americans bought Capehart 400s. Capehart carefully included a list of these prominent owners in a sales pamphlet.[24]

Capehart now was an illustrious personality in the phonograph industry. From everywhere came the encomiums. The ruler of the Elks Lodge in Norfolk, Virginia, testified that the Orchestrope contributed to enjoyment of guests and imparted a "spirit of good fellowship and sociability to our Home." Orchestropes played at Arlington Downs Race Track in Texas, the Paramount Hotel in New York City, Madison Square Garden, the Steeple Chase Pier in Atlantic City, and the Hotel Ambassador in Los Angeles. A study of the industry described "the Capehart" as the "phonographic equivalent of the Steinway in the homes of Mr. and Mrs. prosperous American." Marshall Field III purchased one for his villa near Rome. The French automobile manufacturer, André-Gustave

William B. Pickett

Homer E. Capehart with sons and sales managers

H. Earl Capehart, Jr.

Homer E. Capehart touring his factory

Citroën, listened to a Capehart phonograph, as did George B. Warner of Warner Brothers. The King of Siam installed one in the Bangkok palace, Vincent Astor on his yacht *Nourmahal.* Carl G. Fisher, builder of the Indianapolis Speedway and developer of Miami Beach, possessed one Capehart in his residence and a gyro-stabilized Capehart on his yacht *Shadow K.* R. J. Reynolds, Florenz Ziegfeld, John Wanamaker, Jr., and Gerardo Machado, president of the Republic of Cuba, owned Capeharts. In Hollywood, Olson's Music Company sold Capeharts to Clara Bow and Raymond Navaro. Indiana senator James E. Watson had one in his house in Rushville. At the beginning of the Great Depression the Capehart had become the most fashionable phonograph in America.[25]

3

The Wurlitzer Simplex

NOTHING in Capehart's background prepared him for the Great Depression. He had come to expect economic setbacks and downturns, but the situation now was different. This time business conditions and his response to them brought the loss of his company.

Sales in the phonograph industry actually had begun to lag in late 1929, and the Radio Corporation of America converted its Camden phonograph factory to radio production, naming the factory the Radio Center of the World. The trend continued; sales had reached $104 million in 1927, but by 1932, a dismal year, sales had dropped to $6 million, and production had dropped from 987,000 units to 40,000.[1]

Seeing signs of declining sales, Capehart at first did not assess their seriousness. Expansion had been his motto, his hallmark. In November 1929, less than a month after the Wall Street collapse, he told reporters his phonographs were "correctly priced to start with."[2] He intended to continue his strategy of selling to wealthy consumers and kept prices high. But this strategy was difficult. Undoubtedly, Capehart should have cut prices. If the corporation had accepted less than the $785 wholesale for the Capehart 400, and the dealers less than the $1,095 retail, total sales might have increased.

The growing problem of sales prompted Capehart in 1930 to announce an increase in production. The corporation had been forced to lay off employees, and dealers could remedy the situation, he said, if they gave volume to the manufacturer by temporarily increasing inventories. What business needed, he believed, returning to his sales principle, was enthusiasm. This had been lacking but was "now apparent everywhere." To prime the pump, so to speak, he would produce five hundred automatic record changers a day beginning 10 October. The plant was placing orders for materials and equipment to manufacture approximately forty thousand units "yet this year." The depression "we have just passed through," he said, displaying confidence, was nothing more than the normal business cycle.[3]

Unfortunately, optimism was no longer the answer. His business arrangement with Charles M. Niezer soured. After finishing the Fort Wayne factory, Capehart had allowed the banker to take back the promise of a $101,000 long-term mortgage loan, which meant, as Capehart recalled, that he himself had to find the money from working capital. The Tri-State Bank of Fort Wayne lent the corporation $100,000, seemingly an advantage, but actually an invitation to disaster that, Capehart said afterward, "broke our back." Losses mounted. The corporation by 1931 owed $100,000 to the Tri-State Bank, $400,000 to the Finance Corporation of America of New York, and $150,000 to merchandise creditors. This almost doubled the $370,000 loss of the previous year. The Capehart Corporation had phonographs, plant, and machinery to cover the debt, but nothing liquid. The Tri-State Bank went under. The Finance Corporation of America not only held notes for $400,000 but also $1.5 million of certificates from dealers who had purchased Capehart 400s on installment contracts.[4]

Capehart's corporation now was in difficulty. It had increased preferred stock from four thousand shares worth $400,000 to twenty thousand shares at a face value of $2 million, but was paying no dividends. Only holders of preferred stock, such as Niezer and officers of the banks, could vote when the corporation was not paying dividends. Since Capehart held only common stock, he had lost control.[5]

In February 1932, sixteen months after he had predicted economic recovery, the board of directors dismissed Capehart. Niezer had suffered many losses when the Fort Wayne bank closed, and Capehart recalled that he "sort of went crazy because he'd lost all of his money."[6] The entrepreneur had decided that the market for prestige phonographs was limited. Capehart, too, had discovered limited capacity to influence events. All he could do was stand back. He had resolved patent difficulties and manufactured and sold hundreds of fine phonographs. He held the allegiance of employees skilled in design, production, and sales. But his sixty-five thousand shares of common stock in the Capehart Corporation were now worthless. Aside from a modest savings account, he was, in his words, "just about broke."[7]

The defeat would have stopped the average industrialist, but entrepreneurship was in Capehart's blood, and he demonstrated his inability to see defeat. He sought lessons from the experience. Success, he determined, required caution, knowledge of external influences, and above all a balanced budget and sound finances. He was young (thirty-five), his corporation was continuing to exist, and, notably for a farmhand's son, his name had become a symbol of prestige.[8] With his personal savings he rented the sixty-three-year-old Packard Piano Company plant in Fort Wayne and engaged the services of former employees and skilled phonograph engineers, including Paul U. Lannerd and John R. Mitchell. To abide by the letter of the law he had his wife Irma purchase the Packard Company's name for ten dollars and in June 1932 signed a contract with Lannerd and Mitchell to manufacture and sell a record changer they had been developing when the Capehart Corporation management also had let them go. He formed a new corporation, Packard-Capehart, Inc., and issued one thousand shares of common stock without par value. To avoid confusion with the Fort Wayne company he renamed it the Packard Manufacturing Corporation.[9]

With necessity providing inspiration, Capehart approached the Rudolph Wurlitzer Manufacturing Company in North Tonawanda, New York. The company, Capehart had discovered, had begun marketing a radio with an auxiliary record player. Arriving early one day at the Wurlitzer plant, he found himself passed from purchasing agent to another agent. Finally one of the owners, Farny R. Wurlitzer, called Capehart into his office and began asking questions about the Fort Wayne corporation. At the end of the conversation Wurlitzer signed a contract with the Hoosier phonograph maker for a small number of Packard changers.[10]

In the months that followed, Capehart continued to move in phonograph industry circles, and it was at this time that he came across another interesting industry item: the multi-selector. Developed by the Simplex Manufacturing Company of Chicago and owned by a man named Erickson, it allowed a listener to push a button to select a record. Erickson desired to sell the invention, and Capehart, relying on his reputation, signed a contract in late March 1933 agreeing that in six months he either would buy the multi-selector and the Simplex Company for $50,000 or manufacture and sell a Simplex phonograph for Erickson.[11]

Even in the depths of the depression, the drive to employ the latest technology again paid off. A letter from Wurlitzer arrived, asking if Capehart knew of a coin phonograph that Wurlitzer might produce at North Tonawanda. Capehart replied on 3 April 1933:

> On my return to the office I find your letter in regard to a coin-operated phonograph.
>
> I have just what you need to manufacture in your plant—the best selective coin automatic phonograph I have ever seen. . . .

> I have taken over the sale of this business and would operate it myself if I had the funds.
>
> With the return of beer and good times, you should sell 25,000 units in the next three years, and make a long profit. . . .
>
> I would like to run up to North Tonawanda the latter part of this week and talk the matter over with you in detail.[12]

In the next weeks Capehart joined Wurlitzer and moved to North Tonawanda as vice president and sales manager. Wurlitzer offered Capehart $57,000 for the multi-selector, together with a salary and a percentage of the profits. When sales reached a certain volume he could receive twenty-two thousand shares of Wurlitzer stock.[13]

Capehart's performance during the 1930s, a miserable decade for millions of Americans, was remarkable. He would sell enough jukeboxes to make Wurlitzer the leader in the jukebox industry and make himself a millionaire. When Capehart came to the Wurlitzer Company he had entered a business that had prospered over many years. The firm's founder, Rudolph Wurlitzer, had entered the music business in Cincinnati in 1856 by sending $700 of his savings back to Schoeneck in Saxony to purchase clarinets, oboes, bassoons, and flutes made by local craftsmen. By the turn of the century his company had become famous for its pipe organs, pianos, trumpets, and drums and even produced coin-operated music boxes. It began to manufacture a pipe organ named the Wurlitzer Motion Picture Orchestra, for use in silent movie theaters. By 1910 it offered a new model, the Mighty Wurlitzer. The company also sold the Wurlitzer Military Band—an enormous paper-roll organ for skating rinks and amusement parks—and announced that "increase in patronage should pay for the instrument in a short time, and then yield a handsome profit."[14] Until the end of the 1920s the company had prospered. It had overcome the falling off of coin-operated music box sales in 1922 and the advent of motion-picture sound tracks. Manufacturing and selling pianos and managing millions of dollars in real estate for its retail outlets, it offered reasonably priced musical experiences to the average American.

But by the time Capehart walked into the North Tonawanda plant the company's prosperity had faded. Hard times had begun in 1928 with declining markets and with assets tied up in real estate. Then had come the crash, and Wurlitzer preferred stock fell from a high of $119 per share in 1928 to $10 in 1933. By the latter year Wurlitzer was $5 million in debt and searching for profitable products, any products. It had begun to sell furniture and refrigerators.[15]

To the company's current confusions, Capehart offered a solution. Farny Wurlitzer gave him considerable freedom. Capehart began supervising conversion of part of the plant's assembly line to coin-operated phonograph production. He convinced eight of his regional and district managers to join him and installed a former associate, James E. Broyles, as sales manager.[16]

He again had found the technological edge and a willing patron. With the end of Prohibition the jukebox industry was ready for an attractive invention; the psychological moment was right. Beer and jukebox music helped drown anxieties. By inserting a nickel and pushing a button on the Wurlitzer Simplex, a patron could play any of ten recordings.

One thing led to another. Jukeboxes sold records, and records sold jukeboxes. In 1934 Decca reduced the price of records from seventy-five to thirty-five cents and began to sell recordings by Bing Crosby, the Dorsey brothers, Guy Lombardo, and the Mills brothers. Benny Goodman's "One O'Clock Jump" provided a popular tune, and in 1936 "The Music Goes Round and Round" sold one hundred thousand records. There were other "hits." That year Capehart's Detroit area manager reported that "Beer Barrel Polka" had

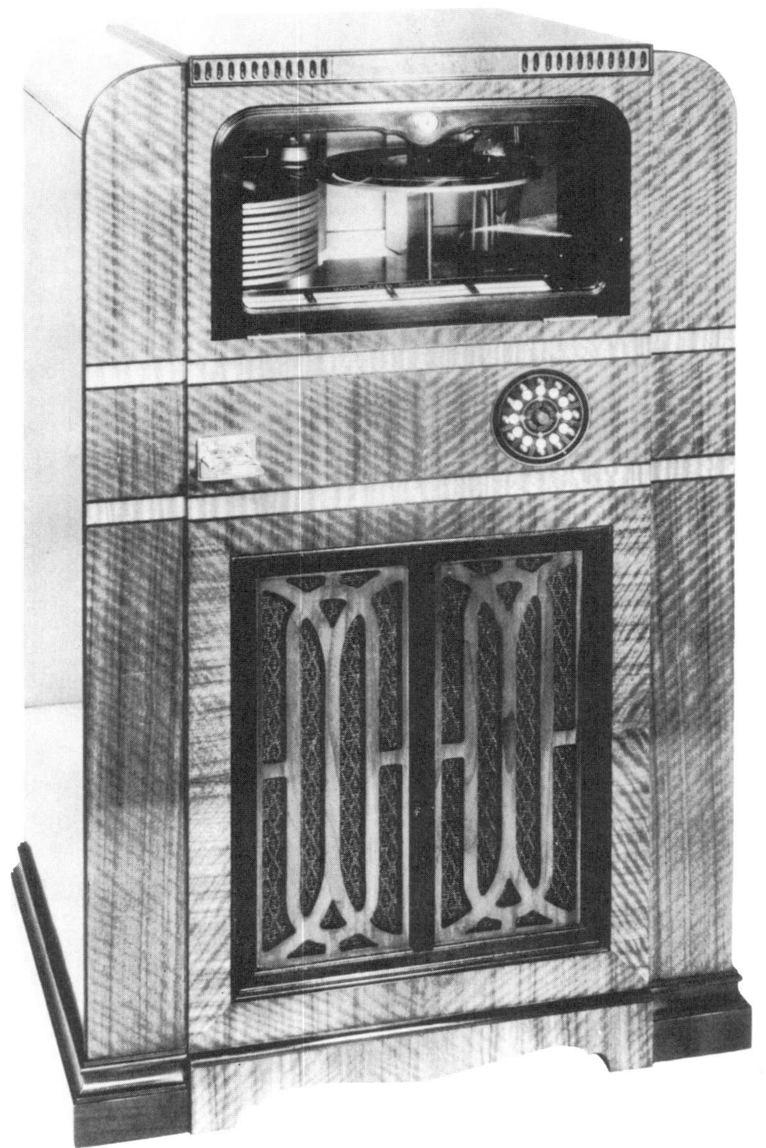

J. Krivine, *Juke Box Saturday Night* (London: New English Library, 1977)

Wurlitzer P-30, 1935

sold fifty thousand records locally. The Orchestrope, Capehart always said, had sold itself. The Simplex, he admitted, did even better.[17]

Success at Wurlitzer came by adapting earlier methods. The Orchestrope had gone through dealers to "locations"—candy shops, restaurants, pool halls, theaters—and was priced at $1,250. The entrepreneur now sold the Simplex through distributors to coin-machine "operators" for between $250 and $300. A local operator, an independent businessman, might buy anywhere from twenty to a thousand jukeboxes and rent them to proprietors of bars and restaurants who desired music for patrons.

The Simplex was very attractive; it was a decorative machine. The early model had resembled a piece of walnut furniture. It differed from a console radio only in that the record-changing mechanism was visible and the coin slot was below the glass door on the left. Ten selector buttons resembling a telephone dial were on the right; below, hidden by a wooden grill, was the speaker. The Wurlitzer cabinet had a hand-rubbed finish, with alcohol lacquer on surfaces where patrons might spill drinks. Capehart's goal, however, was to prevent the Simplex, still a rather somber-appearing device, from resembling a "coffin standing on its end." Direct-mail and trade journal advertising in 1938 pictured a highly visible, if not gaudy, new Wurlitzer 500, according to brochures "the only automatic phonograph cabinet with the spectacular, eye-arresting power of vari-colored light in motion." Its successor, the Wurlitzer 600, came in three combinations of translucent colored plastic: red, amber, and green. Both models played twenty-four selections and had coin slides for nickels, dimes, and quarters. Like Alfred E. Sloan's annual models at General Motors, Capehart placed a more attractive version on the market each year. Operators could return the old ones for a factory discount.[18]

J. Krivine, *Juke Box Saturday Night* (London: New English Library, 1977)

Wurlitzer 600, 1938

H. Earl Capehart, Jr.

Homer E. Capehart with Mr. and Mrs. Thomas H. Sloan of Chicago at the Wurlitzer plant in North Tonawanda, New York

The only real difficulty was keeping the machines in repair. Shop owners frequently had turned broken Orchestropes against the wall. The operators had solved this problem by providing service: replacing worn needles, repairing circuits, and, most important, collecting coins. They received half to three quarters of the income from each location. Capehart therefore introduced more mechanically sophisticated phonographs.[19]

With such leadership Wurlitzer sales soon led the jukebox industry. Salesmanship, Capehart had said, was "getting the other fellow to do what you want him to do," an attribute he believed was shared by any successful individual. As before, he taught his salesmen. He undertook to treat salesmen and distributors better than any competitor, visiting territories, writing broadsides, and meeting to talk over problems. He invited wives to attend sales conventions, made reservations in the finest hotels, and sent flowers to each couple's room. On the convention floor he had a word or two with everyone. Some observers thought he resembled a theatrical producer rather than a jukebox salesman, but he loved crowds and had a genius for promotion.[20]

At Wurlitzer he restrained his proclivities for the theatrical until late in 1936 when the initial Simplex sales boom leveled off. Wurlitzer executives had begun to fear a surplus of old models. Capehart responded with a whirlwind tour of sales conventions in the nation's largest cities. The finale, at the Waldorf-Astoria in New York, was the "Homer E. Capehart Appreciation Banquet" featuring many of the era's top entertainers, including Milton Berle, Gypsy Rose Lee, Benny Goodman's quartet, Guy Lombardo's Orchestra, and Koloah the Sepian dancer.[21] The following year he organized the Wurlitzer Century Club, inviting any operator who had purchased one hundred Wurlitzer coin phonographs to spend three days at North Tonawanda visiting the plant, where he arranged a veritable circus, eating steamed clams and fried chicken under a huge tent, watching a magician escape from handcuffs and coffins, and riding the *Maid of the Mist* beneath Niagara Falls. The occasion was indeed memorable. Twelve hundred people arrived at the same time. Capehart, in straw hat, sports coat, and deadpan expression, led the St. Louis delegation and its German band into the lobby of the Hotel Statler at 2 A.M. The next day, dressed in bib overalls, he pitched softball on the front lawn of the plant. At the banquet he stood beside members of the Wurlitzer family and led a pledge to make the year 1938 the "biggest and best year in coin machine history."[22]

The Wurlitzer Company had clearly made progress since the dark days of 1933. In that year the company sold 266 Simplex phonographs. The next year it sold 3,179. The figures jumped to 15,175 in 1935 and to 44,397 in 1936. Sales dropped to 42,397 in 1937, but the biggest single month of

J. Krivine, *Juke Box Saturday Night* (London: New English Library, 1977)

Wurlitzer 800, 1940

coin machine sales in the company's history came in October of that year when the factory shipped 8,000 coin phonographs worth $2 million. The turning point had been 1936 when the $470,000 loss on 1935 operations became a gain of $550,000. Assets of $13 million in 1935 had grown to $20 million in 1938. In November 1937 holders of preferred stock collected back dividends of $40.25 per share. By 1941, ten thousand businessmen operators managed between 10 and 2,000 jukeboxes apiece and earned $120 a month on each machine. Some 300,000 jukeboxes were making music for America, using 30 million records a year. Three years earlier Wurlitzer, having sold 150,000 jukeboxes, had become the leading supplier for the industry.[23]

By late summer 1938 Capehart could reflect upon his success. By putting Wurlitzer back on its feet he had provided jobs for hundreds of people and income for thousands of distributors, operators, tavern owners, restaurant proprietors, and, of course, racketeers.[24] Particularly gratifying was the fact that he now was wealthy, a result of his contract with Wurlitzer. His income in 1937, including salary, bonus, and commissions, was $68,000. That year Irma's income totaled $44,000 from oil wells in north-central Michigan, the Packard record changer patent, and sale of Wurlitzer stock. Homer and Irma together owned Wurlitzer stock, possibly 20,195 shares, that had increased from $2 a share in 1933 to $20 in 1937. That year Wurlitzer common stock split ten for one with a resulting par value of $10 per share. Assuming that Capehart's holdings were in common stock, his assets in 1938 were worth over $2 million.[25]

It was at this point that Capehart, having succeeded in business—if not his own business, then a well-known, well-established business, the Rudolph Wurlitzer Company—found that he still was not satisfied. His attention turned to his origins in southern Indiana: Pike and Daviess counties. Land was for sale, and he decided to buy a farm. Two miles

H. Earl Capehart, Jr.

Homer E. Capehart at his Daviess County farm, ca. 1939

H. Earl Capehart, Jr.

Homer E. Capehart and his father Alvin, ca. early 1940s

north of the Graham farm in Daviess County, where he had lived as a child, the Metropolitan Life Insurance Company, the Federal Land Bank, and local banks owned a tract from which Capehart bought 900 acres in 1936 and two years later increased his holdings to 1,065 acres. By 1941 his land totaled 1,584 acres, with an estimated value, including improvements, of $226,275. By the mid-1960s he owned 2,265 acres.[26]

The decision to invest in farmland in Indiana had a special meaning for Capehart. He had determined to prove himself, to make a fortune that, he had concluded, could come only in business, not agriculture. Nostalgia for the humid summer haze and tall corn now brought him back.

Moreover, family members still lived there. His sister Bessie, now Mrs. Byron Haskins, resided on a Pike County farm with her husband and seven sons. Homer and Bessie's father, Alvin, lived nearby with his second wife. For the Haskins family the drop in farm prices during the early 1930s had

H. Earl Capehart, Jr.

Homer E. Capehart feeding the hogs on his farm, ca. early 1940s

H. Earl Capehart, Jr.

Homer E. Capehart supervising sandbagging the levy on the west fork of the White River

caused difficulty, and on 1 March 1937 Capehart leased part of his farm to his brother-in-law. Capehart paid Haskins wages, and Haskins supervised the farm.[27]

Equally important, purchasing the farm was a good business move. With land prices depressed he saw a chance to increase his wealth. The soil was sandy, but it was part of a fertile floodplain of the White River. Having worked the land, he knew its sediment and moisture could grow corn. Levees along the east bank could prevent floods. He soon was the leader of the local levee committee, a petition-gathering and lobbying group that, despite his opposition to federal aid in general, by 1939 had obtained federal money for a twenty-two-mile-long earthen wall. Although the farm lost $36,000 in 1937, the following year brought a profit of $26,000.[28]

Another reason for buying the farm appeared in a full-page advertisement in the *Washington* (Ind.) *Herald* on the occasion of the 1937 state cornhusking contest. Homer Capehart, said the announcement, had returned to Daviess County. "Welcome . . . huskers and visitors. It's nice to have you with us in Daviess county. . . . It's great to be with your neighbors. It's great to see old friends." Capehart's Hereford cattle and Duroc hogs would combine "modern up-to-date farm methods with common sense." Capehart had returned to the place of his youth. He soon found that the community admired him and was happy to have him back. He had hoped this would be true and, when it was, began looking in the direction of Hoosier politics.[29]

4

The Cornfield Conference

CAPEHART'S interest in politics had evolved over many years. When he had been a salesman in Green Bay, just after World War I, he had listened to campaign speeches by Sen. Robert M. La Follette, Sr. Politics often were a topic of conversation among business friends in Indianapolis, Fort Wayne, and later in Buffalo. Loss of the Capehart Corporation in 1932 had brought awareness of the limits of individual effort. "The worst aspect of the Depression," Capehart recalled, "was that you couldn't collect your money. Nobody would pay you. They didn't have the money to pay you. And some, maybe they could, wouldn't, because they'd use it as an excuse not to pay . . . it's a depression psychology. It's just bad. It's hell."[1] When the New Deal provided relief to the unemployed and sought to regulate business, he saw the influence of politics on the economy. Government, he concluded, should act to prevent or alleviate economic hardship.

The phonograph entrepreneur could have become either a Republican or a Democrat, but eventually chose the former party. Like his father, he had "almost as many Democratic relatives and friends as . . . Republican." His parents usually voted Democratic, although his maternal grandfather had been a Republican. In the bleak days of 1933, when writing Pike County Democratic officials to seek jobs for his brother Ivan and nephew Harry Haskins, he had contributed to the Democratic party. "The Capeharts are good Democrats," he asserted. By the mid-1930s, however, he had become a Republican. His business contacts reinforced his own conclusions about the nation's future if it remained on its New Deal course. Federal assistance, he believed, had gone too far. He attended the 1936 GOP (Grand Old Party, or Republican party) national convention and about that time began to remark that he had "always been a Republican" or, more accurately, "more often than not I noticed that the people who thought my way" were in the Republican party.[2]

The decision to become active in Republican politics came in part from the ability to sense an opportunity. By late 1937 the New Deal was experiencing difficulties. After an overwhelming electoral victory the previous year, with a large majority in both houses of Congress, Franklin D. Roosevelt's New Deal program had virtually come to a halt. In February conservatives who feared organized labor had joined with New Deal liberals against the plan to reorganize the Supreme Court. In late summer stock prices dropped and unemployment became even more severe than in the months following the Wall Street crash. Washington officials were unsure what to do. Ignoring the advice of the Briton, John Maynard Keynes, who counseled the president not to antagonize businessmen, Roosevelt attacked monopolists, blaming them for the depression. He opposed the reelection of several anti-New Deal Democratic senators and provided opponents another opportunity to compare his opposition to the recent Communist purges in Russia. The New Deal was in disarray.[3]

Across the nation a few people had begun to see a need to galvanize the Republican party. Roosevelt's victory in 1936 over the Republican moderate Alfred M. Landon, by the biggest majority in American history, had given the Democrats their largest Senate majority since 1869 and their largest House majority since 1855. Conservative congressmen and senators in both parties numbered only 28 in the Senate and 110 in the House. According to the editors of *Fortune*, the Republican party had lost its way: its leaders unable to decide whether to adopt Calvin Coolidge-era states' rights, the gold standard, and a balanced budget, or to expel the Old Guard and become liberal. For a brief time party leaders considered joining conservative Democrats to oppose Roosevelt. Sen. Arthur H. Vandenberg of Michigan, a conservative, made the astonishing remark that party labels were not important. Landon's manager, John D. M. Hamilton, said the Republicans needed to realize "they have lost the pulse of the people, the confidence of the great masses of Americans."[4]

Former President Herbert Hoover suggested that Republicans hold a midterm convention in 1938, a chance, Hoover thought, to determine issues for a new platform. The convention never met. Hamilton and the Old Guard favored such a move, but Landon, Senators William E. Borah and Charles L. McNary, Congressman Joseph Martin, Jr., and Col. Frank Knox, publisher of the *Chicago Daily News*, opposed. McNary agreed with Indiana's former senator, James E. Watson, to take no actions that might stir controversy within the party. GOP leaders did agree to create a program committee to study issues. The chairman became Glenn Frank: former editor of *Century*, former president of the University of Wisconsin, and a dark-horse presidential candidate.[5]

As the national Republican party was in trouble, despite the problems of the Roosevelt administration, so was the Indiana GOP. A Democrat, Paul V. McNutt, dean of the Indiana University Law School, had become governor in 1933 and had centralized state government, reducing departments from 169 to 8, and pushed through legislation that placed most expenditure and patronage in his hands. Indiana Democrats entrenched themselves as administrators of relief programs operated by the Works Progress Administration and the Public Works Administration and became known as friends of farmers by dispensing the largess of the Agricultural Adjustment Administration. By the mid-1930s the Democratic party in Indiana had become prosperous, too, from McNutt's "two per cent club," named for the percentage the party deducted from salaries of state employees. All the while Hoosier Republicans were squabbling for control of the state organization and appointments to the national committee. The rank and file was apathetic. Older members supported Watson, their party's aging pro-business spokesman from 1916 to 1933. A dispute over who would be state chairman caused the wealthy Muncie glass jar manufacturer, George A. Ball, to resign as national committeeman in 1938, and it was uncertain where party leaders would find money for that year's congressional campaign.[6]

Fortunately for Hoosier Republicans, Roosevelt's attempt the previous year to increase the number of justices on the Supreme Court in order to avoid further rulings that New Deal legislation was unconstitutional, now combined with the apparent failure of the president's recovery program to give their party a new lease on life. The independent-minded Democratic senator, Frederick Van Nuys, had joined nine members of the upper house's judiciary committee in signing a majority report against Roosevelt's "packing" measure. Gov. Clifford M. Townsend, a Democrat and McNutt's protégé (by this time McNutt had become high commissioner of the Philippines and was in faraway Manila), thereupon read Van Nuys out of the Democratic party.[7]

Such was the situation when Capehart began to take interest in politics, and he seized the moment not merely by joining the Frank committee to discuss national issues, but by moving directly to enter GOP politics in Indiana. To bolster his party's fortunes in his own state he called what he artfully described as a Cornfield Conference.

Someone later asked him where he had gotten the idea for a Cornfield Conference. "I knew from my experience and personality," he responded, "that that sort of thing would be successful and would revitalize anything that was dead." A man whose instincts had put him in touch with all elements of complicated business decisions—employees, dealers, salesmen, servicemen, and especially customers—he had organized a Wurlitzer clambake the previous year that had worked wonderfully. The idea for a similar political rally apparently came during a conversation in February 1938 with state Republican chairman Arch Bobbitt at the Columbia Club on Monument Circle in Indianapolis, an institution with strong ties to the Republican party dating back to the days of Benjamin Harrison. Bobbitt had told Capehart the party was down, workers discouraged, and he had been hoping for a statewide meeting of precinct committeemen. Capehart responded that he had tired of hearing people complain about the New Deal and wanted to do something: "Why not have a clambake on my farm?" As a token of his sincerity he wrote out a check for an amount Bobbitt remembered as $300, "much larger than I had received from anybody for a long time." Before the Cornfield Conference was over Capehart would write checks for $25,000.[8]

Capehart's concern for the Hoosier GOP had an immediate effect. The Angola newspaper publisher, Raymond E. Willis, whose political fortunes had begun to rise, had decided to seek the Republican nomination for United States senator. Little known in national circles, he had written A. H. Vandenberg, Jr., that he had a good chance for the nomination. Then in mid-June he received a letter from his nephew, Hilton P. Hornaday, a reporter for the *Buffalo Evening News*. The young man said he had "confidential" information from Capehart, who was "coming back to Indiana this fall to use his money and his means to put the state back in the Republican column." The jukebox entrepreneur, Hornaday said, would "give his financial backing and support to the man nominated for Senator at the state convention." Capehart's program, to be made public after the state convention in June, would include "a gigantic rally for 10,000 Republicans on his farm in Daviess county this fall." Willis was "very much interested" in Capehart's assistance. Would Capehart, he asked, be willing to put on the rally in Fort Wayne or in Steuben County, of which Angola was county seat?[9] The Indiana Republican Editorial Association supported Willis, and at the convention in June he went on to defeat Watson for the nomination.[10]

The ensuing Cornfield Conference proved an enormous success. Held not on the northern prairie farmland preferred by Willis, but rather on Capehart's farm in the hilly south, it brought together a winning group among Indiana Republicans. It made possible Willis's election as senator, and six years later the opportunity came to Capehart. On the national scene it pointed out the future course for the Republican party. Capehart helped lead the national party out of the wilderness by showing its confused leaders that conservatism, not me-too-ism, was the way to the hearts of many American voters.[11] The rally gave all sorts of national party leaders an opportunity to meet and discuss their problems. Hamilton arranged for attendance of Congressman Martin, chairman of the Republican congressional campaign committee; Sen. John G. Townsend, Jr., chairman of the senatorial campaign committee; Dr. Frank, chairman of the program committee; and Marion E. Martin, assistant chairman of the national committee in charge of women's activities. Former senator James W. Wadsworth of New York agreed to give the keynote address. Invitations went to national committee members, state chairmen, and congressional and gubernatorial candidates in a host of states: West Virginia, Kentucky, Ohio, Illinois, Michigan, Wisconsin, Kansas, Minnesota, North Dakota, Iowa, Kansas, Missouri, Oklahoma, and South Dakota.

Capehart was general chairman with Paul R. Bausman—friend, editor of the *Washington* (Ind.) *Herald*, and leader of the Indiana Republican Editorial Association—vice-chairman and chief assistant.[12]

Asked how his idea had become so important, Capehart recalled, "I handled it exactly like I'd have handled the introduction of a new musical instrument." "The secret," he said, was to "keep writing your name in the sky and if you've got a good product it will be successful, it will draw people to it and they'll buy it." Of course he provided good newspaper copy. Early in July the state committee began releasing publicity advances about the conference and its host who, it related, personified the American farm-boy-to-riches story. Having returned penniless after service in World War I, he had "risen to leadership in the musical instrument manufacturing business. . . . His present interest in the Republican cause is to preserve to American youth the opportunity that was his." His showmanship, known to thousands of coin-machine operators and distributors, so reported the amusement industry journal *Billboard*, was about to "put up the biggest circus tent ever and show the boys some good entertainment in the way of circus acts."[13]

Everything occurred as Capehart planned. Early on the morning of 26 August, a day before the conference took place, he arranged twenty-eight blue-and-white-striped tents on a mowed alfalfa field (not really a cornfield; to be sure, corn had grown there in other years, and green-eared stalks in tassel were in adjacent fields). Tents arose for each of the twelve Indiana district Republican delegations, four for kitchens, one for headquarters, and one each for radio broadcasters, the press, and purveyors of Republican literature. The largest tent would accommodate ten thousand people. Small tents sheltered a first aid station and soft drink concessions.[14]

That same morning festivities had begun in far-off Gary, where the pied piper of the affair, the Wurlitzer Military

H. Earl Capehart, Jr.

H. Earl Capehart, Jr.

Cornfield Conference tents and crowd

Band—a hundred-piece ensemble that only the previous year had won the "best band in the United States" award at the National Band Contest—left its headquarters in three sign-covered buses on a zigzag southward route. The band stopped and played in South Bend, Columbia City, Fort Wayne, Huntington, Indianapolis, Martinsville, Bloomington, and five other communities. Indianapolis Republicans exhibited a huge elephant rented from a circus as an additional attraction at the rally held at the Soldiers and Sailors Monument. An impressive group of politicos from thirteen midwestern "breadbasket" states gathered at the nearby Columbia Club to meet national leaders and plan strategy. Even the Ohio senatorial candidate, young Robert A. Taft, whose schedule would not allow him to attend the next day's rally, had hurried to Indianapolis to meet other regional candidates and obtain advice from such national luminaries as Chairman Hamilton, Senator Townsend, and Congressman Martin.[15]

The next morning, 27 August, at the beginning of the great day, the scene shifted southward to Capehart's farm where a summer haze veiled the sun's first rays and a cooling breeze caused the blue and white canvas of the tents to sway gently. The weather could not have been better. Out on the road to the farm Daviess County men gave parking directions to drivers of eleven thousand cars. By mid-morning the automobiles were stirring clouds of dust. Guests came also by special trains directly to the farm: tracks fortunately ran along the farm's eastern boundary. A train arrived from Buffalo carrying the conference organizer's eastern friends and associates. The mayor of Buffalo, Thomas Holling, a Democrat, stepped down from one of the cars. Queried by reporters, he thoughtfully observed, "I may be properly classed as a good friend of Mr. Capehart and I always like to attend his parties. He has yet to throw a poor one." All the while in the kitchen tents an army of cooks and waiters worked frantically, steaming clams and barbecuing chickens over charcoal pits. When

Capehart rang the noon dinner bell, everything was in readiness.[16]

Dinner at the farm that day was a great occasion. Ten thousand precinct committeemen and county chairmen and their families and dignitaries from out of state sat down at tables covered with dishes of broiled chicken, mashed potatoes and country gravy, corn on the cob, rolls, relishes, and watermelons, all of which delicacies the diners washed down with iced tea and coffee. The huge dining tent resounded with clinking silver and the voices of guests as they paused before devouring five thousand chickens and one hundred thousand clams. Outside the great tent, as in a medieval fair, paraded, ultimately, stuntmen, yodelers, guitar players, a German band, the Wurlitzer Military Band, and thirty-two drum and bugle corps. The farm that day was a cacophony of the diners' conversations and the accompanying bards and minstrels.

H. Earl Capehart, Jr.

Homer E. Capehart welcomes GOP chairman John D. M. Hamilton to the Cornfield Conference.

H. Earl Capehart, Jr.

Homer E. Capehart supervising the decoration of the podium at the Cornfield Conference

Supervising the "Homeric Feast," as *Time* magazine called the occasion, was the happy host, clad in floppy sun hat, long-sleeved white shirt, checked tie, tan trousers, cigar in the corner of his mouth. Reporters observed him shaking hands with Hamilton and standing with arms around Willis. No detail was too minor for his attention; every county committeeman received a warm greeting and handshake.[17]

After the food came the speeches. The speaker's platform stood at the middle of the main tent. Chairman Bobbitt opened the postprandial session, and Indiana's only Republican congressman, young Charles A. Halleck, of Rensselaer, introduced each speaker: Hamilton, Wadsworth, Willis, Capehart, and five others. The new Republicans of Capehart's generation were meeting the old. As late as 1936 Senator Watson had believed that Coolidge should have been the national party standard-bearer in 1928. Now he watched as younger members of the GOP adapted his party to the circumstances of American life ten years later.[18]

The assembled auditors heard Hamilton's familiar charge that President Roosevelt had resorted to a "Russian technique" of staging a purge to "divert our attention from the failures of the New Deal." The economic downturn had come because of a president who attacked the Supreme Court and used extravagant federal spending to regiment citizens, "trying to substitute personal government for the 'American Way.' " The other speakers repeated this litany, albeit with variations to include foreign affairs.[19]

Willis reiterated former President Hoover's view that American problems derived from foreign problems. Appealing to farmers, he decried farm imports, which he said had risen from 347,000 bushels of corn in 1932 to 86 million bushels in 1937, resulting in a price of fifty-one cents a bushel. He opposed, he said, "any entanglement of this country in European politics through adherence to either the League of Nations or that league bureau known as the World Court."

For anyone who doubted his position he restated it: "I am opposed to intervention in Old World affairs in any form." Willis pointed his isolationist appeal at the weakest part of the Midwest Democracy, lower-income urban and rural voters in the southern part of the state. Moreover, many southern Hoosiers were of German ancestry.[20]

The self-professed nonofficeseeker, Capehart, made one of the best speeches that day. He looked to the concerns of a party seeking a return to power. Twelve million Americans were unemployed, he said, and twenty million people were receiving public relief. As early as 1930 President Hoover had called for help to people in difficulty. Six years later Governor Landon had promised relief. The Frank committee had called for Republican responsibility to "youth and age." Revealing a salesman's awareness of the needs of his listeners, Capehart proclaimed that "Roosevelt has spell-bound his believers into feeling that the Republican Party is interested in only . . . the reduction of taxes; the piling up of profit for private enterprise and the protection and ownership of property." The American people had come to believe that Republicans would permit suffering and "NOT take care of the unemployed and will champion NO social legislation." He called for a rally of Americans dissatisfied with the New Deal. Every American boy and girl desired dignity to own a house, hold a position of responsibility in industry, or own a business, "a free business that is serving a real purpose." Every person had a right to the necessities of life. Self-help might be insufficient. "The Republican Party must have the courage to say to the people of America who continue unemployed through no fault of their own, that it will guarantee to them adequate and intelligent relief in whatever form is most appropriate."

Even while presenting himself as a beneficiary of the American dream, Capehart questioned whether it existed in 1938. He proposed to eliminate Rooseveltian inefficiency, a jungle of "red tape, politics, waste and stupid bungling . . . favor-

H. Earl Capehart, Jr.

Dr. Glenn Frank addressing the Cornfield Conference

H. Earl Capehart, Jr.

Homer E. Capehart with Raymond E. Willis at the Cornfield Conference

itism or graft." The Republican party, he said, pointing out the New Deal's most serious failure, would dedicate "its very life to the end that these millions of people who have been able to obtain only government relief employment will be given an opportunity for real employment in private industry—and soon!" He revealed a view rare among Republican businessmen, one that looked to an American society that recognized the place of workers: "Business interests of this country realize that their first responsibility is to labor, and their second responsibility is to their stockholders. If they take care of their responsibility to labor, then labor will take care of their responsibility to the stockholders. It is labor which consumes the largest part of that which the business interests create." Republicanism, he concluded, was Americanism, and any other program was alien. Only employment in private industry was American. "We are not yet a Communistic country, nor a Socialistic country, nor a Nazi country, nor a Fascist country." It was impossible to live "under two systems of government—the American system and the New Deal Experiment."[21]

The speaker, of course, was suitably vague. He did not tell how welfare could be better administered or private enterprise expanded to eliminate relief.

The speech, which Capehart later said made him a sort of "Republican Roosevelt," nevertheless was bound to irritate some listeners. One reporter commented upon the "apparent heresy to Old Guard doctrine," which "disconcerted leaders seated on the speakers platform," including Hamilton and Martin. The party's leaders did not feel comfortable with it.[22]

The Cornfield Conference received enormous publicity. It was emblazoned across the front pages of the *New York Times* and the *Chicago Tribune* the next day. An editorial in the former suggested "a real elephant under the main tent after all, instead of the skeleton of a prehistorical animal that lost his hide with his shirt in 1932."[23]

What were the long-term results of the conference? It is difficult to be sure, for a single conference, however well organized, could hardly have changed the national or even the Indiana party's fortunes. And yet something clearly had happened. Perhaps the conference had galvanized the leadership, national and local, bringing understanding of the possibilities vis-à-vis the Democrats, calling attention to the Democrats' troubles and to the Republicans' opportunities.

The conference nicely publicized the approaching midterm election in November of that year, and the result soon became evident. In Democratic newspapers across the country Charles Michelson, director of publicity for the Democratic national committee, had sought to discredit the gathering. He had asked if the five thousand chickens consumed by Hoosier Republicans had any relation to Hoover's two chickens in every pot. He beheld nothing about which to worry; congressional Democrats could stop campaigning and still have a House majority of eighty or ninety; the "utmost variation" in the Senate could not involve more than "a seat or two."[24] But in the ensuing election GOP representation in the House increased by 80 seats, from 89 to 169. Republican representation in the Senate increased by 8, from 15 to 23. Most of the defeated Democrats were from industrial sections of the East and Midwest and had been ardent New Dealers. Of remaining House Democrats, 80 were at best unenthusiastic about the New Deal, and in the Senate as many as 30 were hostile. Moreover, 45 of the 80 new Republican congressional representatives, House and Senate, were from the Midwest. Voters in Indiana, Iowa, Kansas, Nebraska, and the Dakotas had returned to Republicanism.[25]

In Indiana Capehart's support for Republicanism seems almost to have turned the state around politically. Such large results would appear on the surface to be almost unbelievable. Writers had suggested that if the state GOP could elect a senator and several congressmen, the national party might actually look to Indiana for leadership in 1940. Capehart had attacked government spending, cuts in farm production, appeals to class hatred, and relief programs without jobs. He had harshly criticized Secretary of Agriculture Henry A. Wallace. Less than a week before the election he used a radio broadcast from the farm to address simultaneously 3,872 precinct meetings of Indiana Republicans. In the Senate race that autumn Willis lost to Van Nuys, but by only 5,832 votes. Republicans won seven of twelve congressional seats. They elected James M. Tucker of Paoli as Hoosier secretary of state. The total vote in November 1938 was the largest in Indiana history, with the exception of 1936, a presidential year. Republicans carried every rural congressional district except one and nearly all the rural counties. The state senate remained Democratic, but the GOP gained a majority (51 to 49) in the House of Representatives.[26]

Capehart thus had established his Republican identity. Michelson prophesied, this time correctly, that the name of Homer Capehart would live "whenever politicians seek a rural refuge."[27]

People now began a guessing game about the entrepreneur who had left the state but now had returned to Daviess County. The *Kansas City Star* reported that Capehart desired Hamilton's place as national chairman. The *Columbia City* (Ind.) *Post*, the newspaper of Ralph F. Gates who in 1941 would succeed Bobbitt as Indiana chairman, asked, "What does Capehart want?" It guessed that he wanted to be a national committeeman, a candidate for the Senate, or (the most prized of Hoosier offices) governor.[28]

The salesman-entrepreneur had turned to politics. The mayor of Indianapolis, Charles Jewett, and Capehart's friend Bausman, both beheld his opportunity. John Hastings would recall that Bausman "saw quicker than anyone else the potential that Capehart might have in politics. Bausman was interested in getting a . . . Republican candidate who would win and at the same time deserved to win. I think he became Capehart's original, closest political confidant." Capehart himself liked the prospect. "I was internationally known as a manufacturer of the Capehart phonograph . . . at the time . . . but not too many would know in Indiana," he later explained. "The political thing was a personal thing: they knew the cornfield conference man as Homer Capehart. . . . Whereas the 'Capehart' was a trade name of a musical instrument."[29]

Carefully, Capehart had placed himself in the almost necessary American political tradition: he was not moving toward a goal, but the goal (whatever it might be) was moving toward him. William E. Jenner, who would become Republican state chairman in 1945 and then serve two terms as Capehart's colleague in the United States Senate, put it this way: "The times were right and Capehart stood for fundamental conservatism. In addition, he had money." "From that time on," Capehart would recall, "I was in politics because people forced me into it."[30]

From that time on Capehart was certainly visible in state politics. During a Constitution Day program in Indianapolis he shared the podium with the well-known proprietor of the *Chicago Tribune*, Col. Robert R. McCormick, and said that the federal government should be more "generous with the needy . . . guarantee relief to them . . . take them by the hand, both the old and the young, and pull them up." The truly American procedure was to give employment and initiative. "To kill private industry in America," he said, "is to kill us as a nation." The United States was a country in which "the laborer of today becomes the businessman of tomorrow—the farmhand of today becomes the farm owner of tomorrow, and the poor boy of today becomes the rich man of tomorrow."[31] One reporter on this occasion said that "Capehart stole the show so irretrievably that McCormick" had to cut his speech in half. Shortly afterward Indianapolis newspapers began to refer to Capehart as a man with money and a flare for politics, an outstanding orator, a Republican opponent for Sen. Sherman Minton, even a presidential possibility.[32]

5

Political Fever

THE CORNFIELD Conference marked a turning point in Capehart's life. He began to see that business no longer could contain his energies. The result was a slow movement in the direction of political office.[1] At first it was necessary for the erstwhile Indiana farm youth, become jukebox entrepreneur and official of the Rudolph Wurlitzer Company, to return to his native state. This he did in 1940. As early as January 1939 a letter had gone out to Wurlitzer customers announcing that North Tonawanda factory manager Carl E. Johnson would replace Capehart, and that Milton Hammergren of the company's Cincinnati office would take over as general sales manager. Capehart's hope, he told friends, was to undertake "farming on a big scale in Indiana, oil production, and politics—but maybe you had better not mention politics. I am not a very good politician."[2]

Considering his independence of mind, it was perhaps surprising that he had remained as long as he did at Wurlitzer. He had retained ownership of his phonograph business, the Packard Manufacturing Corporation, in Fort Wayne. Of the 1,000 shares of Packard stock, he and Irma held 998, and the other 2 belonged to friends. Washing machines and vacuum cleaners were possibilities for the Packard Corporation, but he decided to produce what he knew. He put engineers to work making prints, samples, and prototypes for coin phonograph accessories. His contract with his former factory manager, Edward E. Collison, was for "a certain new and improved type of 'wall box,'" a metal container about the size of a shoe box that allowed patrons at tables or booths to deposit a nickel and dial a song on a rotary selector. Collison was a director, vice president, and chief engineer. Capehart was president. He would receive a dollar for each box sold.[3]

The Fort Wayne operation (several men working on designs in a one-room shed) was not the best location to produce wall boxes, and within a few months Capehart leased space in Indianapolis, one of the buildings of the defunct Marmon Motorcar Company, of which his first Orchestrope financiers, G. M. Williams, Hal L. Purdy, and Arthur R. Heiskell, had been officers in 1928. The two-story structure was at the corner of Kentucky Avenue and Morris Street and contained sixty thousand square feet. Capehart announced plans to build

H. Earl Capehart, Jr.

Homer E. Capehart at his desk at the Packard Manufacturing Corporation automatic phonographs as well as accessories. The company, he said, would be in full operation in three to six months with a payroll of two thousand people. A new stock issue, also held by Homer and Irma, increased Packard Corporation shares to eleven thousand.[4]

Indiana Republicans meanwhile were seeking Capehart as a speaker and, indeed, a possible candidate. A year before relocating in Indiana, he had attracted the Bartholomew County Republican chairman who felt fortunate to obtain Capehart to speak at the Lincoln Day dinner. The address, "Lincoln Ideals . . . Brought Down to Date," delivered on the radio in Columbus, Indiana, reiterated the importance of confidence, mentioned the glories of American history, and pointed to perils confronting the ship of state. Lincoln, the speaker said, illustrated "initiative, personal opportunity, a chance to grow . . . and to 'lift himself by his own bootstraps' to the highest office the American people can bestow." The moment was a new time of crisis in which Americans were losing confidence "in themselves, in their leadership, and in their form of government." It never dawned upon Lincoln, Capehart reminded his listeners, to use the presidency to "liquidate and purge those who had opposed him in political or military warfare . . . to stir up class hatred." At another rally in Kokomo about this time he denounced former Democratic governor Paul V. McNutt's reorganization of state offices in 1933. The burden of the address was that McNutt and the Indiana Democratic party boss and national committeeman, Frank McHale, wanted power by any means, at any price; there were similarities between the policies of McNutt and Franklin D. Roosevelt.[5]

For a short while a group of Republicans attempted to persuade Capehart to be a presidential candidate. Investigators for Congressman Martin Dies's Un-American Activities Committee turned up letters from James E. Campbell of Owensboro, Kentucky, to GOP treasurer Felix McWhirter. Capehart was a "natural" for president, Campbell said, and he had a plan that would result in Capehart's nomination. The incident unfortunately associated Capehart with right-wing radicals. Campbell was on the payroll of the New Yorker Dudley P. Gilbert, organizer of American Nationalists, who had attempted to resist a "red revolution" that he believed would break out in the summer of 1938, citing information he had obtained from a well-placed "New York waiter with a 'listening ear.'"[6]

But the Capehart-for-president movement was not confined to businessmen and crackpots. Capehart's friend and publisher of the *Washington* (Ind.) *Herald*, Paul Bausman, who with the Indiana Republican Editorial Association had been instrumental in nominating Raymond Willis for senator, in 1939 appeared at a rally at the state fairgrounds in Indianapolis and proposed to make Capehart a favorite-son candidate in 1940. Between fifteen thousand and twenty-five thousand Republicans had crowded the grandstand and chairs on the racetrack, and in addition to Capehart on the speaker's platform were Glenn Frank, Bertha D. Bauer, the national committeewoman for Illinois, and Frank E. Gannett, the newspaper publisher. Many precinct committeemen were in attendance.[7]

At the rally in 1939, as a year earlier at his Cornfield Conference, Capehart again set out his political views, national and international. Reasserting his theme that the Republican party had never lacked social consciousness, he proposed a platform with something for everyone. Labor was "entitled to" a fair wage, healthy working conditions, reasonable hours, and job security. He favored unemployment insurance, federal "financial and moral support for those unemployed through no fault of their own," and old-age benefits. For businessmen he called for a balanced federal budget and a reasonable return on capital. He called for restoration of the farmer to his "natural position of independence" through protection from imports. As for foreign affairs, he alluded to the fact that Hitler had invaded Poland. He criticized Roosevelt for condemning dictators and consoling Great Britain, France, and Poland. "Never again will our people consent to send our boys to fight Europe's battles. . . . We must stay out of war. That admits of no argument." The increasing boom in employment, he claimed, was "based on the blood of other nations." The European war would make matters worse. Recognizing the political value of fear, he warned against un-American activities, which could range from Fascist or Communist saboteurs to Socialist ideas from Great Britain.[8]

The following week he shared a platform in Vienna, Illinois, with the presidential hopeful Sen. Robert A. Taft. Ignoring both the partition of Poland by Hitler and Stalin and Taft's support of the president's "cash and carry" legislation for shipment of arms and ammunition to Europe, he insisted that voters could not trust a president "who talks of war in April and peace in September . . . who advocates neutrality, but tells you that you do not need to be neutral in thought."[9]

As Republican politics developed in 1940, the presidential nomination, of course, went to the former Indiana lawyer Wendell L. Willkie, by that time a figure in the utilities industry and resident of New York City. The phonograph entrepreneur, now residing in Fort Wayne, soon was preoccupied with the Willkie notification ceremony. As a member of the Hoosier delegation to the Philadelphia convention he had voted for Willkie. At Philadelphia he was the man the Hoosiers designated as their Willkie "notifier." Capehart had first met Willkie in New York City in 1939 at a banquet where the two men were speakers. Although their differences were striking, Capehart's career had resembled Willkie's. Both had grown up in or near small Indiana towns, found success as businessmen in New York State, bought Hoosier farms, and become opponents of the New Deal.[10]

Planning the notification ceremony tested Capehart's skills. He had less than a month to arrange for a quarter of a million people to descend upon Willkie's hometown of Elwood (population 10,798) in the central part of the state, northeast of Indianapolis. Capehart and his friend Bausman determined that if the crowd met expectations the event would cost slightly less than 15 cents a person. (The cost actually would be about twice that much, $75,000.) The cost was to come not from citizens of Elwood or admission charges at the ceremony, so Capehart's responsibility was in part to raise contributions from Willkie supporters across the country.

He set up headquarters in Elwood on 19 July and with Bausman and other members of the committee laid out the town, with blueprints drawn of the stage in Callaway Park, public address systems, parking areas, portable restrooms, and concession stands. Working with Mayor George M. Bonham he convinced a reluctant city council to change the town's four major avenues into one-way streets for the day of the ceremony, leading in before the ceremony, out afterwards. He bargained with a local Democrat who desired to rent parking space for an exorbitant $12,000. To avoid the dust that had enveloped the Cornfield Conference, he had the dirt road leading to Callaway Park oiled. He arranged for thirty thousand chairs in front of the speaker's platform, to keep the remainder of the crowd from surging forward as they cheered the candidate.[11]

As mid-August approached, complexities increased. Willkie sent word that he would give his address not in the park but beneath the front portal of his high school building where the words "The Hope of Our Country" were inscribed. But six trees blocked the view of spectators. Capehart had to have some of them dug up and a platform built over the school's front steps, which cost several thousand dollars.[12]

On the morning of the ceremony Indiana state police were reinforced by officers from Indianapolis and Chicago, a traffic control plane was aloft, and Capehart watched anxiously as fifty thousand cars converged upon the small town. Well-wishers waved and cheered as they beheld bunting-draped buildings and the street lights adorned with photographs of the candidate. By early afternoon two hundred thousand people had arrived.

On the day of the notification the most difficult problem proved to be getting the candidate from his train to the high school, to the platform at Callaway Park, and back to his train. Capehart had arranged for Willkie to remain near the railroad station until his escorts—the Indiana University Band and the Culver Military Academy Black Horse Troop—arrived. Everything went as planned, the motorcade of 250 cars moving in from the station, until Willkie's driver approached the high school, forgot to circle within the school grounds, and followed the police escort car back onto the street where a swarming mob engulfed it. Seeing the predicament from his car behind, Capehart got out, summoned half a dozen policemen, and formed a human wedge to rescue the candidate.[13]

Capehart thus had readied everything for Willkie who, although enthusiastic, failed to take advantage of the great moment. He delivered his speech poorly. People nodded as they listened to the candidate's slurred, stumbling words. The speech also failed to express the sentiments of the audience. Capehart would recall that the crowd was silent when Willkie advocated war if necessary to defend America and asserted that loss of the British fleet would be a peril to democracy. Scattered applause came when he said the draft was "the only democratic way" to secure men for defense. The Republican Old Guard was unhappy to hear support for regulation of utilities and monopolies, collective bargaining, minimum wages and maximum hours for labor, federal pensions, old-age benefits, unemployment allowances, and cooperative buying and selling of agricultural products.[14]

As matters turned out, the Elwood notification ceremony was a disaster. Willkie's inadequacy as a speaker was not the only problem. Arriving on the scene in mid-July, Capehart immediately sensed, too, that the town was too small. And the day of notification was a scorcher; cases of heat exhaustion numbered in the hundreds. But the Elwood ceremony's troubles were not the fault of Homer Capehart. On the great day the organizer was his usual omnipresent self, with long-sleeved white shirt and dark tie tucked in at the second button, dark slacks, and straw hat. He waved his cigar from the back of an open police car. He instructed the police and conferred with Mayor Bonham. Capehart, reporters said, was the "busiest man in the city." One spectator was heard to say, "Don't you know? That's Homer Capehart the man who gave the 1938 Cornfield Conference. He is in charge of this affair." By another account Capehart was "ringmaster." Standing in an open car, he was a second center of attention. One vendor kept shouting, "Look folks, there he is, the Great Capehart!"[15]

The presidential election brought satisfaction to the GOP, for Indiana in 1932 and 1936 had given all its electoral votes to Roosevelt. In 1940 the state gave them to Willkie. Hoosiers did elect the popular Democrat Henry F. Schricker as governor. But it was clear that the New Deal tide had turned. Willis went to the Senate. Eight Republican candidates won seats in the House of Representatives. Lesser state offices passed to Republicans, as did control of both houses of the state legislature.[16]

Capehart now returned his attention to manufacturing. He registered his Packard wall boxes under the trade name "Pla-Mor" and began to sell them in his old national sales regions. The Pla-Mor became the leading selector. His West Coast regional manager, William E. Simmons, recalled that "in less than three years Pla-Mor wall box selectors were on booth walls and counters of thousands and thousands of restaurants and taverns all over the United States." There was $150,000 profit from sales of $1.5 million in 1941 and the first quarter of 1942. The company did so well that Capehart took an annual salary of $18,000. His taxable Packard income during

H. Earl Capehart, Jr.

Pla-Mor remote control on display at the Sportsman's Café and Cocktail Lounge, Los Angeles

1941 totaled $71,000, which with farm income of $29,000 came to a total of $100,000.[17] But in the summer of 1941 he realized that American industry could not continue producing for the consumer market. Within a year Packard was making slip rings for tank and bomber turrets, cartridge slides for the M-1 thirty-caliber carbine, and tank battery boxes.

As one might expect, Capehart was no ordinary war manufacturer. In later years he enjoyed telling businessmen at luncheons that "too many people feel that selling and a salesman is a big, fat fellow with a cigar." "We decided," he said, "that we were going to approach this war material business exactly as we would approach any new product that we might decide to manufacture in normal times." Because the Pla-Mor wall box had no military use, he sent his men to the Chicago and Cincinnati district ordnance offices in search of items that Packard might produce. By the autumn of 1941, Packard engineers were working on a design for a slip ring, an electrical-mechanical commutator for the M-4 medium tank. Capehart took two production-model samples to Washington. When the procurement officer at the Tank Division told them that the army already had a source for slip rings, Capehart persuaded the officer to test Packard rings. The result was a subcontract with Inland Manufacturing Division of General Motors (GM) and with the Pressed Steel Car Manufacturing Company. He signed another with GM to manufacture 350,000 cartridge slides for the thirty-caliber carbine, and another with GM and Pressed Steel to make tank battery boxes.[18]

Capehart estimated that the company could produce 32,500 gun slides and 1,000 sets of tank parts a month, using 750 employees in three shifts. By October, Packard reported dollar volume of war production for the preceding quarter at $750,000. The next year Packard would sign an agreement with eight contractors of carbines and tanks for $15 million. For the 1943 fiscal year, Packard refunded over $400,000 in

Sen. James E. Watson, 11 January 1932

excess profits, and by January 1944 its slip rings were being installed in bomber gun turrets as well as tanks. The company eventually boasted 1,000 employees. By 31 May 1942, the declared value of stock was $5 million. By the end of that year Capehart's taxable salary, plus a bonus of 2 percent on net monthly income, totaled $79,367. Income that year, including the farm, totaled $161,438.[19]

The war work did not reduce involvement in the Hoosier GOP. *Hoosier Republican* pictured Capehart as "somewhat retired," but the "somewhat" was illusory. In August 1941, at a meeting of Daviess County precinct committeemen, he announced his candidacy for the seventh congressional district Republican chairmanship. Active in politics for only three years (and with an uncertain party affiliation prior to 1936), he challenged the longest-serving member of the Republican state central committee, seventh district chairman Ewing Emison. The move was extraordinary. Emison had controlled the seventh district for twenty-two years. As leader of the James E. Watson faction of the party for southern Indiana, he had been national preconvention manager for President Calvin Coolidge in 1924 and four years later national committeeman. When Willis defeated Watson in the state convention in 1938, Emison's seventh district chairmanship faced increasing opposition from a group led by Congressman Gerald Landis of Linton. Then after the 1940 election Emison joined Secretary of State James M. Tucker to oust Capehart's friend Arch Bobbitt as state chairman and replaced him with Ralph Gates of Columbia City.[20] Capehart announced his candidacy for district chairman with the stated purpose to remove the county Republican chairman, Elmer Buzan, his grade school teacher and the man through whom he had purchased his farm in 1936. As it turned out, Capehart's challenge failed. The meeting of the Daviess County GOP was two persons short of the thirty-five necessary for a quorum (Emison was absent), so Buzan kept his office.[21]

But only a battle had been lost, and Capehart soon defeated Emison. The task required imagination and would become part of Hoosier Republican lore. At an all-night party in the Canyon Inn at McCormick's Creek State Park, a function to be held the night before the biennial election at nearby Spencer, Capehart challenged the county chairmen to promise him support. The gathering isolated the county chairmen from Emison's men until time for balloting. Emison to his surprise then found that six of eleven chairmen favored Capehart. He had no choice but to withdraw, and Capehart was elected unanimously.[22]

The elections for representatives to Congress and to the state legislature held in November 1942 became another Capehart triumph. Acting in the role of district chairman, the manufacturer from Fort Wayne visited every county in his district. He was a veritable whirlwind of activity. At each stop he dined with local Republican officials. He urged party workers to set up committees to register voters, telephone them in the days before the election, and provide transportation and babysitters. When everything was over Capehart's seventh district had voted Republican, as in 1940. Hoosier Republicans indeed elected their entire slate of congressmen and dominated both houses of the state legislature.[23]

All the while Capehart was busy with war work. Having received $2.5 million of contracts, the Packard Corporation was becoming well known. A manpower shortage existed, so Capehart undertook to persuade his employees not to change jobs. Harmonious relations between employer and employees, he said, were "perhaps the outstanding factor in meeting the problem of man power and thus increasing production in industry." Recorded music, rest periods, and a social and benevolent organization—the Pla-Mor Club—became parts of company policy. He used money from vending machine profits to purchase flowers for sickrooms and gifts for employees who entered the armed services. He held meetings to inform people about production. He had a group insurance policy, a system of loans of up to twenty-five dollars, free legal service, and encouraged workers to speak directly to company executives. The atmosphere of openness, he felt, stimulated company spirit. A faulty tank slip ring in battle, he told employees, could cost the life of a worker's son. His employees won for Packard the army-navy "E" award for excellence and efficiency.[24]

The secret of his record, Capehart again said, was salesmanship. In a speech entitled "From Music to Guns," which he often gave during this period, he would lift an M-1 carbine for all to see. This, he said, was the gun carried by paratroopers and combat officers, a "very, very interesting gun." Pointing to the cartridge slide manufactured by his corporation, he explained how it fired sixteen thirty-caliber bullets with one squeeze of the trigger. His audience enthralled, he explained how Packard had used principles of private enterprise to convert to war production. "If we are going to build a better city and a better state and a better nation and a better world," he orated, "we business and professional men, we producers and wage-earners are going to have to do the job." "Salesmanship," he told his audience, was the "art of getting the other fellow to do what you want him to do." "I have a very, very strong conviction and feeling," he continued, "that every man and woman in this world, regardless of what business they are in—whether they be doctors, lawyers, bankers, manufacturers, salesmen, foremen of factories, ministers, school teachers"—would be successful "in direct proportion to their ability to sell." For persons who did not have this ability, Capehart told them how to acquire it. "I have never found a better way to learn the art of selling than to take an active part in civic and community affairs and in politics . . . [where] you are dealing with people that are not working for you . . . getting them to do the job through for the jobs' sake, for the love of the work." He introduced this set speech at a meeting of the Indianapolis Rotary Club in the spring of 1943, and by midsummer was touring the state, speaking to civic groups and luncheon clubs. Between May 1943 and March 1944 he spoke to almost ninety clubs and service organizations.[25]

Early in the summer of 1943 talk began to be heard about the United States Senate. The GOP state secretary, Claude Billings, recalled that "we were looking for fresh faces. We had to have them in order to amount to anything. Capehart had enough money that you didn't have to worry about who was going to help finance the campaign."[26]

Capehart was willing and gradually approached a decision. Visiting Washington, he made social calls upon Hoosier politicians: Congressmen Landis and Earl Wilson and former senator Watson. He dined with Republican National Chairman Harrison E. Spangler. An advertising executive from New York, William H. Rankin, began assembling material for a biography; Capehart, he told reporters, was available for interviews. The suspense virtually ended in mid-July at a meeting of southern Indiana Republican leaders when Capehart announced that "if I decide to be a candidate, which I am quite certain I will—I will appreciate your help."[27]

All the while he spelled out his political philosophy: "As a businessman I see everything through the eyes of business—jobs and private employment." In the parlance of midwestern conservatism he referred to the pre-depression economy: "We all went hog-wild in the twenties and forgot that the true values of a nation are in farms and homes and good roads and going factories and the minds of inventors, and not in stocks and bonds that at the very best can only stand for a chance to share in the wealth the real assets of the country produce." Faulty thinking, he asserted, had led Americans to go "hog-wild in the other direction—having somebody from Washington come out and tell us every little thing to do." Billions of dollars were spent to "convince us our national driver's license ought to be taken up, when all we needed to do was pick ourselves up and get back on the right road and run our private enterprises for ourselves a little more carefully than before." Only if the government would allow initiative could the nation be prosperous in peacetime.[28]

Capehart told a group of Indianapolis Republicans in the weeks that followed that the New Deal cure for the depression had been worse than the disease. It had brought "bureaucratic planners" who "would have us believe . . . Communistic principles, many of which already have been discarded by the Russian government." He was referring to the relief payments under the New Deal, attacks against business, high taxes, and foreign entanglements. Businessmen and soldiers, not the Democratic leadership in Washington, were achieving victory for the Allies.[29]

In this manner the businessman from Fort Wayne and North Tonawanda began to turn his attention from problems of manufacturing and sales to those of the state and nation. It was an odyssey from business to politics. And was it all calculation, a meticulous concern for his personal future, a measurement of the opportunity in Indiana that lay open to a man of Capehart's qualities?

While such calculations always were a part of the jukebox executive's approach, there is every reason to assume that Homer Earl Capehart entered politics because he believed in his country's future. Certainly he beheld the opportunity in Hoosier politics; it was a testimony to the incompetence of his state's GOP that other politicians had not seen what the Republicans could do in Indiana, if they put imagination to the task. But Capehart was no mere opportunist. American businessmen had always seized opportunities, that was what had made them successful. In matters that promoted his state's and the country's political future, however, he was an unabashed patriot. He believed that the country needed prosperous businesses and business efficiency in government. A great series of changes had come upon the political scene in the 1930s. Some of these he approved. Others seemed questionable, and some of them downright dangerous. He believed that if he entered politics, he could do something to set the Hoosier state and the nation on the right course.

6

Running for Senator

CAPEHART knew the race for senator in 1944 would not be easy. In Indiana a candidate nearly always had to prove himself, and as a later writer remarked, the larger the electorate the more rigorous the proving. Moreover, the farm boy from Daviess County did not have the right qualifications. Without experience, he was running in a highly political state. The typical Hoosier candidate for the Senate was white, male, Protestant, a graduate of Indiana University, a veteran, and active in the American Legion, community and civic groups, and the local party organization. A lawyer, often county prosecuting attorney, he had been a member of the legislature. Before being elected governor he had served as lieutenant governor. Few politicians were considered eligible for the Senate until they had served as governor.[1]

Capehart's rival for the Republican nomination possessed more of the proper credentials. James M. Tucker of Paoli had grown up in a Republican family, graduated from Indiana University and its law school, and enjoyed a long record of party service. He had worked his way up to state chairman of the Young Republicans. He had served three years as Orange County prosecuting attorney. In 1938 he was elected

Acme Photo

Lieutenant James M. Tucker, November 1943

secretary of state, the only Republican to win a state office that year. Reelected in 1940, he led the ticket. Through control of the Bureau of Motor Vehicles he became a prime dispenser of patronage. As chairman and keynote speaker of the 1942 state convention he had helped his candidate for secretary of state, Rue J. Alexander, defeat Capehart's candidate, James M. Knapp. He also was a veteran. In fact, he had been wounded while serving as executive officer of a landing ship at the amphibious assault at Salerno.[2]

The district chairman from Daviess County nonetheless moved ahead. At his announcement dinner in Washington, Indiana, on 14 January 1944 the president of Capehart's high school class, John Hastings, introduced him and recalled that Capehart's relatives had been among the earliest settlers of Pike and Dubois counties. He spoke of the farm, school, knowledge of people, of selling and manufacturing, and, most important, the extraordinary successes in business. He exaggerated when he told of trips to foreign countries that gave "a knowledge of world affairs." When it was Capehart's turn to speak, the candidate did his very best. America must win the war and bring the boys home, he said. In the postwar era the nation should lead the world out of chaos and confusion "by setting an example" and by showing that "our Representative form of Government gives people more liberty, more individual opportunity and more prosperity than any known form of Government in the history of the world." He called for repeal of every law that "discourages and interferes with business." Foreign markets, he averred, could assist sales far beyond the domestic market. He said that "neither our own people nor the people of foreign countries can buy more unless they are working for good wages . . . jobs make prosperity."[3]

The candidate's proposed program was admittedly vague. The concerns of his depression-period speeches—appeals for good working conditions, reasonable hours, job security, unemployment insurance—were notably absent, wartime prosperity having brought a return to the issues of abundance and reduced government intervention in the economy. He emphasized the need to end federal bureaucracy and regimentation and lower the national debt. He favored a "better method of distribution," high farm prices, and government help in seeking industrial uses for farm products. He called for a nonpartisan policy of care for disabled soldiers and an equitable solution for problems of the aged.[4]

Organization of the 1944 senatorial campaign left nothing to chance. First of all, because he needed a majority of state convention delegates to give him the nomination, Capehart put his campaign manager, State Senator Robert B. Miller of Bloomington, to work. Miller arranged that in every county a loyal supporter reported to a district manager, responsible to one of two regional managers: Harry Youse, lumberman-politician from Markle in the northern part of the state, and Newton Ringer, Republican Legionnaire from Sullivan in the south.[5]

Three other procedures characterized the campaign for the nomination. After party members elected convention delegates in the May primary, Capehart wrote each delegate asking support and inviting him or her to lunch at a restaurant in the delegate's county seat. As soon as the letters reached their destinations he began his tour. Whenever a delegate failed to come to lunch as arranged, the candidate would either telephone or write on the stationery of a local hotel, expressing regret at having missed the delegate and again asking support. He also held meetings with county officials. At a typical meeting in New Castle he said he would "be responsible only to the people of Indiana and not to any political bosses." He referred to himself as the son of a farmhand, credited his country for his rise, and promised to help veterans get jobs. He also attended to the financial needs of the county chairmen, the "pivots" of local organization. Rumor circulated that Capehart gave between $10,000 and $20,000 to the winning pro-Capehart faction in the Marion County (eleventh district) primary. He apparently contributed to eleventh district chairman Jim Bradford's campaign and to campaigns of other leaders.[6]

By the end of May the candidate had won several delegates in northern Indiana, including the fifth district, Kokomo, and the populous first district, Lake County, along with endorsements from the *Indianapolis News* and *Fort Wayne News-Sentinel.* He obtained support of the Indianapolis Republican leaders Joseph J. Daniels and Robert W. Lyons.[7]

Indiana state conventions usually fell on suffocatingly hot days in June, when delegates met at the state fairgrounds, and the convention of 1944 occurred on 3 June. Because Ralph Gates's bid for governor was uncontested, the nomination of a candidate for senator became its principal concern. Actually, there were two Senate nominations: one for two months, to fill out the term of the deceased Sen. Frederick Van Nuys, and the other the regular six-year term.

The outcome of the contests for the Senate was at first uncertain. Convention delegates, however, under their county chairmen (who in those days before voting machines cast all votes orally), liked to vote for a winner. The former state senate president, William E. Jenner, of Shoals, Indiana, whom Capehart had supported for governor four years earlier and was now an air force captain stationed in England, was the party's selection for the short term and Capehart for the long.[8] Everything thereafter came off as Capehart's floor managers planned. The representative of the first district yielded to that of the seventh district, and Hastings made the nominating speech. L. L. "Woody" Jenner, father of the short-term nominee, and Agnes Todd of the eleventh district also made nominating speeches. Allen County (Fort Wayne) set the trend by giving 45 votes to Capehart and 25 to Tucker. The vote was close until Marion County (Indianapolis) cast 194 votes for Capehart and 18 for Tucker. Then St. Joseph County (South Bend), with 71 delegates, went for Capehart,

Bretzman Photo

Captain William E. Jenner, 23 August 1944

Indianapolis Times

Ralph F. Gates, gubernatorial candidate, May 1944

and Tucker stopped the roll call, conceding defeat. The tally ended with 1,004 for Capehart and 584 for Tucker. Capehart had obtained majorities in nine of eleven congressional districts, losing only in Congressman Charles Halleck's second district and Congressman Earl Wilson's (and Tucker's) ninth.[9]

Capehart's nomination in 1944 aptly illustrated the workings of Indiana Republican politics. While he had done everything he could to line up the districts, and newspaper editors had supported him, he also received help from forces that were narrowly factional. Gates had promised to support Tucker, but the latter's attempt when he was secretary of state to obtain Arch Bobbitt's ouster as state GOP chairman had stirred opposition from county chairmen and license branch managers. They now approved Bobbitt's support of Capehart. Having accepted the nomination for governor, Gates dared not alienate anyone, and so Tucker was on the outside. The final blow to Tucker may have come two weeks before the convention when Gates realized that a public endorsement might bring a party split.[10]

Tucker charged Capehart with improper campaign financing. His wealth had enabled him to enter politics. Capehart, it was rumored, had purchased Marion County. At the Democratic state convention in late June, keynoter Ray J. Madden called for the Marion County prosecutor to seek a grand jury investigation. Capehart hastily charged that Tucker had accepted "Democratic 2 Per Cent Club" money to help finance his preconvention campaign. Tucker called Capehart's charge "ill-advised, . . . utterly false and malicious . . . wholly unwarranted." Tucker listed his expenditures and their sources, adding that he had made no contributions to county or district organizations nor had "anyone in my behalf." He had spent $2,865.30, of which $1,000 had been his own money. Capehart reported expenditures totaling over $14,500. He may have spent much more, considering that his reported personal contribution was $13,595.[11]

Happily, no one discovered any illegality in Capehart's expenditures. In those days there were few restrictions on the money a candidate could spend. State law set $12,050 as the maximum but that did not include postage, circular letters, telegrams, telephones, printing, advertising, publishing, traveling, board, convention assessments, or personal expenses. Less stringent federal law set a ceiling of $25,000. What Tucker hated to admit was that his opponent had worked harder. Capehart's early start, many loyal friends, lack of enemies among party leaders, and statewide organization had placed Tucker at a nearly impossible disadvantage.[12]

The GOP nominee's opponent in the November election was the popular Gov. Henry F. Schricker, a formidable campaigner elected to the statehouse in 1940 despite the Hoosier landslide for Wendell Willkie. A banker and former publisher of the *Starke County Democrat* at Knox, Indiana, he had been state senator and lieutenant governor.[13]

Victory, Capehart realized, depended on three intangibles and one contingency: dissatisfaction with the New Deal; the extent to which Hoosiers associated Schricker with such dissatisfaction; Capehart's image as a party regular; and—the contingency—the coattail effect of a Thomas E. Dewey victory in Indiana. Capehart had to seize every advantage, especially the contingency. "When I go to the United States Senate," he told his audiences, "I shall vote as a Republican to organize the Senate along Republican lines, I shall vote as a Republican to uphold Constitutional government . . . to give wholehearted support to every constructive program proposed by a great Republican President—Thomas E. Dewey."[14]

The New Deal issue required some obfuscation. Hoosiers never had believed in all the New Deal measures that assisted city people in the metropolises, such as New York and Chicago. They did not much care for agricultural proposals that assisted the American South, which was not their part of the country. The state was incorrigibly conservative, and much of the talk that accompanied New Deal measures, talk of a new course or new courses, of how capitalism was bad, or how corporations had afflicted the country, fell on deaf ears or else aroused antagonism in Indiana. At the same time Capehart was no doctrinaire and easily had seen the need for many New Deal measures. The campaign made clear that he had moved away from his Constitution Day "American dream" speech about economic opportunity. Assertions to the contrary, he was campaigning on a program far from laissez faire. He said again that government had to help farmers. "Prosperity starts with the farmer and it cannot be extended to other branches of our society until he is prosperous." His program included higher price supports for hogs, a soil conservation service, more farm credit, a "sound" tenant program, and a fair price for farm commodities to "offset the hazards which nature adds to the whims of public demand." As for industrial workmen, he said, they deserved employment at the highest possible wage, but "good working conditions" meant collective bargaining free from "exploitation" from labor racketeers. He favored unemployment compensation.[15]

Having accepted some government intervention, Capehart found it helpful to portray Schricker as a raving New Deal radical. He accused him of having received money from a "Communist-New Deal slush fund."[16] Schricker, he asserted, "gave the people of Indiana definite word that he was in favor of the fourth term and that he would support the policies of the sixteen-year candidate. He cannot support those policies without subscribing to the policies of Sidney Hillman, Earl Browder, and their communist fellow-travelers. . . . It is difficult to understand how my opponent, in view of his Hoosier training, can subscribe to, endorse and support such un-American principles of government."[17] Newspaper advertisements warned of enemies of "our Amer-

Indiana State Library

Gov. Henry F. Schricker

ican way of life" who "permeated" churches, schools, labor organizations, and of course the administration in Washington.[18]

The New Deal-Communist combination was out to destroy private industry and free American labor, Capehart told a crowd in populous, steel-manufacturing Lake County. "Certainly in this war our sons are not fighting our enemies in order that our government can be taken over by some radical, or by communists or socialists."[19] Emulating Dewey, he beheld the possibility of an American president supported by the Soviet Union. Taking his positions, true or not so true, Capehart in 1944 needed to be careful about his position in the party. He was, after all, aspiring to a seat in the Senate and did not possess the usual qualifications, and his opponent had contended that he had bought the nomination. He needed to point with pride to his party regularity, that he was a dedicated member of the Hoosier GOP. He indeed was attempting to revive the party, but he was not, of course, trying to change it. The Hoosier party system had made the state into what it was. Carefully and cautiously, he touted himself as a regular. He also hoped to benefit from riding on Dewey's bandwagon. In 1944 President Franklin D. Roosevelt was again running, but this time for an unbelievable fourth term. Dewey was young and forceful and gave evidence of being a winner, especially in conservative Indiana.

Convinced that once again organization would play a great part, Capehart canvassed the state. As a sales manager it had been his habit to find someone else to drive. Sitting in the back seat, he could take a snooze or watch the scenery. In 1944 it was not uncommon for him to have his driver stop if he saw a farmer out in a field, and taking a couple of campaign leaflets he would climb a fence, walk over to the man, introduce himself, and ask about the prospect for rain, some new kind of seed corn, or what was the best tractor or plow. Happy for a break, the farmer would remember the pleasant time with a plainspoken politician. Arriving in a county seat, Capehart would pass out leaflets at the local barbershop or poolroom. In one town he spotted a middle-aged woman walking alone on the other side of the street. He crossed, tipped his hat, introduced himself, handed her a leaflet, and declared: "I know you're too young to vote, but it's a pleasure to meet you just the same." If no one was in sight he would go into a store and say: "I wonder if we could get some people to gather for, maybe, a sandwich and cold pop?" The tactic usually worked. He visited all ninety-two Indiana county seats.[20]

The possibility of defeat was omnipresent until Schricker's assets at last began to turn into liabilities. The governor's popularity had been enormous and had come from a variety of sources. The son of poor German immigrants, Schricker had benefited from an ability to give speeches to German voters in fluent German. He had many friends in the legislature and again would be elected governor in 1948. Unfortunately, during a war against Germany his immigrant lineage lost its attractiveness. Then the left-leaning Political Action Committee of the Congress of Industrial Organizations threw its support to him, in effect cooperating with Capehart's strategy, and he lost conservative votes among his party's membership.[21] Dissension in the party leadership also hurt; party boss Frank McHale, corporation lawyer, former state commander of the American Legion, and former state chairman, was on the outs with his successor Fred P. Bays. McHale believed Bays to blame for party setbacks since 1938. He may have inspired the national committee to write Bays in October 1944 asking why President Roosevelt's name was "seldom mentioned"; this at the time when German voters were condemning Bays for aligning himself with Roosevelt.[22]

Capehart won in November, but the race was close. He trailed the national and even the state tickets. Of 1,651,385 votes cast for senator, he received 829,489, or 50.2 percent.

Dewey received 875,891 or 52 percent of 1,672,091 votes cast for president. Gates won the governorship with a margin of 46,581. Jenner won by 81,833. Dewey's margin over Roosevelt in Indiana was 95,224; Capehart defeated Schricker by only 21,723. Capehart received fewer votes than Dewey in all Hoosier counties, fewer than Gates in all but six, and fewer than Jenner in all but two. It is important to note, however, that he had defeated the most formidable state Democratic candidate.[23]

Capehart's shrewd analysis of the three needs and the contingency of his campaign had paid off. And by making a county-by-county canvass, going personally to the voters, he had done his very best. He estimated he shook one hundred thousand hands. He suffered defeat in four of the six urban industrial counties. He carried Allen County (Fort Wayne) by 52.6 percent, but lost in Lake County (Gary-Hammond) with 37.7 percent, in Marion (Indianapolis) with 49.2 percent, in Vanderburgh (Evansville) with 44.5 percent, and in Vigo (Terre Haute) with 44.8 percent. In the rural areas he made up these losses.[24]

7

First Term

UPON TAKING office in Washington, D.C., in January 1945, Capehart necessarily was a question mark, even to those many Hoosiers who had voted for him. They could not be quite certain what he would do once a member of the Senate. There was a distinct possibility that his interests and concerns, as exhibited on the hustings, would come to nothing in the upper house. He looked not unlike a cartoon character of his time, the reputed "Senator Snort." Snort, to be sure, was drawn more like the southern perennials of the 1920s and 1930s than the representative of the Hoosier GOP. Liberals enjoyed portraying the senator as a modern-day Babbitt, and there was some truth to the characterization. The former jukebox tycoon looked the part: his two-hundred-pound, large-boned, five-feet-eleven-inch frame was poorly concealed by his expensive dark blue or gray suits.

Appearances and portrayals to the contrary, Capehart worked hard at being a senator, something he generally enjoyed. His supposed prototype, Snort, always was drawn with a huge book, *The Old Rocking Chair Got Me*, on his desk. This was not Capehart's mode. Far from it. He arrived at his office (Room 140 in the Senate Office Building) at 8:00 A.M.,

Acme Photo

Homer E. Capehart being sworn in as senator by Vice President Henry Wallace, January 1945

an hour before his staff appeared. When Congress was in session he remained until after dark, seven days a week.[1]

He was aware that his business experience and lack of training in the law had not prepared him for the duties of his new office. Soon impatient with the hours of haggling, hairsplitting, and compromise in committee meetings, he confined his attention to strategy and direction of his work. "I loved organization," he later remarked. "I loved administration."[2] His staff helped him respond to constituents, lobbies, and the press. His administrative assistant was Ray Donaldson, a young Harvard-educated attorney from Washington, Indiana, who had just completed four years in the army. Charles Egenroad, political writer for the *South Bend Tribune*, became the senator's sounding board, devil's advocate, and alter ego and could write a speech or press release that the senator could read without mispronouncing the words.[3]

He retained control of his business assets in Indiana but could not supervise them as he wanted. He turned over the presidency of the Packard Corporation to its general manager, William Struby. As chairman of Packard his annual salary of $50,000 was an important supplement to his $12,500 as senator. The end of the war brought reconversion of Packard to coin receptacles and jukeboxes. The former proved a profitable item. Decreased profits forced cuts in jukebox production, and within two years the company stopped making them.[4] He turned over his farm to his brother-in-law, Byron Haskins. The war had assisted farm prices. When European farmers got back into production, American farms languished, including the Capehart farm.

All the while he sought to alter the Truman administration's approach to government. He scorned the Employment Act of 1946 for its principle of making the government responsible for economic stability. A gesture, he called it. Obtaining maximum employment, production, and purchasing power was, he said, the task of private enterprise. The government should confine its economic activity, he said, to balancing its budget. Seeing no difference in financial matters between an individual, a corporation, or a nation, he decried spending by any of them that exceeded income. Similarly, he decried government intervention in labor disputes. Such activity again involved the president in matters best left to private enterprise and labor. "The only substitute for our private enterprise system is that the government will own and operate all businesses, and we will all work for the government. Once we all work for the Government we will find that the worst private industry boss is better than the best governmental boss."[5]

He feared inflation, but when President Harry Truman called a special session of Congress in October 1947 to regulate some commodities and food, ration scarce consumer products, and, if needed, control wages and prices, Capehart opposed the plan. "Inflation cannot be curbed, except temporarily, through rationing and price control. Price control, even if continued forever, would not produce a single pork chop, a single bushel of corn, a single bushel of wheat. Those things are produced back home, on the farms." He wondered when his Democratic colleagues would realize that "we do not grow corn on the floor of the United States Senate."[6]

Still, Capehart was no extremist. Like businessmen in other eras, he accepted what he considered appropriate government intervention in the economy. He saw continuing need for aid to farmers, schoolchildren, veterans, the elderly, the unemployed, and blacks. He supported better distribution of commodities, industrial uses for farm products, and measures to conserve soil, provide farm credit, and protect tenants. He continued to advocate a Veterans Economic Development Corporation, "preplanning" public works, unemployment compensation, social security, and markets overseas. He supported federal aid to education.[7] He voted for the Housing Act of 1949. This is not to say that he advocated federal support for important groups of Americans: urban slum and ghetto inhabitants, the physically or mentally handicapped, chronically ill, rural poor, migrant workers, or technologically unemployed. He believed that the federal government should not pass laws against racial segregation in the South. But he was no racist. He favored antidiscrimination proposals in federal housing legislation, voted for extension of the Fair Employment Practices Commission (FEPC) and, after proposing an amendment to meet some southern objections, for cloture to halt a filibuster in 1946 over a proposed permanent FEPC.[8]

What liberal critics called lack of compassion for the have-nots in American society resulted from a different approach by the Hoosier senator to federal policy, based on different assumptions about the nature of the problem, which he believed was short term, economic, and often outside Washington's jurisdiction. With inflation surging in December 1946, he introduced a bill to freeze prices. He was willing to help labor; he considered labor part of the "team" that had made possible the Allied victory during World War II. In March 1945 he had asked President Franklin D. Roosevelt to increase wages in the steel industry, "more in line with the current cost of living." Later he advocated increasing the minimum wage and conceded that it was "a terrible indictment of American business that such a bill is necessary."[9] Intervention in labor-management relations was acceptable, if the public welfare otherwise would be hurt. When trainmen and engineers walked away from their jobs in May 1946, causing the most complete transportation stoppage in the nation's history, he introduced a wide-ranging bill; the president could take possession of railroad property or services essential to public health, safety, or security.[10]

And, of course, Capehart's brand of conservatism appealed to prosperous, white, small-town dwellers and farmers, business and professional people, and suburban taxpayers, many of whom voted for him. They supported his opposition to a cabinet-level Department of Welfare because they agreed it would bring "additional federal regulation and control" and "deprive the individual, private agencies and local communities of their opportunities." National health insurance "must necessarily result in impersonal care and treatment" and could cost the taxpayers as much as $4 billion a year. He opposed early versions of the Wagner-Ellender-Taft Act providing loans for slum clearance, housing, and rent subsidies for low-income families. His constituents, he knew, agreed that "one of the greatest human rights we have, is that of owning property . . . whatever we care to do with it. Under rent control millions of people are denied the right to do with their property as they see fit."[11]

Hoosier voters especially admired his defense of American business. Capehart, one lobbyist said, "had a greater consciousness of . . . the need for businesses to make profits than almost any senator whom I have ever known."[12] The Taft-Hartley Act was, he believed, the most important legislation passed in the Eightieth Congress. He liked its provisions forbidding union coercion of workers and outlawing jurisdictional strikes, the closed shop, and secondary boycotts. As chairman of the Newsprint and Paper Shortage Subcommittee of the Special Committee to Study and Survey the Problems of Small Business Enterprises, he encountered the postwar shortage of newsprint. The subcommittee drafted legislation to make newsprint purchasers immune from antitrust prosecution. It suggested that the Federal Trade Commission investigate jobbers and asked the Department of the Interior to open the Alaskan forest pulpwood reserves to development by private capital.[13]

The senator's most publicized activity in behalf of businessmen came in the spring of 1948, after the Supreme Court declared illegal the basing point system in the cement industry. The system had allowed manufacturers to charge a set price for the same product—cement, steel, metal products, sugar—shipped to buyers within a given radius from a city designated as the basing point. The Court's decision left shippers without price guidelines. Capehart listened to industry representatives who insisted that the system was the best available. The only way to avoid price discrimination and encourage competition, they said, was to require each buyer in a basing point area to pay the same freight charge. Otherwise, each producer would have a monopoly because of his lower freight charge in his area.[14] Congressional Democrats saw the opportunity to publicize Capehart's pro-business outlook. Congressman Wright Patman asserted that "selfish, greedy, big interests . . . in favor of maintaining a basing point pricing system, had exerted mesmeric powers on Senator Capehart," surrounding him with an "invisible fog." Capehart described Patman as "almost a perfect demagogue."[15] The Indiana senator lost his chairmanship of the basing point subcommittee when the Republican Eightieth Congress ended in December 1948. By then its hearings probably had brought a less militant stance by the Federal Trade Commission, whose counsel, Edwin L. Davis, admitted he did not see a violation of the law in every basing point case.[16]

Capehart assuredly was a solid Republican. The years as a businessman had convinced him that private enterprise was necessary for prosperity. Depression and war were over. The federal government, consequently, had an interest in business efficiency, increased investment, and employment in real work. Three of his bills to encourage the aviation industry—a study of causes and characteristics of thunderstorms, a measure to limit liability for deaths and injuries caused by aircraft, and a bill to record ownership of aircraft engines—became law.[17] The millions of Americans who continued to live in poverty, discrimination, malnutrition, or the problem of growing numbers of people who lived inside large cities—unresponsive, rural-dominated state legislatures and the flight of tax money to the suburbs—were not his concern. Responsibility of the federal government, he felt, was not to remedy injustice or distress for individual Americans. The task of Washington was to help businessmen build a strong national economy and, with it, a higher standard of living.[18]

As a member of the right wing of the congressional GOP during the presidencies of Truman, Dwight D. Eisenhower, and John F. Kennedy, Capehart in fact seemed the archetypical midwestern conservative. Considered one of the senators least likely to cooperate with the administration on any issue by President Truman's counsel Charles Murphy, Capehart in an average year, 1949, supported the Republican majority on votes 88 percent of the time—ranking with his colleague William E. Jenner's 91 percent and Nebraska Sen. Kenneth Wherry's 92 percent. Sen. Robert A. Taft, "Mr. Republican," scored only 79 percent. The average of all Republican senators was 76.3 percent. The Truman program, Capehart told his Senate colleagues, was unattractive. "I speak very little on the floor of the Senate," he said, but "I am delighted and anxious to vote against the great majority of the President's program."[19] His record, of course, made him a member of the congressional bloc of midwestern Republicans and southern Democrats that had begun to dominate Congress in 1938, during the Roosevelt era, and determined the fate of much legislation during the Truman and even the Eisenhower years.

Conservative that he was, Capehart was not as far to the right as his Republican colleague, Jenner. Slender and handsome, Jenner had longed to be governor of Indiana and considered Washington an alien place. As GOP state chairman in 1945 and 1946, he had depended upon the organization to run his campaign. An abundance of energy and a sharp-tongued humor made him a formidable orator. He frequently combined a warm smile with recrimination. His strident but earthy style attracted supporters. But he could be, as one reporter put it, "completely irresponsible and intellectually vacant." He contributed mightily to the atmosphere in which Sen. Joseph R. McCarthy of Wisconsin later embarked on a hunt for Communists in the American government. He described Gen. George C. Marshall, architect of victory in World War II, as a "living lie" and "a front man for traitors." Marshall, he claimed, was "either an unsuspecting stooge or an actual co-conspirator with the most treasonable array of political cut-throats ever turned loose in the executive branch of the government."[20]

The former phonograph entrepreneur, in contrast, understood the need to respond to the problems of the time. Heavy-set, round-faced, and affable, Capehart won votes by traveling the state and county roads, making appearances on courthouse squares, and shaking hands. His speeches were often predictable. Capehart, Jenner said, told people what they wanted to hear. But the views of the man from Daviess County were far less simple and never ludicrous. He admired General Marshall. And after sharing in the anticommunist talk that set the scene for the red-baiting campaign of McCarthy in the early 1950s, he moved away from it.[21]

The frequent public identification of Capehart's views with those of Jenner arose from the fact that on many occasions early in their careers the two men had supported each other and continued to do so for a while in the Senate.[22] Seeking to be a party regular, Capehart had assisted with Jenner's bid for the governorship in 1940 and was grateful for Jenner's assistance in 1944. Seeing the advantage of standing with him whenever possible, in 1946 he helped Jenner to his first full term in the Senate, a contest the Hoosier party leader won by a margin of 150,000 votes.[23]

But his desire to throw in his lot with Jenner got Capehart into trouble during the election campaign of 1948. As the year began, everything seemed fine. Capehart was elected president of the Indiana Society of Washington, and a Capehart-for-President Club formed in Indianapolis, a spontaneous organization that, though flattering, Capehart discouraged. He became vice-chairman of the Republican Senatorial Campaign Committee. He urged support again for Thomas E.

Indianapolis Times

William E. Jenner campaigning for the gubernatorial nomination, 28 September 1939

Indianapolis Times

William E. Jenner and Homer E. Capehart in the Senate

Indianapolis Times

William E. Jenner with Sen. Joseph R. McCarthy

Indianapolis Times

Gov. Ralph F. Gates, 28 February 1945

Dewey, and there were rumors that he would be the new secretary of commerce.[24] The trouble came when Jenner decided once more to seek the governorship. Although Capehart supported the decision, Gov. Ralph Gates announced that he favored Walter Helmke of Fort Wayne, who charged that the senators were trying to control state government. In the resulting confusion Helmke and Jenner both lost the nomination. Hobart Creighton of Warsaw, speaker of the general assembly, became the Republican candidate and then lost in the November election.[25]

Dewey's defeat convinced Capehart that while he must be wary of Jenner, he needed also to sharpen his conservative image. He remembered that Dewey was "a little aloof, was not particularly easy to approach, and was confident he was going to win." The New York governor had tried to obtain liberal votes from the Democrats. The senator's chances for 1950, he decided, would hinge on his ability to distinguish himself from such Republican moderates.[26]

The first term established Capehart as a suitable representative of his Indiana constituents. Conservative, but not reactionary, he spoke for common sense as Hoosiers understood it. He spoke also, it is clear, for himself, for his roots in rural southern Indiana, for the enduring values of hard work, and for the virtues of seizing the moment. Considering that the attraction of the New Deal had begun to wear thin in the late 1930s, and even more so that life in the United States, not least in Indiana, had changed remarkably with the prosperity of the Second World War, the program of Homer Capehart had almost a national attraction. His conservatism was in the mainstream of postwar America. When he began to turn more conservative, however, he would almost depart from the dictates of judgment, and for a while toward the end of his first term, it now is evident, would move in the wrong direction. Eventually his good judgment would overcome this problem.

8

Midwestern Conservatism

DURING the years immediately after the end of World War II, down to the time of the Korean War, the country enjoyed a newfound prosperity of peace, but underlying everything was a fear that the tranquility could not continue without some respite from communism. Indeed there was feeling that world communism (the phrase became fashionable at that time) might overwhelm democracy. Homer Capehart felt these winds of fear, and because he was basically a conservative he did not even have to trim his sails to deal with them as he began his efforts to win reelection in 1950. He needed only restate his views over the many years: that those Americans who helped themselves and worked hard would triumph, so long as their country allowed them thus to fulfill the American dream. The need for the country, he believed, was a conservative stance, assuredly toward the citadel of world communism, the Soviet Union, without, and toward Communists and fellow travelers within. It turned out to be a successful approach.

Capehart clearly stood for nationalism in foreign affairs. From his entry into politics in the late 1930s he had been a nationalist. As World War II began to appear on the horizon he had opposed "any entanglements of this country in European politics" through either adherence to the League of Nations or the World Court. Hitler's invasion of Poland in September 1939 seemed not to faze him. Americans would not send their boys to "fight Europe's battles." For a while Pearl Harbor had transformed Capehart's views. He was one of sixteen freshman senators who signed a letter to President Franklin D. Roosevelt supporting the United Nations Organization (UN). His first Senate address had called upon Americans to "assume new obligations in the world economy . . . new duties with regard to organizing, and perhaps enforcing, peace in the postwar world." Foreign and domestic interests were "so interlaced," he remarked, "that the line between them is no longer distinct."[1] But he was suspicious of wartime diplomacy and only a week after Roosevelt's death

Photo by Zeigler, 3131 Signal Photo Platoon

Homer E. Capehart with machine-gun squad in Italy, 4 June 1945

in mid-April 1945 Capehart condemned the conferences at Tehran and Yalta, inserting in the *Congressional Record* a diatribe about secret diplomatic agreements and asking that the organizational meeting of the United Nations in San Francisco be open to the public and have complete reports to the Senate.

In the next years Capehart's positions on foreign affairs became ever more conservative. He was certain that the Soviet system was hostile to American purposes. In meetings with Gen. Dwight D. Eisenhower and Prime Minister Winston S. Churchill, he discovered that "no unity of plans had been achieved with Russia" and that the latter nation controlled an area that had produced 45 percent of Germany's food. "Berlin time," he said, was changing to "Moscow time," and narrow-gauge railroads were changing to Russian broad-gauge. The food of Eastern Germany could not be "shipped across the demarcation line." Stalin had demonstrated bad faith.[2]

He saw little need to assist Western Europe. After returning from a five-week, eighteen-thousand-mile European tour with members of the Interstate and Foreign Commerce Committee, he desired no assistance across the Atlantic. The Allies should "insist on a form of government in the nations of continental Europe which would create a so-called middle class and raise the standard of living." In 1946 he attempted to reduce the proposed $3.75 billion loan to Great Britain that administration officials considered the " 'key' to American foreign economic policy." He advocated $1.5 billion, enough to finance that country's adverse trade balance.[3]

Similarly, the world economy did not seem to him an impressive arrangement. When the reciprocal trade bill of 1945 passed Congress, he remarked that only if the administration was more interested in the welfare of America than in the welfare of the world, "the act will work." If American labor competed with slave labor of other parts of the world, "the act isn't going to work." He wondered where the United

Homer E. Capehart, Winston S. Churchill, Ambassador John Winant, and Senators Albert Hawkes, Burton Wheeler, and Ernest McFarland, London, Number 10 Downing Street, May 1945

G. Felici

Homer E. Capehart and other senators at the Vatican in 1945

States would "get the money" and "when we will stop going into debt." Only reluctantly did he vote for the measure that assured American participation in world trade and helped bring postwar economic recovery, the Bretton Woods agreement.[4]

To be in favor of the United Nations Organization might appear an exception to his conservative nationalism, but closer scrutiny shows that his support for the organization was weak at best. He believed it offered little advantage to the United States. The UN had rallied the Allies against the Axis, but he worried that it could interfere with the American national interest. He voted for the Charter, but only because he believed "no man has a right to vote against anything, no matter how feeble it may be, if it is aimed to eliminate war."[5] But he opposed the Baruch Plan for United Nations control of atomic energy. He disliked it even with its veto-proof, on-site inspections. If the atomic bomb was going to be in the hands of an international organization, he said, "It will be there for the purpose of being used for emergency demands—which may be against us."[6]

He supported military aid for Greece and Turkey but not the global commitment of the accompanying Truman Doctrine. American capacity to extend aid to other nations was limited, peace best assured by a strong United States. "Russia is preparing for war against the United States," he said, "but America can prevent World War III before the shooting starts," by production at home and minor assistance for rehabilitation abroad.[7] The need for aid had been occasioned by failures of Democratic foreign policy. "Only a few months ago the Russians were our great partners and allies. . . . Now we are told they . . . are trying to gobble up little Turkey and Greece, . . . the American people are confused, and it is easy to understand why."[8]

When President Harry Truman in early 1948 asked Congress for appropriations for the Marshall Plan, Capehart would have none of it. "No nation was ever as well prepared for war," he told an audience at the Sons of Indiana of New York award dinner. "We have 14,000,000 trained men from World War II who can be called back into the Army tomorrow. We have the atomic bomb, the largest Navy in the World, a fine Air Force and the same tools, dies, and jigs that we had in World War II. The real threat," he charged, was "timid leadership, leadership that wants to appease." He joined a five-member Republican strategy board (chaired by Sen. Joseph Ball of Minnesota) to explore "various west and midwest Republican ideas" for amending the European Recovery Plan. "Government administrators in this country," he said, "would make mass purchases with government funds which they would then turn over to European governments." His proposed substitute was a "businessman-to-businessman program" with a lower price. This measure failed, and he voted against the Marshall Plan. The following year he attempted unsuccessfully to cut the plan's second-year appropriations from $5.8 to $3 billion. He would not vote to "make a success out of state socialism" in Great Britain and Western Europe with the dollar earnings of a free enterprise system.[9]

He favored American adherence to the North Atlantic Treaty in 1949 but not the concept of collective security. He supported the measure that tied the United States to defense of nations outside the Western Hemisphere in peacetime because he thought the treaty would allow the United States to be the "policeman of democracy." The United States should establish military bases in North Africa and other points. He did not favor distributing arms to European nations. If the North Atlantic Treaty Organization had "contained an arms program I would have voted against it," he said. "I am opposed to sending arms to Europe."[10]

The United States, he assumed, could largely withdraw to its own shores and at the same time impose peace abroad. Victory over Germany, he forgot, had made the Red Army liberator of Eastern Europe. At the Tehran and Yalta conferences the United States had necessarily recognized Eastern Europe as a Soviet security area. Stalin knew Americans were weary of war, possessed few nuclear weapons, and were unlikely to use them. American military demobilization meant freedom to impose his will in Eastern Europe and perhaps elsewhere.[11] Instead of blaming Roosevelt and Truman all the time, Capehart might have tried to focus public attention on realities of the postwar world: the need to consider ways of living with a Soviet presence over the long haul. American setbacks were, after all, less the result of mistakes by American presidents than of forces beyond their control.[12]

It was at this time that Capehart also began to distance himself from postwar bipartisanship. As vice-chairman of the 1948 GOP Senatorial Campaign Committee, he watched Truman defeat Gov. Thomas E. Dewey of New York, after the Republican candidate refused to attack the president's foreign policy. Capehart rebelled against the bipartisan leadership of Arthur H. Vandenberg. He joined six other Republican senators against the confirmation of Dean Acheson as secretary of state. Partisanship, he believed, was the only answer.[13]

Incidentally that also meant salesmanship. "I don't care how good our program is, or how good our record in Congress is," he told a group of Republicans in Omaha, "until this party learns how to sell itself, it will never win another election. I've been in business 25 years, and I wouldn't hire one of you as a salesman. If I wanted a sales manager I'd hire Harry Truman."[14]

At this juncture, with the loss of the presidential election in 1948, and his feeling that following Vandenberg had proved a complete waste of time, Capehart began to combat not only international communism but communism at home. He threw his support to anyone, such as Sen. Pat McCarran of

Associated Press

Homer E. Capehart with Senate Republican Steering Committee. Sen. Robert A. Taft is in the middle.

Nevada, who would seek to buttress the country's internal security. He even accepted the expostulations of the junior senator from Wisconsin, Joseph R. McCarthy, when that demagogue discovered the internal Communist issue in 1950.

Years earlier, the Indiana senator had begun looking in the direction of anticommunism at home—internal security. At the Cornfield Conference in 1938, he had said that only private industry would keep the United States from resembling a Socialist, Communist, Fascist, or Nazi country. Later he beheld "subversive threats to private enterprise." The New Deal would have people believe in communistic principles. Gov. Henry F. Schricker, he said, supported "the policies of Sidney Hillman, Earl Browder and their communistic fellow travelers." Immediately after World War II, Republican advertisements warned of enemies to "our way of life" who "permeated" labor organizations, schools, churches, and the government in Washington. William E. Jenner joined him in condemnation of anti-American, "even anti-God" Communist supporters "of the man who wants to be President for sixteen years." Campaigning for Jenner in 1946, he said two ideologies were clashing. "One represents Communism and more and more government regulation; the other stands for free enterprise and a minimum of regulation. These ideologies cannot be mixed."[15]

Then came serious and startling postwar discoveries of Communist espionage in the United States and elsewhere. During the war a Soviet atomic spy ring had operated in Canada, and its existence, revealed late in 1945, moved anti-communism to center stage. Capehart was alarmed. During the Senate debate in early 1947 over confirmation of David E. Lilienthal as chairman of the new Atomic Energy Commission, he said that "atomic power should not be entrusted to one about whom there is the slightest question of doubt concerning his leanings toward a central or dictator-type government."[16] Hearings in the House of Representatives in 1949-50 and two trials of the former New Deal official Alger Hiss seized attention of newspaper readers. Hiss had been deputy director of the office of special political affairs in the State Department and a member of the department's delegation at the Yalta Conference. His brother was a member of the law firm of Secretary of State Acheson. In August 1948 two former Communist party members, Elizabeth Bentley and Whittaker Chambers, testified before the House Un-American Activities Committee (HUAC) that they had known him as a fellow Communist. President Truman called the hearing a red herring, an attempt by Republicans to distract attention from failures of the Eightieth Congress. When Hiss sued Chambers for slander, the latter brought new evidence. The statute of limitations had expired for espionage, but the Justice Department proceeded with an indictment for perjury. The first trial ended in a hung jury in July 1949; the second trial would find Hiss guilty on 21 January 1950.

The senator from Indiana proceeded to exploit the Hiss conviction. Voting against the nomination of Acheson as secretary of state, he had described him as one of the Hisses and other "world lawyers." When the Soviet Union detonated a nuclear device, in August 1949, quicker than American officials had expected, and the Communists of Mao Tse-tung took over the government of China, Capehart accused Truman of a cover-up.[17] The president, he said, had lied to the American people when he used the term red herring. Reciting from the trial transcript and from records of the HUAC investigation, Capehart espied "a secret conspiracy to deceive and mislead" in which "others may not have been guilty of espionage, or even of perjury, but they are definitely guilty of laxity, negligence, and disloyalty." He listed four occasions, beginning in February 1947, when the president had discounted Communist infiltration or denied he was protecting Communists. Truman, he said, "should now come forth and apologize." Acheson should resign.[18]

Capehart, it is now clear, was helping open an unfortunate period in American history that would be named for his senatorial colleague from Wisconsin. On 7 February 1950 Capehart spoke out on the Senate floor. He insisted that the Democrats were no different from British Socialists, Communists, and other left-wingers. The administration, he said, had allowed Socialists to creep "in the back door" and take over practically all of Asia while the United States was "spending billions upon billions of dollars to stop the Communists from going into Europe." Two days later McCarthy told a Republican meeting in Wheeling, West Virginia, that "he had the names of 205 Communists in the State Department." Later that month it became known that a British nuclear scientist, Klaus Fuchs, had turned over to Russian agents details on the manufacture of atomic bombs. What difference, Capehart asked, if people accused by McCarthy had a few good points when, after all, some of them were Communist sympathizers and fellow travelers?[19]

The national mood was moving to the GOP, and the outbreak of war in Korea was for Capehart a stroke of political fortune. "Our job," Jenner said shortly thereafter at the state GOP convention, "is to save America, and we dare not fail." The state's veterans and conservative press rallied to the party. The American Legion, fearing that the leaders of the Communist bloc would take advantage of American weakness, called for wartime mobilization and enforcement of laws against Communists in America. The *Indianapolis Star* in endorsing Capehart accused the Democrats of appeasing the Soviets and protecting the Hisses.[20] Jenner charged that the Korean War completely discredited "the global Truman doctrine." Capehart complained that Americans were "standing alone" in Korea after having furnished European nations "billions and billions of dollars." With twenty-six other senators, he signed a remonstrance composed by Sen. Ralph Flanders of Vermont asking for "total engagement of our psychological and spiritual force" to bring the Russian people into contact with the American people in hope of avoiding the "appalling expenditure of life and treasure with which we are faced." Capehart scorned Truman's description of the Korean War as a police action. It was, he said, war. "We are fighting Communists." Congress in September passed the McCarran Internal Security Act. It required registration of Communist groups, emergency detention of persons likely to be spies or saboteurs, and tightened laws against sedition and espionage.[21]

All this did not mean the Hoosier senator could be confident of reelection. The Democrats at their state convention nominated Assistant United States Attorney General Alexander Campbell to run against him, an excellent choice considering the national concern about Communists. A native of Fort Wayne, member of the Indiana University board of trustees, and trustee of the First Christian Church of Fort Wayne, Campbell was the strongest possible candidate on the internal security issue. He had prosecuted eleven leaders of the Com-

Indianapolis Times

Alexander Campbell

Indianapolis Times

Alexander Campbell waves to crowd as he accepts the Democratic nomination for the United States Senate, 27 June 1950.

munist party for advocacy of violent overthrow of the government and had presented evidence when the New York grand jury was investigating charges against Hiss.[22]

Capehart's first moves to secure reelection had come the year before when he joined Jenner to take control of the Hoosier Republican party. The youthful chairman of the eleventh district, former chairman of a Republican veterans group and favorite of the Capehart-Jenner wing, Cale Holder, became the new state chairman. The Capehart and Jenner people then organized the state, opened a Citizens' Committee for Capehart, and announced a fund drive. Activities had begun in July 1949, and the senator's official announcement came at the GOP kick-off dinner in mid-October. Sen. Kenneth Wherry of Nebraska spoke in his behalf at the Indiana Republican Editorial Association's meeting. The *Chicago Tribune* of 28 January 1950 celebrated the Hoosier senator. Robert A. Taft inserted a laudatory editorial in the appendix of the *Congressional Record.* Capehart's political coffers began to fill.[23]

The incumbent campaigned furiously. His wife and children saw him only late at night, after he came home exhausted, or when they met him at the airport or took him to a train.[24] A reporter who said he covered ten thousand miles through Indiana in fifty-five days did not exaggerate. He made appearances in practically every county. His outlays are unknown, but spokesmen from both parties admitted he spent considerably more than Campbell. The Capehart organization had spent $90,000 before the candidate was even nominated.[25]

His winning margin in November 1950, it turned out, was 103,278 votes, much better than the 60,000 he expected. He took 53.3 percent of the vote, up from 50.2 percent in 1944. He increased his margin in nearly half of Indiana's counties where he received votes of farmers and white-collar workers. Some observers blamed "unimaginative and ineffective" Democratic leaders. Others pointed to rain and concluded

F. Clyde Wilkinson Photo

Homer E. Capehart and his Senate staff celebrate his fifty-third birthday on 6 June 1950.

H. Earl Capehart, Jr.

Homer E. Capehart buys campaign issue of newspaper, 1950.

that Republican party faithful had gotten the voters to the polls before the statewide downpour. But it was clear that hard work had combined with anticommunism to bring victory. Local concerns did not outweigh the international issue.[26] The administration's decision to send troops to Korea and Gen. Douglas MacArthur's success with the Inchon landing in September 1950 rallied support, but by election day consumer prices had begun to rise and the People's Republic of China had begun to send troops across the Yalu River into Korea.[27]

And so one thing led to another during the years after World War II. The senator's inherent, basic nationalism had come to the fore. He saw the troubles in foreign policy and concluded that it was the new foreign foe that lay at the center of many of them. But he refused to say that all of the nation's woes were coming from abroad and as the years passed came to believe that internal subversion—the same sort of forces that McCarran and then, with much more ability to mislead Americans, McCarthy had become concerned about—was working its malign will against the hopes and dreams of his fellow Americans. Capehart did not need to change the foundation of his outlook. He was pursuing the same Americanism, the same nationalism, with which he had grown up in the Republican Indiana of the turn of the century. A combination of self-reliance and hard work, he maintained, had taken the nation so far, ever since the American Revolution, and this was now threatened by Communists abroad and at home.

In this respect, it is fair to say, McCarthy in 1950 and in subsequent years, down to his death in 1958, did not come to meet Capehart. The Indiana senator went out to meet him. Capehart was overjoyed to discover a man who could fight the Communists, and having worked in tandem with the flamboyantly anticommunist Jenner to gain control of the state GOP, took the Wisconsin senator at his word, rather than looking to see if behind the word was anything except ambition, recklessness, and the ability to make the headlines day after day.

How much was the Indiana senator responsible for the excesses that marked this saddening period in American politics? Capehart understood the rhythm of American politics. He knew an issue when he saw it. No one can deny that Capehart contributed to McCarthy's rise, and before Senate colleagues censured him in 1954, McCarthy gravely damaged civil liberties, discrediting dozens of fine civil servants. He embarrassed the nation.

It is worth noting, however, that Capehart was different from the Wisconsin senator and for that matter, from Jenner, who became McCarthy's principal lieutenant. The senior senator from Indiana was a political conservative. Anticommunism was a response, albeit an unfortunate one, to his fear that the United States was losing its position in the world and that Americans one day might lose their way of life. The diplomatic and economic uncertainties of the mid-twentieth century brought an understandable effort by the GOP to distinguish its platform from that of the Democrats as a means of reestablishing itself and its philosophy as a source of national policy. As part of this undertaking, Capehart seized upon anticommunism as a negative but in 1950 an effective means of harkening to an idealized past, the rural Indiana of his youth when, he remembered, life was hard but the resourceful individual survived.

9

A Republican President

BY THE beginning of the 1950s opposition to the executive branch had become the accepted stance for Republicans in Congress. For years, since 1933, the GOP had been on the outside looking in. White House Democrats were careful to include Republicans at receptions for visiting dignitaries and occasional meetings of congressional leaders. But on major issues they sought cooperation, not advice.

As a member of the Senate during what turned out to be Harry Truman's last two years, 1951-52, Capehart let it be known that he had stopped cooperating. Perhaps partly for this reason only three bills that he wrote or of which he was coauthor became law. They established the strength of the Marine Corps at four hundred thousand, set up a federal mortgage administration, and gave Korean War veterans preference in federal housing. To his joy, however, the Senate voted against much of the Fair Deal. This did not mean that Capehart was doctrinaire in his opposition to the president. Prices began to soar, less because of Capehart's opposition to price controls than from a running argument between the executive and legislative branches.[1] President Truman, Capehart said later, was "solid in many respects, a man who fought for what he believed in." The fighting quality appeared when the president refused to ask for price and wage controls and then failed to use those authorized by Congress. The Capehart amendment to the Defense Production Act allowed prices to remain at their high January 1950 level, but the president threatened to veto it. Capehart thereupon sent a letter to the White House expressing support for modified wage, price, and rent controls. Truman brushed off the letter as a "strictly political document" intended to support the Capehart amendment. Capehart obtained support from his colleagues and the amendment remained.[2]

The Korean War reinforced Capehart's opposition to bipartisan foreign policy. As early as March 1950 he announced he would "reserve the right . . . to oppose or to favor any piece of legislation that comes to this floor."[3] Gen. Douglas MacArthur's dismissal, Capehart said in April 1951, was "the worst—in a long list of mistakes that have resulted from the stultifying international policies laid down by Dean Acheson and European influences." He supported all MacArthur's proposals, including a blockade of mainland China, allowing Chinese Nationalist troops to invade the mainland, and bombing Chinese staging areas in Manchuria.[4] Following MacArthur's congressional address in which he said melodramatically that old soldiers "never die" but rather "just fade away," Capehart was asked to join Senators Robert A. Taft, Hubert H. Humphrey of Minnesota, and Herbert Lehman of New York for a radio debate. During the broadcast, when the two Democrats reaffirmed support for the president, Capehart accused them of Communist sympathies. When the show was over Humphrey angrily approached Capehart. "I deeply resent this type of vilification, character assassination, and malicious unfounded statements," he said. "I want no more of it." Caught off guard and perhaps instinctively sensing a threat, Capehart lost his composure, grabbed Humphrey's arm with his left hand, and clenched his right fist menacingly. Lehman, coming from behind, pinned Capehart's arms, and the Hoosier senator leaned forward, pushing Lehman backward. Taft then stopped the scuffle. The incident left Capehart unrepentant. He voted to limit United States ground troops in Europe to four divisions and to cut economic aid by $250 million. He continued to call for Acheson's resignation.[5]

The counterpart of Capehart's opposition to Truman's foreign policy was his support for Taft. Capehart admired Taft's intellect and disliked the ambition of Gen. Dwight D. Eisenhower, a newcomer to the GOP. Nomination of Eisenhower would mean "the end of the Republican party," he said. Eisenhower had failed to take a stand, was an amateur in politics "like Landon and Willkie," and approved Democratic foreign policy as had Thomas E. Dewey (including "appeasing the Russians in Europe" and "abandoning Chiang Kai-shek to the communists in Asia"). "Unless we nominate Taft the New Deal is going to take over the Republican party."

When Eisenhower defeated Taft at the national convention, Capehart was disappointed but recovered. He saw too many advantages in a Republican president, even one with whom he disagreed, and announced he was "ready to do anything to help the whole ticket."[6] Putting the party first thereupon paid dividends. Eisenhower swept Indiana by 335,000 votes. George N. Craig, former national commander of the American Legion and pro-Eisenhower Republican candidate for governor, won by 233,701. William E. Jenner, who did his best to appear an Eisenhower supporter despite his failure to reconcile himself to the general's defeat of Taft, won by 109,436, defeating Henry F. Schricker.[7]

During the two Eisenhower terms, 1953-61, Capehart reached the height of his national influence. Since he appeared to be one of the major obstacles to the new president's domestic legislative program, this might have seemed surprising. Along with George W. Malone of Nevada, John W. Bricker, Herman Welker of Idaho, Joseph R. McCarthy, and Jenner, he also seemed to oppose a considerable amount of

Eisenhower's foreign policy. Less apparent is the fact that while he and Eisenhower were never close, they developed a mutual respect. The president set out to win over the Taft wing of the party, and Capehart had a capacity to forget political squabbles. Although Capehart scored eleventh from the bottom among GOP senators in support of the president's legislative program, he became increasingly pro-Eisenhower, and during his first term eighteen of the Hoosier senator's bills, amendments, or resolutions became laws.[8]

Several issues had seemed at first to separate the new president from the Hoosier senator. Eisenhower had favored reciprocal trade and foreign aid. He had called for extension of several New Deal programs, including unemployment insurance and public housing. He proposed to use the power of government to prevent economic downturns, asking the chairman of the Council of Economic Advisers to keep in "a high state of readiness" plans for preventing recession, including projects for soil conservation, public power, roads, public buildings, defense construction, and shipbuilding. But to the demand of Republicans in the Senate for lower taxes through a $10 billion cutback in the defense establishment, Eisenhower had responded that "the American public wants security ahead of tax reduction."[9]

The most striking difference between Eisenhower and Capehart was their outlook on the activities of Senator McCarthy. The president considered McCarthy a distasteful and even dangerous character. After a loyalty review program in which hundreds of government employees lost their jobs, Eisenhower in the spring of 1954 took another action. The Republican party, he said in a letter to his friend Governor Craig, "has got once and for all to make up its mind whether to follow the ludicrous partnership of the Old Guarders and the McCarthyites (one of my friends called it a 'marriage of convenience') or whether it is going to stand behind the program of the Administration and the middle-of-the-road phi-

Associated Press/Dwight D. Eisenhower Library

Dwight D. Eisenhower and Republican Senate leaders, 3 February 1953

Courtesy Dwight D. Eisenhower Library

Dwight D. Eisenhower signs the Housing Act of 1954 on 2 August 1954.

losophy in which we firmly believe."[10] The president undertook to bring about McCarthy's political demise. "The McCarthys, the Jenners, the Brickers and the rest of them can do what they want as far as I am concerned," he said. "I'm going to get this Republican Party of ours to be progressive or else—and that's that!"[11]

Perhaps testimony to the effectiveness of the man in the White House, Capehart gradually warmed to the president, who had not mentioned Capehart's name but no doubt considered him at the time to be one of "the rest." Eisenhower held regular meetings with congressional leaders, worked through his White House congressional liaison team with committee chairmen and leaders, and showed willingness to compromise. The feeling was reciprocal. Capehart always had been attracted to successful men and so, for that matter, had Ike. After Eisenhower's victory in November 1952 the senator had sent congratulations. He complimented the general's first State of the Union address as "a forthright statement of sound policy in every respect." The president had made a "grand start," he said, and would provide direction in which the American people "can have confidence." Eisenhower's Republicanism, after all, was not much different from Capehart's Cornfield Conference proposals or his 1944 campaign program. The Hoosier senator even went beyond what the president wanted in calling for standby wage and price controls in case of another emergency like the Korean War. He supported the Public Housing Act of 1954.[12]

It was therefore not difficult for Capehart to move away from McCarthy. Capehart had far more in common with Eisenhower than he did with the Wisconsin senator. Cooperation between Capehart and Eisenhower stemmed from the fact that both men were essentially conservative. Both advocated reducing taxes, spending, and the bureaucracy, looked to a balanced budget, and sought open access to markets and materials. In the period from 1953 to 1957 the *New*

Republic recorded no progressive votes by Capehart on key issues. But as one historian has shown, Eisenhower never really clarified the value he claimed to attach to liberal issues. Enabling each person "to do more to look after himself," he said, "restores the feeling of self-dependence and self-respect and enhances the value of the individual as an active citizen of our country." His discussions of economic action to prevent a depression were only prudent planning for an emergency. Like Capehart, he condemned "left-wingish, pinkish influence" in American life. Both men were in this sense nationalists.[13]

Capehart was by outlook and experience a builder rather than an obstructionist. This did not mean he had abandoned anticommunism. "We cannot condemn the one man who people think is trying to do something about Communism," he said. "They are not going to stand for that." None of the Senate Republican leaders spoke out against McCarthy until after the November 1954 midterm elections in which the GOP lost its majorities in both houses of Congress. Capehart joined the GOP Senate leadership in voting against censure of McCarthy. But now he criticized the methods of the senator, deciding that McCarthy had "gone overboard," that he had "some little substance to go on, but spoiled it all by his tactics." "I don't know that I ever turned against him [McCarthy]," Capehart later recalled. "I just discontinued supporting him and helping him."[14]

The similarity of view between the president and the Hoosier senator became particularly important after Taft died of cancer in July 1953 and Capehart took his place on the Foreign Relations Committee. Soon Eisenhower was enlisting Capehart in support of a commission on foreign economic policy headed by Clarence B. Randall. The president dispatched his brother Milton and a delegation of officials on a thirty-six-day tour of ten Latin American republics in June and July 1953. Any changes in American policies and programs, he felt, should contribute to "the meaningful unity we all desire." Milton Eisenhower's thirty-five-page report of November 1953, later the basis for his book entitled *The Wine is Bitter*, included recommendations for cultural exchange, economic cooperation, and a consistent trade policy.[15]

Capehart became enthusiastic about the United States' trade with Latin America. He and his friend, Sen. Burnet R. Maybank of South Carolina, ranking minority member of the Banking and Currency Committee, had introduced a resolution to study the possibilities for expanding trade. The resolution passed unanimously, and Capehart began organizing a congressional study of trade and ways to finance it. "Basic to the sound functioning of international trade," he said, "is international monetary stability and an effective banking structure."[16]

One thing led to another. A citizens advisory committee of 131 leaders in banking, manufacturing, labor, and farming, headed by Roy C. Ingersoll, president of the Borg-Warner Corporation, donated research staffs to the Capehart project on trade and held a two-day conference in Washington. The committee submitted reports to Ezra Solomon of the University of Chicago School of Business, who prepared a draft report. Other officers of the committee were Alan H. Temple, executive vice president of the National City Bank of New York; Robert C. Graham, Capehart's childhood acquaintance in Washington, Indiana; Vance Brand, vice president of Borg-Warner; and William Simon of Washington, D.C. Members included Henry P. Bristol, chairman of the board of Bristol-Myers; Eisenhower's friends Gen. Lucius D. Clay, chairman of the board of Continental Can, and Paul G. Hoffman, chairman of the board of the Studebaker Corporation; Victor Emanuel, president of Avco Manufacturing; Allan B. Kline, president of the American Farm Bureau; John L. Lewis, president of the United Mine Workers; and George Meany, president of the American Federation of Labor.[17]

Indianapolis Times

Homer E. Capehart shakes hands with Ambassador Victor Andrade of Bolivia.

Associated Press/Dwight D. Eisenhower Library.

Dwight D. Eisenhower shakes hands with Homer E. Capehart after signing bill authorizing an Air Force Academy, 1 April 1954.

To find out for himself what Latin Americans thought were the blocks to commerce, Capehart gathered a thirty-member entourage that included Senator Bricker (chairman of the Interstate and Foreign Commerce Committee); Sen. J. Allen Frear, Jr.; and Congressman Brent Spence, chairman of the House Banking and Currency Committee. The group departed on 18 October 1953 and traveled until 9 December. The group traveled twenty-one thousand miles, visited fifteen countries, and attended ninety-three meetings with businessmen and sixty-three conferences with foreign officials, not to mention inspection trips. Capehart enjoyed himself immensely. There was even a glimpse of the aftermath of an attempted overthrow of the Bolivian government and forty anxious minutes stuck between floors in an elevator in Cochabamba. Capehart told the Chamber of Commerce in Buenos Aires that the peace and prosperity of the world depended on trade because "trade means jobs and jobs mean trade." The biggest problem of any country, he said, was "keeping its people employed, keeping them busy, rendering services, manufacturing, processing and producing things. That's the substitute for war, in my opinion." Upon his return he presided over the meeting of his citizens advisory committee, one of the "biggest gatherings of prominent businessmen under one roof at the same time in the history of Washington." After he returned he was for all practical purposes the leading congressional expert on Latin America.

The report of his mission to Latin America was published in 1954 and went beyond Milton Eisenhower's report of the previous November. Manufacturing in Latin America, the report said, had increased by two-thirds since 1946. Virtually all the hemisphere's countries desired to be self-sufficient in basic industry. The difficulties were a shortage of private capital that tended to involve government in business, producing a trend toward socialism, maldistribution of wealth, and low per capita income. There was lagging agriculture, inadequate

Indianapolis Times

Homer E. Capehart in 1954

power and transportation, and declining and unstable prices for raw materials. The result was import controls and frequent dollar shortages. The committee discovered resentment that both European allies and former enemies had received American gifts. The group also discovered that low-priced European goods, ironically, had a competitive advantage over American products. It recommended purchase of more Latin American goods and services, maintenance of tariff rates for five years or more, and no import quotas. It also encouraged private investment, credit, and fair prices. Americans, the report said, should improve living standards in the southern hemisphere.[18]

Working with the Randall Commission, the citizens advisory committee received high marks from the White House. Following the recommendation of the report, the Export-Import Bank in 1955 lent $300 million to Brazil to provide foreign exchange and approved a loan application for a public water system in Asunción, Paraguay.[19]

Capehart was pleased. The Latin American diplomatic corps, including more than a dozen ambassadors, accepted his invitation to attend an Indianapolis 500-mile auto race party on 30 May 1955 that the *Indianapolis Star* called the "most important event of the Speedway social season." The Latin Americans reciprocated in July by inviting twenty-five hundred guests (three hundred of them Hoosiers) to the Aztec Gardens of the Pan-American Union in Washington to honor Capehart. At this second occasion Mary Martin sang "Back Home Again in Indiana." There were two fountains of pink champagne, two fifty-foot-long tables of food, fifteen bartenders, and a ten-piece orchestra. Helen Hayes, appearing in Washington at the time in *The Skin of Our Teeth*, attended with playwright George Abbott. The eighty-eight-year-old Sen. Theodore Francis Green, Rhode Island Democrat, danced the mambo. A reporter noted that Capehart stayed in the receiving line for three hours. He had achieved international prominence.[20]

Capehart's Senate bills to help businessmen also were successful. During his second term his legislation assisted the sale to private industry of twenty-eight government-owned synthetic rubber plants and helped set up the Small Business Administration, transferring to it the lending authority of the Reconstruction Finance Corporation. He introduced no new programs, but he expanded old ones, especially those concerning veterans, servicemen, and housing. Eighteen of his bills became law, including those expanding home improvement loan guarantees of the Federal Housing Administration (FHA) and defense and military housing assistance, and altering the housing act to provide more military housing. A Capehart amendment increased the maximum amount of federally sponsored mortgage insurance from $1.5 billion to $3.5 billion. Finally in 1954 the House version of his bill to establish an Air Force Academy passed.[21]

His most time-consuming and valuable domestic undertaking was investigation of corruption in the Federal Housing Administration. The purpose of the FHA, established in 1934, was to encourage financial institutions to lend for mortgages and home improvements. As chairman of the Banking and Currency Committee Capehart brought to light consumer fraud, windfall profits for contractors, and high rents for unsuspecting apartment dwellers. His probe had begun after disclosure that the head of the Housing and Home Finance Agency had opened an investigation of fraud in FHA programs. Capehart received from the White House a list of persons who the Internal Revenue Service believed had received windfall profits. After a preliminary hearing in Washington in April 1954, Capehart took his subcommittee on tour of seven of the nation's major cities, conducting thirty-three hearings in forty-three days, with more than a thousand witnesses.[22] The subcommittee found the cost of construction often was much less than FHA-issued mortgages. Instead of returning the savings, builders received windfalls, and rents were set high because they were based on estimates. One

Indianapolis construction firm received $686,583 on an investment of $24,180 in seventeen FHA-insured apartment projects that cost the government $12 million. The subcommittee estimated that nationally as much as $1 billion had been taken in windfalls. The parallel Senate and executive branch investigations accomplished their purposes, and Eisenhower reported in October 1954 that the attorney general had obtained two hundred indictments. Twenty-one federal officials in the FHA were dismissed by the administrator.[23]

The Hoosier senator soon found himself spokesman for White House-supported legislation.[24] The military housing program for armed forces personnel in 1955 actually carried his name. It was one of the 1955 housing amendments, replacing the so-called Wherry program. Under the latter, private developers had built and operated family housing adjacent to military bases. The government leased land, guaranteed mortgages through the FHA "military housing insurance fund," and assured reasonable rent. Authorized in 1949, the Wherry program was having difficulty because of shifting military personnel requirements. Eisenhower was concerned that the government was losing money on Wherry housing, at the same time making a few people "very rich." The Capehart program, in effect until 1962, allowed construction by private contractors using FHA-guaranteed private financing. Instead of remaining in private hands, housing was operated, maintained, and amortized over twenty-five years by the military. The armed forces became landlords, but the program resulted in decent, low-cost "Capehart" housing for servicemen and their families.[25]

By 1956 the Hoosier senator's service to the administration and his nation overshadowed his earlier isolationism and diminished the stigma of association with McCarthy. At the outset of the Eisenhower administration when the Hoosier senator voted in favor of the Bricker Amendment requiring

Indianapolis Times

Homer E. Capehart and wife Irma, 10 March 1955

that nontreaty international agreements have congressional approval, the president may have had doubts about Capehart. And he probably was displeased when Capehart voted against increasing military assistance. But the Hoosier senator's vote in favor of the Formosa Resolution of 1955, authorizing the president to use force to protect the island from Communist invasion, was in keeping with his later support of the president's foreign policy, as was his rebuke of McCarthy's opposition to the Geneva summit conference of 1955.[26] Capehart in 1956 opposed Jenner when the latter criticized Eisenhower for failing to condemn the Soviet Union's suppression of the Hungarian uprising as he had condemned the simultaneous British, French, and Israeli invasion of Suez. "Death, destruction and deportation" in Hungary was deplorable, Capehart said. But "it was more in the nature of civil war . . . a clash between two brands of communism," while Egypt was a "clear-cut case of aggression from without." The distinction was not as clear as he claimed, but his main point was a valid one. Senators, he said, should support the administration in trying to "avoid conflict by settling controversies through the peaceful means provided by the United Nations."[27]

In such ways, out of conviction and increasing admiration for the president, Capehart prepared his campaign for a third term. In 1950–52 he was virtually a reactionary. He had a sense of Communist conspiracy. Then new political circumstances, common sense, and a commonsense president changed his mind and led him to considerable achievement.

10

Third Term

THE EISENHOWER fifties were a good era both for the country and the GOP, a time of almost no inflation and of large economic growth. The Republican party flourished, and Eisenhower easily won reelection in 1956. The Hoosier senator also ran well that year.

Return of Indiana's senior senator for a third term occurred in part because of the popularity of the president. The Republican president swept Indiana by 398,903 votes, helping elect a Republican governor, Harold Handley, by 227,475, and nine Republican congressmen out of the state's eleven. Capehart carried all the industrial counties: Allen, Lake, Marion, St. Joseph, and Vanderburgh, this despite the fact that in the past, industrial Indiana had not admired him.[1]

Victory came also because Capehart was becoming a GOP moderate. The Republican right wing, he said, possessed "no program and no ideas. They are just against; while Ike and the rest of the Republican party are in a position of a receiver going about rebuilding a bankrupt company into a going concern." "I did not know Ike four years ago. I know him now. And I have learned to like him because of his capabilities and his grasp of the American system."[2]

His Democratic opponent, too, was no match for the erstwhile farmer-salesman-businessman. Capehart defeated another farmer and a secretary of agriculture in the Roosevelt and Truman administrations, Claude R. Wickard: sixty-three years old, a native of rural Carroll County, and a ruddy-faced individual who, one reporter said, "looked like a farmer." After growing up in a small town similar to Washington, Wickard had gone to Purdue and returned home to enter politics in 1933 as state senator from Carroll, Clinton, and White counties. The following year he joined the Agricultural Adjustment Administration in Washington and in 1940 succeeded Henry Wallace as secretary of agriculture when the latter became the Democratic nominee for vice president. He left the cabinet in 1945, eased out by Truman. To the surprise of the president, Wickard had asked, outright, for the Rural Electrification Administration. He served out the balance of the Truman years in this minor post.[3]

Capehart presented himself as a farmer, if only to offset Wickard's claim, and rested on his record in the Senate for sponsorship of farm legislation. He even advanced new programs to assist the farmer. He made an interesting proposal for farm-product marketing that called for $100 million a year for research to discover ways to double the market for farm products.[4] The senator pointed to the boom in demand for citrus fruit that resulted from the quick frozen-food process and talked about a grain-alcohol substitute for gasoline. One hundred million dollars, he said, was less than one-third of the $365 million expended that year for storing surplus crops and ten times the $12 million then expended annually for research by the Agriculture Department. Current programs, he said, concentrated on cutting production instead of "boosting the demand so farmers can produce all their land will yield." He proposed an "international food community board" to distribute surplus grain "to the needy throughout the United States and the world." An industrial agricultural products administration would explore the use of farm products in industry, make contracts with research institutions, and operate pilot plants to develop manufacturing processes

Courtesy Dwight D. Eisenhower Library

Homer E. Capehart and Dwight D. Eisenhower at the GOP national convention in 1956

Indianapolis Times

Homer E. Capehart, Irma, and grandson Jimmy Pearson, 1956

to the point where it would "be profitable for private industry to take over." It would pay for inventions and expand research funded by the United States Department of Agriculture at such places as Purdue University.[5]

All the while he did what he could to hold down squabbling within the Hoosier GOP. "We will win in 1956," he told friends, "if we can get back that old spirit of unity and co-operation." Virtual warfare had been raging since 1952 between Governor Craig's faction and that of Handley and Jenner. Because of his move into the Eisenhower camp there was even some danger of his being caught on the losing side at the state convention. His strategy was to declare his candidacy early, steer away from controversies, and obtain the services of John Hastings as chairman of an independent Citizens' Committee for Capehart. Hastings announced that the committee would raise "possibly $100,000" and pointedly said he did not believe Craig nor any other Republican would run against Capehart. Meanwhile the senior senator sought Jenner's support. He attempted to bring the factions to a harmony luncheon at the Columbia Club. Such dignitaries as state chairman Alvin Cast and national committeeman Ralph Gates were present.[6] To make absolutely sure that he would win in November, Capehart waged a whirlwind campaign, traveling to every locality, urban and rural, that he could, shaking every possible hand. Once again he became a political whirling dervish. In fifty-six days he drove, rode, or flew ten thousand miles. The campaign began in August with a watermelon feed for fifty Republican candidates and officials on the lawn at the Capehart farm. Dressed in dark blue slacks, striped tie and blue shirt, the candidate drove a hay wagon filled with such notables as Handley, Crawford Parker, who was the candidate for lieutenant governor, Alvin Cast, Capehart's friend and now State Supreme Court Justice Bobbitt, and Congressman William Bray. Thereafter he made three hundred speeches, nine talks a day. Their tone appar-

Indiana State Library

Claude R. Wickard

ently was right. As *Fortune* magazine reported, "he has never lost the gallusy, porch-settin', just-up-from-swilling-the-hogs manner that has made it so easy for many of his supporters to keep right on identifying themselves with him." The message, too, came across. Speaking off-the-cuff he sometimes stuttered around but by the time he finished waving his arms he had presented his issues: prosperity and progress under Eisenhower.[7]

Such peripatetic and even frantic activity combined with a strong national ticket and the senator's moderate politics made it virtually impossible to lose. He defeated Wickard by a margin of 212,481 votes, 109,203 more than his comfortable 1950 victory, 190,758 more than his narrow win in 1944.[8]

Unfortunately, the senator had little opportunity to relish victory. The triumph of 1956 proved evanescent, for reasons both personal and public. Capehart encountered a series of physical problems. For many years he had pushed himself, working incessantly. His strong physical makeup, the huge frame and farm-hardened body, had served him well. But he had never taken care of himself, and he worked harder in his fifties than most younger men. There was a slight and carefully unpublicized heart attack in 1957. He had to cut short a trip to Latin America in November 1959 because of a severe fever and in following months again suffered from heart problems. In late 1960 he went into the hospital with a bruised vertebral disc, an affliction so painful that he missed the opening sessions of the Eighty-seventh Congress and then attended for a while in a wheelchair. Complicating matters, Irma fell on the steps of the Capitol and injured her knee, and phlebitis and pneumonia followed, delaying surgery.

Meanwhile, in January 1960 the worst personal blow of Capehart's life occurred. His son Tom and daughter-in-law Nancy, both aged thirty-six and the parents of four children, took passage on an airliner that crashed into Montego Bay, Jamaica. Because of his outgoing personality and business acumen, Tom resembled and was perhaps closer to his father than the senator's other two children. He had been on a trip to investigate possibilities for a new Packard manufacturing contract in Colombia. The tragedy devastated Homer and Irma.[9]

During this third term there were also unceasing political troubles. The nation's atmosphere was changing. Voters were moving away from the conservatism that had marked the initial years after the Second World War. The economy during the 1950s produced a vision of a better life for everyone, and people began to believe that even more was possible in part through federal legislation.[10] Such a view was outside Capehart's experience. In rural southern Indiana the years before the First World War were lean and hard, the idea of a cornucopia opening for everyone was absurd.

Perhaps for this reason nearly every one of Capehart's legislative proposals failed. A five-point economic program introduced to increase the "general economy"—to bring full employment, generate tax revenue, and create an atmosphere in which "small business and small people" could grow—was rejected by Raymond J. Saulnier, chairman of the Council of Economic Advisers, and Secretary of the Treasury Robert B. Anderson, both of whom felt that it would give relief to the wealthy and to businesses, not increase national income. Refusing to give up, he supported private power companies in their attempt to end tax-subsidized competition from rural electric cooperatives. He advocated legislation to tax businesses at only 30 percent of their first $100,000 of income.

He likewise made no progress in his efforts to force a balancing of the federal budget. In the spring of 1959 he appeared on the Dave Garroway television program to ask for a balanced budget ("either curtail expenditures to fit within the $77 billion requested by President Eisenhower or increase taxes to meet the additional outlays"). He added that "the folks at home don't want any more taxes." The following year when Eisenhower, under pressure from the arms lobby, increased the budget to $79.8 billion, the unhappy Capehart undiplomatically remarked that President Eisenhower should have cut expenditures. "This could have been done by curtailing the bureaucracy."[11]

There was conflict, of course, between any desire to balance the national budget and efforts to obtain federal assistance for Indiana, but Capehart responded to his constituents seeking federal help for the long-term unemployed and farmers suffering from flood damage or low prices. He tried to amend the Douglas Depressed Areas Bill so that the proposed $390 million revolving fund could be used for loans only in areas of "chronic unemployment." Otherwise, he complained, Indiana cities and towns would receive no aid. After returning from aerial inspection of thousands of acres of flooded cropland in June 1958, he advocated $45 million for flood control on the upper Wabash. A bill already passed by the House contained money for Mansfield Reservoir in Parke County, and he supported it in the Senate. Until the end of his third term he continued to advocate his $100 million program to find industrial use for farm products, attempting to make it part of the 1960 GOP national platform.[12]

He continued to favor federally supported housing. His support of housing financed by the FHA made money available to middle-income homeowners. He helped write the Housing Act of 1959. At first he proposed an authorization of $1.35 billion, including a two-year urban renewal program, money for college housing and classrooms, housing for the elderly, and an increase in FHA insurance. The president vetoed this largess as too expensive and asked Sen. Prescott Bush of Connecticut to introduce another bill written by administration officials. Capehart could only grumble that "the president had been misled by his advisors." He voted, however, to sustain the veto, and after a trip to the White House supported the $1.05 billion substitute bill, which passed.[13]

His attitude toward civil rights legislation remained ambivalent. He voted for the Civil Rights Acts of 1957 and 1960, but favored jury trials in contempt cases arising from civil rights activities. He refused to vote for cloture to shut off filibustering and voted against requiring school desegregation and ensuring voting rights. He spoke out against breaking state Jim Crow laws, "even though the laws also are wrong." Justice Department officials, he claimed, helped sponsor the freedom rides in the Southern states "to cause riots, to violate laws in an organized way."[14]

On labor issues at this time he stood against "real evils which have crept into labor unionism." He continued to support the union shop, but wanted laws that would weaken the hold of union officials. He voted against extending unemployment compensation, supported a bill to allow state courts or labor relations agencies to handle disputes declined by the National Labor Relations Board, and supported legislation reducing the workers covered by the Fair Labor Standards Act. His record, in short, caused workingmen to turn against him.[15]

After the end of the Eisenhower years the Hoosier Republican not surprisingly became one of the most persistent critics of President John F. Kennedy. In preceding years a gulf in experience and outlook had separated the Indiana senator and the ambitious young Democrat from Massachusetts. As fellow members of the Committee on Foreign Relations the two senators had confronted each other over defense spending. Part of the disagreement may have had its origins in Capehart's antagonism toward Kennedy's brother Robert, which had arisen when Capehart became a member of the so-called rackets committee, a bipartisan panel with John L. McClellan (Democrat, Ark.) as chairman and Robert Kennedy as counsel. The committee was in its third year when Capehart became a member. He soon complained about "dirty pool" when the younger Kennedy scheduled Milton Hammergren, who had succeeded Capehart as vice president of the Wurlitzer Company, to testify as the first witness in hearings about racketeering in the jukebox industry. When the *New York Times* pointed out that Capehart had been Hammergren's predecessor the Hoosier responded that he had not seen any racketeering in the industry up to the time he left Wurlitzer. Testimony before the committee did not contradict him, but it revealed Hammergren's dealings with organized crime in selling jukeboxes. Angry with what seemed an attempt to embarrass him, Capehart fought fire with fire and demanded that Robert Kennedy "reveal the names of witnesses who offered political help to his brother [John] if he would go easy on them." He later criticized the Kennedy-Ervin Labor Reform Bill as "sorely inadequate to correct the conditions which the rackets committee has revealed." Passage of the bill, he asserted, "is supposed to help Sen. Kennedy's aspirations for the presidency. It may help him with some labor leaders, but the people as a whole are not likely to be impressed." Robert Kennedy in 1960 published a book about the Senate rackets committee investigation entitled *The Enemy Within*, which contained a false assertion that one of Capehart's assistants had been indicted for attempting to influence a witness.[16] All this made nearly impossible any cooperation between Capehart and the new Democratic president who took office in January 1961.

For Capehart the New Frontier also marked a resurgence of the New Deal. Once again he was fighting countercyclical spending. "It is idle to talk of cutting taxes unless there is a corresponding reduction in government spending," he said. He warned against federal aid for local projects. The Kennedy administration did not have a "modern Aladdin's lamp from which it gets the money it wants to spend and spend and elect and elect." That money, he said, came from taxpayers. He voted against an administration bill to raise farm price supports while reducing crop acreage, another to authorize $2.5 billion in aid to education, and another for $4.88 billion for housing over four years. He thus opposed the programs that, combined with Eisenhower's anti-inflation measures, continued economic prosperity through the 1960s.

The times went out of joint by the early 1960s, and Capehart knew he had lost much national influence. In the Eighty-sixth Congress only four of his bills became law. Two concerned banking, one extended the voluntary home mortgage credit program, and one provided health benefits for federal employees. In the Eighty-seventh Congress his proposed legislation fared even worse: only one of his four successful measures—to amend and extend the Export-Import Bank Act of 1945—concerned a public issue. The other three were commemorative (medals for Bob Hope and Sam Rayburn and provision for observing the centennial of the Homestead Act).[17]

In his third term, as one could have expected, Capehart took part in debating the major issues of foreign policy. The Foreign Relations Committee was a body that William S. White once labeled "incomparably the world's most powerful legislative group in the field of foreign affairs," and the senator was well aware of his importance as a policymaker. The responsibility, perhaps, and his support for the president caused him to cast off his earlier nationalism, at least for a while.

He visited Latin America again in 1957 as a delegate to the annual economic conference of the Organization of American States in Buenos Aires. In Asunción a boulevard was named for him to honor his help in obtaining funds to build the city's public water system. After touring Brazil, Peru, Chile, and Ecuador, he returned to report that he had seen improvement since 1954. "Trade has increased with the U.S.A. and our political relations are most cordial." Trade with Latin America, he said, "accounts for 26,000 jobs in Indiana alone." "I was an isolationist," he explained. "I still would like to be one. But when the Russians got the A and H-bomb, jet-propelled bombers and the intercontinental ballistic missile, our whole posture of defense had to be changed."[18]

In the autumn of the same year in which he made his second journey to Latin America, 1957, he undertook the most dramatic of his foreign excursions, a six-week trip to Western Europe and the Soviet Union. "I'm going to find out as much as I can about exact conditions there," he said, "so we can help decide if we're right or wrong in our analysis of foreign affairs." Irma accompanied him on the trip that included visits to Copenhagen, Oslo, Stockholm, Helsinki, Berlin, Warsaw, Prague, and Moscow.

During this ambitious trip the Soviets launched *sputnik*, the first earth-orbiting satellite. Russian scientists and technicians, Capehart explained, had been made "heroes of Soviet society," receiving "capitalistic incentives" such as fine apartments, summer houses, and automobiles. The Hoosier senator otherwise was not impressed. Socialist society, he said, lacked consumer goods. There was "total lack" of information by which people could "check on the truth or falsehood of government propaganda." He thought the United States still could deter war. He was not, he said, worried about *sputnik*. "The United States," he said, "is not behind Russia in any phase of endeavor—including the military, missiles, economy, and education."

That year, 1957, the Middle East was still in turmoil, and in Czechoslovakia the senator had beheld the Skoda works producing tanks and other armament for Middle Eastern countries, notably Egypt, which earlier had arranged to trade its cotton for East European arms. He therefore favored the appropriation in support of the Eisenhower Doctrine of $200 million in aid to countries of the Middle East. It was "realistic," he said, to protect Middle Eastern oil "because all of Western Europe depends upon it." He voted for the $3.6 billion foreign aid bill of that year.

The Middle Eastern issue plagued American foreign relations, and Capehart carefully supported the administration. After President Eisenhower in July 1958 ordered marines to prevent the fall of Lebanese President Camille Chamoun, the senator made national headlines with a statement that the president's action would help keep Russia out of the Middle East, oil flowing to Western Europe, the Suez Canal open, and our word with allies. "We went into Korea shooting," he said. "Here we are going in to avoid war. We're calling the bluff of Russia." In 1959 he announced his support for the administration's mutual security assistance proposal, for $3.9 billion. He also approved the president's firm stand against Nikita Khrushchev's announcement that without an American agreement the Soviet Union would sign a separate agreement with East Germany that would exclude the West from access to Berlin. He received warm thanks from the White House, and, according to public opinion polls, from a majority of Hoosiers.[19]

During the presidential race in 1960 he rebutted charges by Senator Kennedy that the Eisenhower administration had allowed a dangerous "gap" to develop between American and Soviet strategic missile capacity. Would the Soviet Union, Kennedy had asked, "have 500 intercontinental ballistic missiles by the end of 1960, as against 30 intercontinental ballistic missiles of the United States and 1,000 by the end of 1961 against 70 in the possession of the United States?" Kennedy's claims, Capehart responded, were part of a "concerted effort on the part . . . of a few senators on the opposite side of the aisle to discredit 100 percent the President of the United States; to sell our defense establishment short; and to make statements which, in my opinion, could give comfort to the enemy." He pointed out that Kennedy had said that "the Russians were ahead of us," and had said it "at least thirty-five times." Democratic senators such as Wayne Morse of Oregon and those from states with large military and aerospace industries—Henry Jackson of Washington, Stuart Symington of Missouri—supported Kennedy, but Capehart was steadfast. He asserted—correctly, it turned out—that the senators were on the wrong track, that the United States was strong. "We have the bombers and the atomic bombs and the hydrogen bombs," he said, "to destroy Russia." He might have added that the United States also had the missiles. The so-called missile gap existed, to be sure, but it vastly favored the United States. Information to this effect became public early in the Kennedy administration.[20]

Capehart's defense of Eisenhower foreign policy during the latter 1950s, one must concede, was a remarkable performance. At one point the senator described one of Kennedy's speeches as "a good high school debate" and said that the Massachusetts senator had "promised something to everybody in the world." Kennedy could only retort that he was "complimented by the fact that the Senator from Indiana has not complimented my speech." Capehart again received thanks from the president, this time for vigorous and outspoken support and for being "a personal champion of mine when one thing or another bobs up on the Senate floor. The party needed," the president added, "a lot of rough and ready and effective fighters like you."[21]

Reluctantly, however, Capehart in Eisenhower's last months in office turned critical of the president's foreign policy. American policy, he believed, had begun to go awry. Responding to White House announcements of a visit by Khrushchev in the autumn of 1959, he said that "it leaves me flat. The Kremlin hasn't kept a peacetime promise made to us since the Democrats first recognized Russia back in 1933." The following spring he discovered that only the chairman and ranking members of the Foreign Relations Committee had been briefed when the U-2 spy plane flown by Francis Gary Powers went down inside the Soviet Union on 1 May 1960. Capehart was angry about the entire affair. "The Eisenhower administration should take Congress into its confidence. Perhaps we could be of some help. God knows they need help, if I can read the record and the times correctly." He refused to participate in the committee's report on the episode and voted against Eisenhower's foreign aid proposals that year. When the Japanese government canceled its invitation for a state visit by Eisenhower, Capehart suggested that American presidents abandon "personal diplomacy and stay in the U.S.A."[22]

Latin American policy, in his opinion, had begun to falter. He attacked Eisenhower for opposing such "little Latin American dictators" as the anticommunist but notoriously corrupt and tyrannical Rafael Trujillo of the Dominican Republic, while inviting Khrushchev, "the biggest dictator of them all," to visit the United States. When the new Cuban premier, Fidel Castro, solidified his hold by using firing squads to execute his opponents Capehart saw a "bearded monster" stalking close to the American mainland. Shortly, he said, Castro would be attempting invasions of Panama, Nicaragua, and the Dominican Republic. The president, he advised, should "take the necessary action to overthrow the Castro government" before the regime made "Cuba 100 per cent Communist and a Russian satellite."[23]

With Kennedy as president, however, Capehart could find nothing to support. As senior Republican on the Foreign Relations Committee he voted against the Peace Corps Bill, saying that "there isn't anything good about it. It is just giving a group of selected young people a foreign joy ride." Foreign aid, he now asserted, returning to his view in the year 1948, should be "loaned" to foreign corporations, not governments, and spent in the United States to alleviate unemployment. He blamed anti-Americanism in South Korea on lack of a "strong, positive U.S. foreign policy" and questioned support of UN forces in the Congo against Moise Tshombe's Katangan separatist revolt.[24]

He especially condemned administration policy with regard to Cuba where the failure of the American-sponsored invasion in early April 1961 appeared to justify his opposition: in the disastrous attempt at the Bay of Pigs, fourteen hundred Cuban exiles were captured by the army of Castro. Kennedy's announcement that "there will not be under any conditions an intervention in Cuba by United States armed forces" brought indignation. "Khrushchev can say he won it for Castro," Capehart said. "Therefore, we can't help, I am sorry to say, losing face throughout the world." He criticized the Democratic president for permitting shipments of Soviet arms to Cuba and failing to enlist supporters of the overthrown Fulgencio Batista regime. "The thing was bungled very, very badly," he announced on the floor of the Senate, "and I'm amazed at some of the things that we did or failed to do." There must be a way, he said, to eliminate Russian control in Cuba.[25]

Cuba now became Capehart's cause célèbre. During the ransom of the captives of the Bay of Pigs disaster, arranged by the Central Intelligence Agency under an implausible claim that a private organization had raised enough money to pay for the tractors and medical supplies that Premier Castro demanded, he inquired whether the White House had "authorized the so-called Castro tractor committee." When Kennedy replied weakly that he had done so only in his capacity as a private citizen, Capehart was not mollified; in Castro's mind, he said, the deal was "part and parcel of the so-called invasion that failed here a couple of weeks ago." Capehart asked his staff to see whether it violated the Logan Act of 1799 that forbade private citizens to deal with a foreign government. He sponsored a bill to prevent tax exemption on private contributions for the tractors and asked for hearings. He told White House staff member Lawrence O'Brien that "the president should call in some of us to discuss these things. . . . Why let Castro blackmail us by exchanging his own flesh and blood?" Then he gave perhaps his best advice: "Let's relax for a year and ignore Castro and Khrushchev." He felt reassured when *U.S. News and World Report* published a survey relating that communism in Cuba was the chief concern of the American people and that editorial opinion opposed the tractor deal.[26]

Capehart was once more in opposition during the Cuban missile crisis of October 1962. But by that time his luck in politics was running out. The signs of trouble that had appeared soon after his victory in 1956 became too evident to ignore or attempt to group with other signs that said everything was much as it had been before. The senator was already encountering physical troubles, and to the tragedy of the deaths of his son and daughter-in-law in the plane crash had been added the political difficulties. The combination spelled defeat in the senatorial election of 1962.

11

Defeat

By the beginning of the 1960s it was clear that Homer E. Capehart's political fortunes were in decline. In the last year or two of the Eisenhower administration he had opposed measures sponsored by the president, the leader of his own party. Eisenhower gave way to a Democratic president, a young Senate colleague for whom he had little respect. Then, in addition to such difficulties, the senior senator from Indiana had almost tired himself out attempting to hold the GOP factions together within his own state. He had gotten his start in Hoosier politics by bringing together the dissidents. He had proved himself a remarkable peacemaker. Times now had changed. One problem would be resolved within the state organization only to have another appear.

In the early 1950s Capehart's ally, Gov. George N. Craig, had been acutely embarrassed when his chairman of the state highway commission, Virgil Smith, and close advisers Elmer W. Sherwood and William E. Sayer were convicted of land profiteering and soliciting and taking bribes and were sent to jail. The so-called "highway scandals" were perhaps the logical extension of a system in which the party regularly had solicited kickbacks from patronage employees. This arrange-

Associated Press

Sen. William E. Jenner delivers speech defending Sen. Joseph R. McCarthy, 16 November 1954.

ment had gone on for years, and no one had thought much about it. With the retrospect of later years, when party organizations across the country either disintegrated or were glued together in fragile manner by contributions from large illegal contributors or else from political action committees, the Indiana system of taking a percentage of the wages of each state employee did not appear altogether unreasonable. It nonetheless sanctified an essential illegality and encouraged party leaders to look away from others, and Craig's governorship thus got into trouble. The resultant scandal that tarred the governor's administration reflected upon his sponsor, Capehart.[1]

Another problem had been what to do about Jenner. Capehart sought to get along with him. The task, however, was finally impossible.[2] Jenner was far more conservative than Capehart, and far more outspoken, often in obnoxious ways, as when he had described Gen. George C. Marshall as "a front man for traitors." The senator from Shoals, Indiana, was also, and quite unlike Capehart, unhappy in the upper house and seemed constantly looking for some other office, either the governorship or, as in 1956, a federal court appointment. Jenner developed an interest in appointment to the district court in Chicago and unhappily withdrew only when he discovered that as a senator he could not constitutionally be a candidate. Differences between the two Hoosiers, which began with Eisenhower's nomination in 1952, became almost irreparable in 1956. Jenner berated Capehart for supporting Eisenhower's program and called him a "New Deal sonofabitch." He referred to the president's foreign policy as "nauseating" because Secretary John Foster Dulles "secretly carries on a planned retreat before the communist advance." In mid-October 1956, in the heat of the campaign, he again attacked Eisenhower's foreign policy, telling audiences openly that it had "never been anything but a global giveaway. It is still a giveaway." Perhaps the last straw came when he remarked to

Hoosier GOP leaders that he would rather belong "to a losing Republican party which is faithful to the Constitution than to a winning Republican party which makes deals with those who would betray America." He predicted the "ignominious defeat of Capehart and other Republicans in Indiana next November."[3]

At last Jenner took himself out of politics. Exactly what influence Capehart may have had in the junior senator's unexpected decision in late November 1957, not to run for reelection is unknown, but the *Indianapolis Times* columnist Irving Leibowitz speculated that "powerful forces are trying to enlist the support of Congressman Charles Halleck, Senator Homer E. Capehart and the White House in a long range program to 'dump' Senator William E. Jenner and win control of the party in Indiana." According to Leibowitz the purpose of the plot was to convert the state GOP to Eisenhower's "modern Republicanism" by removing Jenner from the state scene, giving control of the organization to Halleck and Capehart. While these things may not have been true, Capehart did tell reporters about Jenner's prediction that he, Capehart, would lose in 1956 by two hundred thousand votes and remarked that "too many Republicans are helping the Democrats try to discredit the Eisenhower administration." Privately, he sent a clipping to the White House quoting Jenner's boast of not being a modern Republican because "my parents were married." By this time Capehart was publicly rebuking Jenner. "It is not logical," he announced, "to fear communism inside the United States and then vote against defense." Jenner's decision not to run in the election of 1958, taken "for personal and family reasons," came soon afterward, a clear relief. When journalists asked Capehart to comment he recalled his remark at the time he found himself caught in the revolution in Bolivia: "As a member of the Republican Party in Indiana, I was well qualified to start a revolution, fight a revolution and end a revolution."[4]

With considerable difficulty Capehart had won out over Jenner, perhaps in part because the junior senator had possessed a sort of self-destruct mechanism. But soon after Jenner's decision not to run, another imbroglio arose concerning the state GOP. When Harold W. Handley announced his intention of running for Jenner's seat, Capehart told the GOP leadership he disagreed with Handley's political philosophy and doubted his chance for success in the middle of his term as governor. The state committee held a luncheon for the nine Republican congressmen including Halleck and Capehart. Afterward, Chairman Robert Matthews asked reporters to leave so party leaders could discuss strategy. Unaware that the public address system was still turned on, Capehart announced in his booming voice that the Hoosier GOP was "split right down the middle" between "federal and state government. I represent the federal and Handley the state. You're continually beating the brains out of us Republicans in Washington. Don't deny it. There are speeches made here constantly that everything is wrong in Washington." He asked Handley and "Old Guard Republicans to stop 'picking on' the president and other modern Republicans." Halleck joined the fray, saying angrily that Matthews had made a speech in Halleck's district in which he said "Indiana doesn't want modern Republicans." He warned that "when someone undertakes to read me out of the party, I don't understand what the h... they're talking about."[5]

The discussion appeared in the press the next day and for a while everything in Indiana politics turned to chaos. Chairman Matthews neither resigned nor changed his tactics. Capehart charged Governor Handley with purging four Brown County precinct committeemen from state jobs and making an unnecessary trip to Washington to seek defense contracts. In return Capehart was not invited to a farewell dinner for Jenner organized by the state chairman. Handley took the senatorial nomination despite Capehart. The senior senator then sought to mend party fences by offering to campaign for Handley, who did not accept Capehart's assistance until late September. The Democratic senatorial candidate in 1958, Vance Hartke of Evansville, won the election by 242,000 votes. The GOP suffered additional blows in 1959 as Democrats swept to victory in statewide mayoral elections. In 1960 the Democrats took control of the statehouse.[6]

All the while demographic changes within the state were working against the Hoosier senior senator. According to *Indianapolis News* political writer Edward Ziegner, the Democrats had elected Hartke to the Senate in 1958 and elected Matthew Welsh to the governorship in 1960, because the state was slowly losing its image of being rural and conservative.[7] In 1962 there were 157,000 more registered voters than in 1956, and some were young suburbanites who had turned away from the Republican party. Many had voted for Kennedy in 1960. Much of the increase had occurred in the twelve most populous counties. It was important for Capehart to do well in those counties.[8]

Capehart contemplated this new challenge. Should he move in a liberal direction, to enlist the new urban voters? His record and long membership in the midwestern conservative bloc was well known. He decided to straddle the situation, to show the liberal tendencies which he assuredly possessed. He wanted to show that his association with Jenner had made him seem more conservative than he really was. Alas, the attempt to appeal to the new liberal voters backfired. It took away his traditional supporters, many of whom began to consider him "indecisive," an individual who "played politics too much."[9]

Capehart made yet another error when he decided to turn over his 1962 campaign to the Hoosier GOP organization, which, as he should have suspected, was not united. He had moved in his own man as party chairman, Thomas Gallmeyer of Fort Wayne, but had been unable to ensure that the membership was loyal. Or it may just have been an unwillingness to work hard when Capehart was the candidate. In times past, when Capehart was running, party members had known that the senator could raise money from his own resources, that is, his own pocketbook, and had tended to let him do that. For whatever reason, in 1962 there was not much activity.[10]

Obtaining the nomination for a fourth term, it turned out, was easy. The task was to defeat his Democratic opponent, Birch E. Bayh, Jr. Capehart's opponent in 1962 did not seem unbeatable. Bayh was thirty-four years old. The son of an army colonel, he had been born in Terre Haute but lived most of his early years in Washington, D.C. Upon the death of his mother, while his father was overseas during the Second World War, he had moved to the farm of his grandparents near the mining community of Shirkieville, a few miles northwest of Terre Haute. After graduating from high school he enlisted in the army and served with the occupation forces in Europe. Upon return he entered the Purdue University School of Agriculture. He became known as a debater, participated in boxing, and was senior class president. For a short time thereafter, long enough to be considered a farmer, he managed his grandfather's 450 acres near Shirkieville. He was elected to the Indiana House of Representatives in 1954, served four terms, and became successively floor leader, minority leader, and speaker. Of the representatives in the 1961 general assembly he was voted by Indiana reporters as "most able." Meanwhile he courted and married Marvella Hern, whom he met at a national debate contest while at Purdue. He graduated in 1960 from Indiana University School of Law.[11]

Capehart's plan for the campaign was simple. "If President Kennedy is popular by campaign time, I'll run on my own record in the Senate," he said. "If he is unpopular and his program bogged down, I'll run against the administration. The people of Indiana like me, because they always know where I stand." The contest gave Hoosiers an apparently clear choice.[12] As a reporter for the *Indianapolis Times* put it, "Bayh is a liberal, pledged to virtually all of another young liberal's

New Frontier. Capehart classifies himself a 'progressive conservative,' and he has voted against or spoken against virtually all of the issues in the Kennedy program." Bayh was enthusiastic about the Peace Corps, Capehart against it. Bayh sought medical care for the aged, Capehart said it would bring socialism. Bayh favored federal aid to education and slum clearance, Capehart feared loss of local control over schools and felt the cities should cope with their own slums. Bayh favored the Kennedy farm program and the plan to increase trade by reducing tariffs, Capehart criticized both.[13]

The election should have turned upon Cuba. In fact, both Kennedy and Bayh supposed privately that the revelation of missiles in Cuba in October 1962 had handed Capehart the election. In an Indianapolis speech for Bayh the president referred to the Hoosier senator as one of "those self-appointed generals and admirals who want to send someone else's son to war." An adviser, however, heard him exclaim, "Would you believe it? Homer Capehart is the Winston Churchill of our time."[14]

But Capehart made too much of Cuba. As Halleck recalled, the senator "put all his eggs in the Cuban basket." To make things worse, his prescience during the crisis created a dangerous overconfidence, convincing Capehart's campaign staff, the GOP rank and file, the senator himself, and even Hoosier journalists, that the senator's reelection was assured. Meanwhile the energetic Bayh redoubled his efforts. Bayh's campaign manager, Larry Conrad, recalled that "rather than saying Birch Bayh says so and so, we ran pictures of John Kennedy and said, 'Back the president in Cuba—Vote for Bayh!' "[15]

Capehart had appeared in national headlines by predicting two days ahead of the fact that President Kennedy would call up reserves to deal with Cuba. The senator was justifiably indignant about the administration's belated handling of the missile crisis. But Bayh accused him of revealing a Foreign

Harris & Ewing, Washington, D.C.

Birch E. Bayh, Jr.

Relations Committee secret briefing. In a public debate with his young opponent the incumbent lost his temper over this issue, grabbing Bayh's lapels. It was reminiscent of the altercation a decade earlier with Herbert H. Lehman and Hubert H. Humphrey.[16]

Instead of Cuba, Bayh addressed issues close to home, the need for reapportionment of the state legislature—to prevent federal intervention—and property tax relief. He supported a "judicious" federal tax cut, updated depreciation allowances for business, expanded world trade, and reduced federal controls on farmers. He demonstrated a mastery of Capehart's voting record, exposing the senator's opposition to increases in the minimum wage in 1947, 1949, 1960, and 1961, asserting that Capehart had failed to propose one single piece of legislation for working men and women. When Capehart responded that he had voted to increase the minimum wage several times Bayh answered that he had not done so in 1947 and reminded listeners that Capehart voted seven times in 1960 for amendments to limit coverage or reduce the amount before finally voting for an increase to $1.25. He attacked Capehart as either vacillating or against civil rights and showed that on four occasions Capehart had voted to uphold a filibuster and six times had voted in 1960 against civil rights measures. Capehart claimed that eighteen years in the Senate had provided him seniority and qualifications sufficient to deal with the nation's problems; Bayh insisted that the aging senator was behind the times.[17]

The older man soon was on the defensive. Former President Truman charged in Evansville that Capehart had pleaded with him to end a coal strike in 1946 because it was costing the senator personally $10,000 a day. The charge was frivolous. Capehart became angry and replied that he "never had any interest in a coal mine . . . or any shop or factory that used coal. Nothing could be further from the truth." All to no avail; Truman's assertion was what people remembered about

Indianapolis Times

Homer E. Capehart, 20 September 1962

a man who admittedly was wealthy. Finally, Bayh called attention to the senator's occasional imprecisions. Admittedly it was turn about; it was something, after all, that he, Capehart, had done in 1950 to Alex Campbell, the man who had prosecuted Alger Hiss. When Capehart praised the regime of Trujillo and explained it was not enough for a dictator "to be anti-Communist, because so was Hitler," Bayh expressed shock. He asked why Capehart had talked of invading Cuba when it would have cost thousands of American lives, made a martyr of Castro, and touched off nuclear war. After the Cuban quarantine had ended and Capehart announced that the president had done what he, Capehart, had been advocating all along, and that Bayh should "apologize for calling me a warmonger" and "apologize to the President, too," Bayh responded quickly that such criticism made the president's job more difficult. "If my opponent had his way," he said, "we'd have been at war a year ago without the support of any of our Allies, who would have turned against us." Unlike Capehart, said Bayh, "I do not consider my own political future as important as the country's." The president had taken "the right action at the right time."[18]

All the while Bayh managed to focus much attention on appearances. To Capehart's disadvantage the candidates were opposites in style. Bayh took spot commercials on radio and television and used a contemporary show tune to introduce himself with the words, "Hey look me over." He exuded confidence.[19] Capehart was the caricature of an old-fashioned senator: overweight, bespectacled, cigar-smoking, sparse hairline above his large round face, and double chin. The senator's speeches seemed to reflect his appearance and played into the hands of his opponent. Making a fist with one hand and then the other during speeches, he would pound his right fist into his left, then open both hands and spread his arms. He would act coy: "I don't intend to, but I might get a little politics into this speech." He believed in "good common horse sense." Bayh made an excellent platform appearance. Before a speech he would move through the audience to shake hands. He opened his speeches with a flurry of jokes and anecdotes.[20]

The combination of Capehart's liabilities was too much. After longer service in the Senate than any other person ever elected by Hoosier voters, he met defeat. Even in the rural areas he received only 17,000 more votes than Bayh. In these eighty-seven counties, each with fewer than 100,000 votes, he took only 51.33 percent, compared with 56.2 in 1956, 54.2 in 1950, and 53.5 in 1944.[21]

The event's meaning was uncertain. Next day the *New York Times* ran a page-one story under the caption, "Capehart Unseated as Bayh of Indiana Confounds Experts." Radio Moscow commented that the defeat of Capehart for senator, and former Vice President Richard M. Nixon for governor of California, showed that the "foreign policy of the present United States government does not enjoy great popularity among the broad masses of the electorate." But the Indiana election was too close to be a commentary on policy. Bayh had won by 10,944 votes in a turnout that set an off-year record, 905,491 votes to Capehart's 894,547.[22]

Defeat brought tears. It had been a long time, all the years of striving, the hard work, the successes, the almost unconquerable feeling that he had done the right thing, taken the correct path, done what a good Hoosier should do. He had "made it" in a wonderful way, up from the farm in southern Indiana, and accomplishment had made him believe his instincts were right, that he could not err, that nothing could stand in his way. At last he had failed, and at the hands of a young man barely out of law school who had no experience in national affairs, who waged a campaign on local issues, and allowed his managers to take a Broadway tune and make a campaign song out of it. There was humiliation here, to be defeated in this way.[23]

It was perhaps impossible at that moment for the senator, facing retirement, to understand that it was time for him to leave the Senate and return to Indiana, to Indianapolis and a half-day's drive from the farm in Daviess County, where he could receive friends and reminisce about Washington experiences and live with memories of influence and authority.

12

Retirement

HOMER CAPEHART during his years of retirement lived with his wife Irma in a large and comfortable house in Indianapolis on North Pennsylvania Street. The Capeharts were pleased to have time together.[1] Irma had not shared her husband's enthusiasm for politics. She had not been comfortable with the public attention he had attracted. Their son Earl recalled that his mother was frequently a pessimist and "would go along with the moves or the changes, but with a certain amount of disappointment and complaining."[2] Still, Irma loved her husband and their life together. She had provided a balance, a different point of view. Although plagued with illnesses, she had made a good life for her family, guiding the children, cooking and cleaning, seeing to it that the family went to church. She had looked forward to vacations with family and friends in Miami, to the Kentucky Derby, sometimes an excursion. She and Homer agreed that each child should receive a college education. Earl graduated from DePauw and Harvard Law. Tom obtained an electrical engineering degree from Purdue. Pat majored in political science at the University of Maryland. In retirement Irma in a sense came into her own, even more important than in the past, for now it was her task to be a support in adversity.

For a man like Capehart, retirement naturally did not mean relaxation, and he at once became busy, sometimes very busy, with a number of activities. He served as court-appointed receiver for the $26 million International Barber and Beautician's Union pension fund, for which he recovered $3 million during litigation against the fund's managers. Although members lost dividends and interest, they got back what they had put in. He was director of seven businesses or charitable institutions, including the United Service Organizations (USO). He made trips to South America as a business consultant, in one instance representing a California family seeking reimbursement for land expropriated by the Argentine government. Ever the impresario, he staged a national farm power show in September 1965, an event that attracted 150,000 people to his farm. Weekdays, he could be found at the large desk in his office at the Board of Trade Building in Indianapolis, a huge, multicolored map of the world on the wall behind him, dictating letters to his secretary. He bought the old Van Camp estate, where he had done yard work as an eighteen-year-old on North Meridian Street, and promoted the construction there of the Stouffer Inn (which has undergone several changes in ownership and name), a large red-brick building with limestone trim that had a restaurant on top where he sometimes dined at a table next to the windows that looked south down Meridian.[3] As he viewed the Soldiers and Sailors Monument in the distance he could sense the extraordinary changes of life in the capital of the Hoosier state that had occurred in his lifetime. On such occasions he could recall the scene before high-rise bank and insurance buildings and the bulky domed stadium changed the skyline. In his mind's eye it was possible not to see the lines of fast-moving automobiles and the downtown core of office buildings. He could reminisce about the coal-smoke and horse-and-buggy days when he first traveled to Indianapolis in 1915-16 after selling baking powder for the Rumford Company. Then, as he finished his prime rib and reached for an El Producto, he would reflect on the changes and his role in them, his eyes gleaming as he looked out on the old from high up in the new.

But his greatest pleasure was helping with the upbringing and education of twelve grandchildren, including the four children orphaned by the deaths of Tom and Nancy.[4] He often brought them together on the farm in Daviess County, a property that had grown to 2,100 acres and where he went on weekends. There he would instruct his farm manager, John Shawhands, about the corn, hogs, and steers, and perhaps "go to town," the Washington of his high school days and of his return during the Great Depression, where people still recognized him and came up to shake hands and have a few words with "the senator." During the farm visits he lived in a rambling wood-frame, one-story, ranch-style building he called the Lodge, on a knoll surrounded by a big yard. Beyond the fence were cornfields and pastures with grazing cattle. On hot sultry summer afternoons he enjoyed watching the grandchildren play ball or ride horseback on the lawn while waiting for dinner. At 6:00 P.M. on the weekends everyone gathered around the huge table, waited while the senator said a prayer, and, finally, served themselves from bowls and plates, eating the delectable, now almost historic produce of the Capehart farm: fried chicken, corn on the cob, mashed potatoes with milk gravy, and watermelon. The head of the clan looked on, enjoying the scene but sometimes asking the children whether they realized what momentous events had occurred in this same location many years earlier and how they had contributed to the future of the nation.[5]

Politics remained in his blood. Not long after his defeat he returned to Washington, D.C., for a brief visit with the congressional Republican caucus. He sat for a while in the back of the room, chewing his cigar. Then he spoke. Why, he wanted to know, were they all taking themselves so seriously? "Don't you know," he asked, "that the people back home don't even know you are here?" He received applause from his former colleagues. He attended the GOP national convention in 1964 and spent time reminiscing with friends.[6]

During this time Capehart undertook association with colleges and universities, recounting his experiences to college students at Indiana University in Bloomington and receiving an honorary doctor of laws degree at Indiana Central University (now University of Indianapolis).[7]

The years passed, and age took its toll. More physical problems arose. He suffered from feebleness and a continuing heart problem and had surgery for an aneurism of the aorta. The senator broke his hip in an accident at the house in July 1979. The trauma of surgery was too much, his condition worsened, and the end came on the evening of 3 September.[8]

How, then, to sum up Capehart's career? Homer Earl Capehart, one must conclude, had helped to change American life. By the time of his death the United States had reached what historians now see was its pinnacle of world influence. Some of his activities, bringing with them a beneficial alteration of material and political culture, helped this along. Others had interfered and brought unfortunate consequences. The nation had grown rapidly after the 1890s and the war with Spain. Visitors to Indiana towns could go down side streets near the courthouses and see the little houses that remained from the nineties and the earlier large Victorian frame and Italianate residences of the 1880s and earlier, the houses that Capehart had known in his youth. They possessed cupolas, fancy bargeboard and sawtooth decoration, pilasters, and verandas. Then the bungalow period of the First World War came, and after it the Georgian replicas and Tudor copies of real estate developments in the interwar years. Vast suburbs and shopping malls inspired by automobiles came after the Second World War. This was the America that Capehart represented. He could almost feel the country's strength as he watched the population rise from eighty million at the time of his birth, to one hundred million during the First World War, to double and more by the 1970s. Sensing first the economic opportunities, then the political, he had taken matters in hand and went off in what he believed were the necessary directions.

Life in America was not always improved by these movements, but as senator from Indiana he had gotten things done, most of them what the people of his state desired. With his unthreatening manner, friendly confidence, belief that he could help people reach goals—that his purposes were theirs—he won respect, then loyalty. Whether it was a new automatic phonograph factory, a Republican cornfield rally, or a celebration for the party's nominee at Elwood, Capehart could find people to help. He knew better than to stay in Indianapolis and talk to other men who smoked cigars. He went out in his own automobile to the counties, to cigarette and chewing-tobacco areas, and convinced people to devote time to politics and then, beginning in 1944, to vote for him.

His appearance was rough-hewn, his wit not always sharp, his view of the world frequently harsh and sometimes pessimistic, but he never stopped seeking how to do something better. A man without formal training in mathematics, mechanical engineering, music, management, patent or corporate law, agronomy or animal husbandry, domestic or international politics—the areas of knowledge in which he spent his life—he respected knowledge, understood its power, and in the areas he considered important was always seeking answers. Perhaps inevitably, considering his background, he made mistakes, some of them large. They included belief that the United States without additional commitments or spending could prevent the spread of Soviet and Chinese communism in the world, refusal to support the Marshall Plan for European recovery, lack of confidence in the durability of the

American political economy, failure to see that the abundance of America—his vaunted opportunity—was much less available to Americans who were handicapped or suffered discrimination, and, most regrettable, excessive partisanship and willingness to use unfounded anticommunist accusations. But he also displayed prudence and courage. His cautious, pay-as-you-go approach and awareness of the limits in governmental affairs—something he had learned in business—might have helped head off difficulties caused by the fiscal policies of President Lyndon B. Johnson and his successors, especially Ronald W. Reagan. In foreign affairs he properly doubted that the Soviet Union was as large a threat as President Truman claimed, defended Eisenhower's national security policies, and distrusted Kennedy's handling of Cuban policy.

Capehart's unpolished manner and way of putting things in imprecise or overly simple terms sometimes made him appear naïve. Commentators remarked on his capacity to simplify and insinuated that, while perhaps appealing to the average Hoosier, it revealed a failure to understand. An unvarnished man, they said, had brought naïveté to public office, an innocence that, combined with driving ambition, made him easily swayed by partisans and ideologues such as the Indiana Republican Editorial Association, Indiana and Midwest veterans organizations, and Senators William E. Jenner and Joseph R. McCarthy. Capehart, according to this view, failed to see the danger posed by the right-wing Republicans who desired to rid the nation of New Deal-Fair Deal policy by whatever means.

Capehart, however, was not nearly as simple as he appeared. A man of capitalist convictions, during the mid-1930s he feared big government and any tendency toward diminishing opportunity.[9] He knew free enterprise firsthand, as a practitioner, and had accepted it despite its flaws, including the 1920s speculation and profiteering. When the flaws helped bring the crash of 1929 and the Great Depression, events that shook his confidence in the promise of America, instead of rejecting the system he turned his considerable resources and energies to politics. His purpose, no different in essence from the New Deal, was to preserve the system by reforming it. If certain of his methods were incorrect, he nevertheless held to his worthy goal, working for twenty-five years to move the nation toward it amidst the unprecedented confusion of new international responsibilities. The meaning of America, he had decided, was that individual effort counted.

Notes

Abbreviations used in the notes of this book are:
HEC—Homer Earl Capehart
CMM—Homer Earl Capehart Manuscript Memoir, 1943, in the Homer E. Capehart personal papers in the possession of H. Earl Capehart, Jr., Indianapolis
HECP—Homer Earl Capehart personal papers in the possession of H. Earl Capehart, Jr., Indianapolis
IUOHP—Indiana University Oral History Project. Tapes and transcripts of the Capehart project at the Lilly Library, Indiana University, Bloomington, Indiana
CMSS—Homer Earl Capehart papers, Indiana Division, Indiana State Library, Indianapolis
CR—*Congressional Record*

Chapter 1

1. Beulah Gray, "Half of Capehart's Life Spent in Near-Poverty," *Washington* (Ind.) *Herald*, 3 July 1950 (special Capehart campaign edition). When Capehart left the Senate after being defeated by Birch Bayh in 1962, he had served longer than any previous senator elected by the people of Indiana. Daniel W. Voorhees, a Democrat, served twenty years (1877-97) but was elected by the Indiana General Assembly. Sen. James Eli Watson served only sixteen years. CMM, 31, 32, 35, 36.

2. Thomas C. Capehart may have been the son of a landowner, slaveholder, and fish processor in Bertie County, North Carolina. County records show a Thomas, son of George Capehart, who owned both land and slaves. Transfer Book, Jefferson Township, 1891-95, Auditor's Office, Pike County Courthouse, Petersburg, Indiana; John Bennett Boddie, *Southside Virginia Families*, 2 vols. (Redwood City, Calif.: Pacific Coast Publishers, 1955-56), 2:142.

3. Jack B. Haskins, interview with author, 10 Sept. 1971; HEC and Bessie Haskins, IUOHP, tape 1, p. 33; HEC, IUOHP, tape 6, p. 175; Transfer Books, Jefferson Township, Pike County, 1885-90, 1899-1903.

4. CMM, 36, 47, 55, 57; Marie Arrington Davidson, comp., *Andrew Foster Kelso* (Twin Falls, Idaho: n.p., 1957), 18.

5. Paul Capehart, interview with author, 12 Aug. 1971; Transfer Book, Jefferson Township, Pike County, 1907-11; *Washington* (Ind.) *Herald*, 3 July 1950; Marion C. Borders, IUOHP, tape 1, p. 12, tape 2, p. 38.

6. Robert Hyatt, interview with author, 10 Aug. 1971.

7. Mrs. John Sellman, interview with author, 8 Oct. 1969; *The Washingtonian* (Washington, Ind.: Washington High School, 1914), 44.

8. *The Washingtonian*, 1914, p. 109; 1916, p. 33; [Homer] Earl Capehart, Permanent-Final High School Record, Washington High School. John S. Hastings would become a prosperous lawyer and was one of the earliest supporters of Capehart for the Senate. The senator in 1957 arranged an appointment for Hastings to the U.S. Court of Appeals in Chicago. John Hastings, IUOHP, tape 1, p. 8.

9. HEC, tape 6, pp. 172, 174-77; [Homer] Earl Capehart, Permanent-Final High School Record, Polo High School, Polo, Illinois.

10. HEC, tape 2, pp. 8, 11, 12.

11. CMM, 92.

12. Ibid., 94-96.

13. Ibid., 97. On his father's mechanical ability Capehart's son, H. Earl Capehart, Jr., once remarked: "He has no mechanical ability whatsoever. He has none. I have never seen my father do any mechanical work at all. I have never seen him even hammer a nail in a board . . . he doesn't know how to fix anything and knows virtually nothing about mechanics or engineering." H. Earl Capehart, Jr., IUOHP, tape 1, pp. 19-20.

14. Certificate of the World War I Army Service of Homer E. Capehart, Indiana Commission on Public Records, State Archives Division; HEC's army service record, Form 724-1 A.G.O., 12 Mar. 1920, ibid.; *Twelfth U.S. Infantry, 1789-1919: Its Story—By Its Men* (New York: Knickerbocker Press, 1919), iii, 29, 31, 261, 301.

15. HEC, tape 2, p. 23.

16. CMM, 104.

17. "How Case Capitalizes Tractor Contest Award," *Printer's Ink*, 13 Oct. 1921, pp. 133, 136; *Moody's Manual of Railroads and Corporation Securities: Twenty-first Annual Number, Industrial Section* (New York: Poor's Publishing Co., 1920), 299-300.

18. CMM, 110, 115-16, 125; HEC, interview with author, 11 July 1969.

19. George E. Gill, "A Brief History of the Packard Manufacturing Corporation" (unpublished manuscript, 1944), 12, HECP; Frank Hoke, "Two Heads Are Better: The Story of Holcomb & Hoke Manufacturing Company" (unpublished manuscript, 1958), 3, Frank Hoke personal papers, Indianapolis; Amendment to the Articles of Association, The American Box Ball Company, 29 May 1913, Office of the Secretary of State of Indiana, Indianapolis.

20. Annual Domestic Report to the Secretary of State of Indiana, Holcomb and Hoke Manufacturing Company, 21 July 1921, Indiana Commission on Public Records, State Archives Division; James Irving Holcomb, *Salesology of the Butter-Kist Popcorn and Peanut Machines* (Indianapolis: Holcomb and Hoke Manufacturing Co., 1923), 79.

21. Holcomb, *Salesology*, 42, 172, 248.
22. HEC, tape 2, p. 37.
23. CMM, 128-32; Carlton and Earle Mueller, IUOHP, tape 1, p. 2; *Indianapolis News*, 22 Sept. 1956; *Green Bay Press-Gazette*, 4 Oct. 1922, microfilm, CMSS. For the Baker-Capehart Agency see HEC, tape 3, pp. 42-43; H. Earl Capehart, Jr., tape 1, pp. 2, 13; Hoke, "Two Heads Are Better," 9, 16.

Chapter 2

1. *The Talking Machine Journal* (Apr. 1928): 49.
2. HEC, *Creative Selling* (Fort Wayne, Ind.: The Capehart Automatic Phonograph Corporation, 1929), iv, 3, 28, 47, 56.
3. HEC, interview with author, 11 July 1969; "The Capehart," *Fortune* 23 (Feb. 1941): 64.
4. Oliver Read and Walter L. Welch, *From Tin Foil to Stereo: Evolution of the Phonograph* (Indianapolis: H. W. Sams, 1959), 269, 327-30. The first home record changer to receive much attention was an Orthophonic Victrola in 1927. The phonograph was acoustic with an electric turntable and changing mechanism. Ibid., 314.
5. Frank Hoke, "Two Heads Are Better: The Story of Holcomb & Hoke Manufacturing Company" (unpublished manuscript, 1958), 16, Frank Hoke personal papers, Indianapolis; HEC, IUOHP, tape 3, p. 50.
6. Hoke, "Two Heads Are Better," 18; Kenneth F. Valentine, IUOHP, tape 1, p. 14; Gerald C. Crary, letter to author, 30 Oct. 1971.
7. CMM, 134; William E. Simmons, letter to author, 2 Sept. 1969.
8. Annual Domestic Report to the Secretary of State of Indiana, Marmon Motor Car Company, 14 Sept. 1927, Indiana Commission on Public Records, State Archives Division; CMM, 134.
9. CMM, 136; HEC, tape 3, p. 54.
10. Report to the Secretary of State, Caswell-Runyan Company, 2 July 1928, Indiana Commission on Public Records, State Archives Division; Articles of Incorporation, Capehart Automatic Phonograph Corporation, 4 Feb. 1928, ibid.; Report to the Secretary of State, Capehart Automatic Phonograph Corporation, 3 Apr. 1929, ibid.; HEC, tape 3, p. 55; CMM, 136.
11. *Fort Wayne News-Sentinel*, 13 June 1929; *The Capehart Orchestrope*, Capehart Automatic Phonograph Corporation, pamphlet, HECP.
12. "Capehart Music," The Capehart Corporation, Fort Wayne, Indiana, pamphlet, microfilm, CMSS; HEC, tape 3, p. 60; "From Music to Guns," Capehart speech, 4 Jan. 1944, Box 154, folder 6, CMSS; CMM, 137.
13. Simmons, letters to author, 19 Aug., 2 Sept. 1969; Crary, letter to author, 30 Oct. 1971.
14. HEC, *Creative Selling*, 58, 66; Kenneth F. Valentine, IUOHP, tape 1, pp. 7, 9; *Fort Wayne News-Sentinel*, 13 June 1929; *Fort Wayne Journal-Gazette*, 14 June 1929.
15. Valentine, tape 1, p. 17; HEC, *Creative Selling*, 75.

16. "The Capehart," 64; Crary, letter to author, 30 Oct. 1971. Capehart phonograph ads appear in *The Billboard*, 15 June 1929, p. 162 and *Radio Broadcast* (Dec. 1929): 102.

17. CMM, 137-38; Valentine, tape 1, p. 2; HEC, "From Music to Guns."

18. HEC, tape 5, p. 138; CMM, 138; Articles of Incorporation, Capehart Corporation, 27 May 1929, Indiana Commission on Public Records, State Archives Division; Report to the Secretary of State of Indiana, Capehart Corporation, 1 July 1929 through 30 June 1932.

19. *Fort Wayne Journal-Gazette*, 14 June 1929; *The Capehart Amplifier* 2 (Oct. 1929), HECP; HEC, interview with author, 1 Dec. 1971.

20. *The Capehart Amplifier.* The export division of the corporation retailed Capehart phonographs overseas at $1,450. William Merchant, IUOHP, tape 2, p. 44; Kin Hubbard, ed., *A Book of Indiana* (Indianapolis: Indiana Biographical Association, 1929), 642, 671; *Fort Wayne News-Sentinel*, 27 Nov. 1929.

21. *The Capehart Orchestrope*; *Fort Wayne News-Sentinel*, 13 June 1929; HEC, tape 8, p. 211.

22. HEC, interview with author, 1 Dec. 1971.

23. The Capehart Corporation sales brochure, 1931, microfilm, CMSS; Read and Welch, *From Tin Foil to Stereo*, 296, 297, 314; "The Capehart," 119; Capehart Corporation Sales List, 1930, microfilm, CMSS; *The Capehart Orchestrope*.

24. HEC, interviews with author, 28 Sept., 1 Dec. 1971; "The Capehart '400,' " microfilm, CMSS; Capehart Corporation Sales List, 1930; HEC, *Creative Selling*, 80; "Pride of Possession" (brochure), microfilm, CMSS.

25. Letter from D. R. Winstead, Exalted Ruler, Norfolk Lodge No. 38, B.P.O.E., 1 Sept. 1928, in *The Capehart Orchestrope*; Read and Welch, *From Tin Foil to Stereo*, 296; *Fort Wayne News-Sentinel*, 27 Nov. 1929.

CHAPTER 3

1. Roland Gelatt, *The Fabulous Phonograph: From Edison to Stereo* (New York: Appleton-Century, 1966), 251, 254-55, 325.

2. *Fort Wayne News-Sentinel*, 27 Nov. 1929.

3. Ibid., 3 Oct. 1930; Kenneth Valentine, IUOHP, tape 2, pp. 33-34; "The Capehart," *Fortune* 23 (Feb. 1941): 122; William F. Merchant, IUOHP, tape 1, p. 61.

4. HEC, IUOHP, tape 8, p. 208; Valentine, tape 1, pp. 19-20; CMM, 142.

5. Articles of Amendment to the Articles of Reorganization of the Capehart Corporation, 21 Oct. 1931, Indiana Commission on Public Records, State Archives Division.

6. HEC, tape 3, p. 75.

7. HEC, interview with author, 1 Dec. 1971.

8. His son, H. Earl Capehart, Jr., now a prominent Indianapolis attorney, was ten years old at the time and remembers that "the business was not doing well in Fort Wayne during the depression . . . my mother told us that we were going to have to be more frugal . . . we had Buicks and Cadillacs and that sort of car and my father, I know, ended up with a Ford . . . but

he didn't keep the Ford very long." H. Earl Capehart, Jr., IUOHP, tape 1, p. 20.

9. CMM, 144; John R. Mitchell, Paul U. Lannerd Contract with Irma Capehart, 1 June 1932, Minutes of the Packard-Capehart, Inc. Directors, HECP; Articles of Incorporation, Packard-Capehart, Inc., 13 June 1932, ibid.; Mitchell, Lannerd License Agreement with Irma Capehart, 18 June 1932, ibid.; George E. Gill, "A Brief History of the Packard Manufacturing Corporation" (unpublished manuscript, 1944), ibid., 34; Articles of Amendment to the Articles of Incorporation of Packard-Capehart, Inc., 3 Nov. 1932, Minutes of the Packard-Capehart, Inc. Directors, ibid.

10. HEC, tape 4, p. 95; Farny R. Wurlitzer, interview with author, 24 Aug. 1971.

11. Oliver Read and Walter L. Welch, *From Tin Foil to Stereo: Evolution of the Phonograph* (Indianapolis: H. W. Sams, 1959), 312-13; CMM, 146.

12. HEC to Farny R. Wurlitzer, 3 Apr. 1933, Correspondence Files, Wurlitzer Company, North Tonawanda, N.Y.

13. Merchant, tape 2, pp. 48-49; HEC, interview with author, 1 Dec. 1971.

14. *Wurlitzer at One Hundred* (Wurlitzer Company, North Tonawanda, N.Y., 1956, pamphlet), 8-9; Lloyd Graham, "The Story of the Rudolph Wurlitzer Family and Business" (North Tonawanda, N.Y., 1956, unpublished manuscript), 105-6, 107-9; "Chronology of Important Events in the History of the Wurlitzer Company," A. D. Palmer, Jr., Historical File, Wurlitzer Company, North Tonawanda, N.Y., 149-50, 204; Read and Welch, *From Tin Foil to Stereo*, 312-13.

15. *Moody's Manual of Investments: American and Foreign: Industrial Securities* (New York: Moody's Investors Service, 1933), 1537-38; Graham, "Story of the Rudolph Wurlitzer Family," 148, 149, 151.

16. The Packard Manufacturing Company would remain in existence only on paper as holder of the Lannerd-Mitchell patents. Minutes of the Packard Manufacturing Corporation Directors, 22 Apr. 1933, HECP; CMM, 147; HEC, tape 4, p. 97. Capehart lived in an upstairs apartment a few blocks from the plant until he could move his family from Fort Wayne. In preparation for their arrival he rented a large house in Snyder, a Buffalo suburb twenty minutes from the office. HEC Employment Record, Wurlitzer Manufacturing Company, North Tonawanda, N.Y.; Clock No. 1202 Data Card, ibid. Regional and district managers who went with Capehart to Wurlitzer included W. F. Merchant of Fort Wayne, W. E. Simmons of Los Angeles, W. R. Deaton of Greensboro, N.C., J. A. Darwin of New York City, W. C. Mossbarger of Minneapolis, O. F. Kramer of Oklahoma City, R. Q. Kramer of Atlanta, and J. H. Payne of Pittsburgh. *Heads Up!* 1 (Oct. 1938), Wurlitzer Company, North Tonawanda, N.Y.; HEC, interview with author, 22 Aug. 1971.

17. "Multi-Selector of the Wurlitzer Simplex," Wurlitzer pamphlet in personal papers of William E. Simmons, Hollywood, California; Graham, "Story of the Rudolph Wurlitzer Family," 158; Geoffrey Parsons, Jr., and Robert Yoder, "A Nickel a Tune," *Reader's Digest* (Feb. 1941): 113; Gelatt, *The Fabulous Phonograph*, 267, 272.

18. William F. Merchant, interview with author, 11 Dec. 1970; *The Billboard*, 16 July 1938, pp. 64-70.

19. Graham, "Story of the Rudolph Wurlitzer Family," 158; E. H. Petering to All District Managers, 3 Nov. 1938, E. H. Petering Correspondence Files, Wurlitzer Company, North Tonawanda, N.Y.; CMM, 152-53, 162.

20. CMM, 159-60; HEC to All District Managers, 22 Oct. 1938, Correspondence Files, Wurlitzer Company, North Tonawanda, N.Y.

21. CMM, 167; Program for the Wurlitzer Appreciation Banquet, 6 Dec. 1936, microfilm, CMSS.

22. Pictorial Report, First Annual Convention of the Wurlitzer Century Club, HECP; HEC, "From Music to Guns," Capehart speech, 4 Jan. 1944, Box 154, folder 6, CMSS; Program from First Annual Convention of the Wurlitzer Century Club, 25-27 Aug. 1937, microfilm, CMSS.

23. Graham, "Story of the Rudolph Wurlitzer Family," 111-14; *Prentice-Hall Capital Adjustments: Stock Dividends, Stock Rights, Reorganizations* (Englewood Cliffs, N.J.: Prentice-Hall, 1970), W-117; Read and Welch, *From Tin Foil to Stereo*, 316; T. Murray, "You Pay before You Play: Coin Operated Phonograph," *Nation's Business* (June 1940): 30, 110.

24. Although there is no evidence that Capehart had dealings with gangsters, testimony about Wurlitzer's dealings with racketeers in Chicago and Gary comes from various sources. Merchant, tape 2, p. 71. Capehart's successor as general sales manager at North Tonawanda was Milton Hammergren. Hammergren would admit to selling 550 jukeboxes to Chicago gangsters. "We didn't like it," he said, "but we had to sell juke boxes." *New York Times*, 11 Feb. 1959; U.S. Congress, Senate, *Hearings before the Select Committee on Improper Activities in the Labor and Management Field, February 10, 1959*, p. 16546.

25. HEC, United States Individual Income Tax Return for 1937, HECP; Irma V. Capehart, United States Individual Income Tax Return, 1937, ibid. The estimate that Capehart still held 20,195 shares is computed by subtracting 1,805 shares sold in May 1936 at $20 a share, from his original 22,000 shares. *New York Times*, 7 Mar. 1937; HEC Employment Record, Wurlitzer Manufacturing Company.

26. Transfer Books, 1935-39, 1941, 1962-67, Auditor's Office, Daviess County Courthouse, Washington, Indiana. Capehart remembered paying about $150 an acre for the farmland. HEC, interview with author, 15 July 1972.

27. Capehart-Haskins farm agreement, 1 Mar. 1937, microfilm, CMSS; Jack B. Haskins, interview with author, 10 Sept. 1971; HEC, tape 5, pp. 126, 131.

28. William E. Simmons, letter to the author, 2 Sept. 1969; HEC, tape 6, p. 165; *Washington* (Ind.) *Herald*, 3 July 1950 (special Capehart campaign edition); Ray S. Donaldson, IUOHP, tape 1, p. 3; HEC, interview with author, 5 July 1971; HEC, United States Individual Income Tax Return for 1937, HECP; HEC, Annual Individual Gross Income Tax Return, Indiana, 1938, ibid.

29. *Washington* (Ind.) *Herald*, 27 Oct. 1937; Farm Inventory, 31 Dec. 1937, microfilm, CMSS; List of checks, 1937, HECP. For HEC's desire to show off his accomplishments in his boyhood surroundings see Marion C. Borders, IUOHP, tape 1, p. 12 and H. Earl Capehart, Jr., tape 1, p. 18.

Chapter 4

1. HEC, IUOHP, tape 3, pp. 74, 188, tape 7, p. 198. He later recalled, "If we hadn't gotten into this terrible depression and I hadn't, as a result of it, been forced out of Capehart Corporation, I possibly would never have been a senator." HEC, tape 6, p. 147.

2. CMM, 19, 188. Capehart remembered writing these letters but denied that he personally was ever a Democrat. He found his friend and neighbor, Thomas L. Holling, Democratic mayor of Buffalo, to be politically attractive because as a successful businessman he sought efficiency in government. *Buffalo* (N.Y.) *Evening News*, 12, 18 Aug. 1937; HEC, interview with author, 25 Apr. 1972.

3. James MacGregor Burns, *Roosevelt: The Lion and the Fox* (New York: Harcourt, Brace, 1956), 307, 320, 326–27, 332, 360.

4. Donald Bruce Johnson, *The Republican Party and Wendell Willkie* (Urbana: University of Illinois Press, 1960), 12-13, 15; James T. Patterson, *Congressional Conservatism and the New Deal: The Growth of the Conservative Coalition in Congress, 1933-1939* (Lexington: University of Kentucky Press, 1967), 82, 202; Milton Plesur, "The Republican Congressional Comeback of 1938," *Review of Politics* 24 (Oct. 1962): 527-28, 532; "The Republican Party: Up from the Grave," *Fortune* 20 (Aug. 1939): 97, 104.

5. Capehart became a member of the 215-member Frank Committee, which early in August met in Evanston, Illinois. It warned of a breakdown in the nation's economy and "disintegration of responsible and effective government." The committee set out to identify "stimulations, regulations, and freedoms" that would sustain productivity. Membership List of the Republican Program Committee, OF 856, file: "Republican Party, 1935-1945," Roosevelt MSS, Roosevelt Library, Hyde Park, N.Y.; Malcolm Moos, *The Republicans: A History of Their Party* (New York: Random House, 1956), 405; *Saturday Evening Post*, 10 Dec. 1938, p. 22.

6. James T. Patterson, *The New Deal and the States: Federalism in Transition* (Princeton, N.J.: Princeton University Press, 1969), 134–35; *Peru* (Ind.) *Daily Tribune*, 23 Sept. 1938; John D. Barnhart and Donald F. Carmony, *Indiana: From Frontier to Industrial Commonwealth*, 4 vols. (New York: Lewis Historical Publishing Co., 1954), 2:484–85.

7. Iwan Morgan, "Factional Conflict in Indiana Politics during the Later New Deal Years, 1936-1940," *Indiana Magazine of History* 79 (Mar. 1983): 37-43; Patterson, *Congressional Conservatism*, 274.

8. HEC, tape 5, pp. 120-21; Arch Bobbitt, IUOHP, tape 1, p. 1; *Washington* (Ind.) *Herald*, 5 Aug. 1938; Felix McWhirter, IUOHP, tape 1, pp. 1, 2, 4. After underwriting the finances for the affair, Capehart appealed to his regional managers for donations. William F. Merchant, IUOHP, tape 1, p. 73.

9. Raymond E. Willis to Hugh A. Butler, 2 July 1938, Box 78, Willis MSS, Indiana Division, Indiana State Library; Willis to A. H. Vandenberg, Jr., 20 May 1938, ibid.; Hilton P. Hornaday to Willis, 11 June 1938, ibid.; Willis to Hornaday, 13 June 1938, ibid.

10. Barnhart and Carmony, *Indiana: From Frontier to Industrial Commonwealth*, 2:485.

11. For the Cornfield Conference as symbol of the conservative Republican resurgence see Joe Martin, *My First Fifty Years in Politics* (New York: McGraw-Hill, 1960), 82; "G.O.P. Picnic," *Newsweek*, 5 Sept. 1938, p. 8; Plesur, "Republican Congressional Comeback," 525, 542, 554-55; "The Republican Party," 33-34. This resurgence led to the bipartisan congressional coalition of conservative Democrats and Republicans that gained control of the Eightieth Congress in 1947.

12. *Indianapolis Star*, 2 July 1938; *Cincinnati Times-Star*, 9 Aug. 1938.

13. HEC, IUOHP, tape 9, p. 231; *Indianapolis Star*, 2 July, 25 Aug. 1938; *The Billboard*, 20 Aug. 1938, p. 66.

14. HEC, "Details of the Cornfield Conference," Indiana State Central Committee Handout, 2 July 1938, microfilm, CMSS; *New York Times*, 28 Aug. 1938.

15. Robert A. Taft to Raymond E. Willis, 28 Aug. 1938, Box 78, Willis MSS; John Hamilton to Taft, 25 Aug. 1938, Box 118, file: "Political 1938, Republican National Committee," Taft MSS, Library of Congress.

16. *Buffalo Courier-Express*, 27 Aug. 1938; HEC, "Details of the Cornfield Conference"; *Indianapolis Star*, 28 Aug. 1938.

17. *Indianapolis Star*, 25 Aug. 1938; *New York Times*, 29 Aug. 1938; *Spokane* (Wash.) *Spokesman Review*, 28 Aug. 1938; "G.O.P. Picnic," 8; "Homeric Feast," *Time*, 5 Sept. 1938, p. 12; *Newsweek*, 5 Sept. 1938, p. 8.

18. *Indianapolis Star*, 27 Aug. 1938; *New York Times*, 28 Aug. 1938; James Eli Watson, *As I Knew Them* (Indianapolis: Bobbs-Merrill Co., 1936), 254-56.

19. *Indianapolis Star*, 28 Aug. 1938; *New York Times*, 28 Aug., 4 Sept. 1938.

20. *Indianapolis Star*, 28 Aug. 1938.

21. HEC, speech, "Dealing with the Relief Problem," 27 Aug. 1938, Box 154, folder 6, CMSS.

22. HEC, interview with author, 25 Apr. 1972; Morgan, "Factional Conflict," 53-54, 59.

23. *New York Times*, 29 Aug. 1938.

24. *Westchester County* (N.Y.) *Weekly Press*, 8 Sept. 1938.

25. Democratic National Chairman James A. Farley called it "the great turnover." Patterson, *Congressional Conservatism*, 288-90; Plesur, "Republican Congressional Comeback," 543; Samuel Lubell, *The Future of American Politics* (New York: Harper and Row, 1965), 195; Edward H. Ziegner, "Indiana in National Politics," in Donald F. Carmony, ed., *Indiana: A Self-Appraisal* (Bloomington: Indiana University Press, 1966), 41; James H. Madison, *The Indiana Way: A State History* (Bloomington and Indianapolis: Indiana University Press and Indiana Historical Society, 1986), 295-308.

26. In their report to the Democratic national chairman, Indiana Democratic leaders spoke of conservative farmers disillusioned with crop control, of the WPA make-work programs that helped make farm labor scarce, and of the wages and hours law that hurt small business. These measures, along with government leniency toward sit-down strikes, spending programs that antagonized independent voters, and the attempted presidential purge of Democratic senators opposed to packing the Supreme Court, they said, gave the Republicans "effective ammunition." Indiana

Democratic State Committee, "Results of Indiana Election, 1938," OF 300, Box 86, file: "Farley, 1938, Ind.," Roosevelt MSS; *Indianapolis Star*, 5 Oct. 1938; Barnhart and Carmony, *Indiana: From Frontier to Industrial Commonwealth*, 2:486.

27. *Westchester County* (N.Y.) *Weekly Press*, 8 Sept. 1938.

28. *The Billboard*, 20 Aug. 1938, p. 66; *Kansas City Star*, 4 Oct. 1938; *Columbia City* (Ind.) *Post*, 29 Aug. 1938; *Evansville* (Ind.) *Courier*, 2 Oct. 1938.

29. John Hastings, IUOHP, tape 1, p. 20; HEC, tape 9, pp. 220-21. Capehart about this time started a collection of Abraham Lincoln photographs and busts—an assortment which would by 1956 number some 150 and which, he claimed, was the "most complete collection of Lincoln photographs in the United States." *Indianapolis News*, 11 Feb. 1956. The Lincoln National Life Insurance Company in Fort Wayne now owns the collection.

30. William E. Jenner, interview with author, 20 Sept. 1971; HEC, tape 9, p. 216; *Indianapolis Star*, 18 Sept. 1938.

31. *Indianapolis Star*, 18 Sept. 1938; Jenner, interview with author, 20 Sept. 1971. Indeed, HEC had hit a chord with the voters. As one writer has said, "the legendary hero of America is the self-made man." Irvin G. Wyllie, *The Self-Made Man in America: The Myth of Rags to Riches* (New Brunswick, N.J.: Rutgers University Press, 1954), 6.

32. *Indianapolis Star*, 18 Sept. 1938; *Evansville* (Ind.) *Courier*, 2 Oct. 1938.

Chapter 5

1. Farny R. Wurlitzer, interview with author, 24 Aug. 1971; HEC, IUOHP, tape 5, p. 13.

2. *Buffalo* (N.Y.) *Courier-Express*, 5 Jan. 1940; HEC to all Wurlitzer customers, 20 Jan. 1939, microfilm, CMSS.

3. Packard Manufacturing Corporation Stock Book, 6 July 1940, HECP; Minutes of the Packard Manufacturing Corporation Directors, 8 July 1940, ibid.

4. Minutes of the Packard Directors, 21 Sept., 12, 31 Dec. 1940; *Indianapolis Star*, 15 Sept. 1940; Articles of Amendment to the Articles of Incorporation of the Packard Manufacturing Corporation, 30 Dec. 1940, HECP.

5. HEC speech entitled, "Lincoln Ideals . . . Brought Down to Date," 13 Feb. 1939, delivered over radio station WIND, HECP; *Columbus* (Ind.) *Evening Republican*, 24 Jan. 1939; *Indianapolis Star*, 18 Apr. 1939.

6. *Indianapolis Star*, 24 May 1939; Felix M. McWhirter, interview with author, 1 Aug. 1972.

7. Capehart commented that the Indiana Republican Editorial Association supported him as it did Raymond Willis. He knew all the officers of the association and considered them friends. HEC, interview with author, 25 Apr. 1972; Arch Bobbitt, IUOHP, tape 1, p. 7.

8. *Indianapolis Star*, 23, 24 Sept. 1939; HEC speech, 23 Sept. 1939, Hoover MSS, Herbert C. Hoover Library, West Branch, Iowa. HEC's speech earned

a note of praise from Herbert Hoover. Hoover to HEC, Oct. 1939, Post-Presidential papers, Capehart Correspondence, Hoover MSS.

9. *New York Times*, 1 Oct. 1939.

10. Both Arch Bobbitt and Capehart recalled that they went to Philadelphia as Taft delegates but shifted to Wendell Willkie on the last ballot. HEC, interview with author, 25 Apr. 1972; HEC, tape 5, p. 141. Capehart's sudden prominence had its drawbacks. In his daily column Maurice Early wrote: "Old-timers secretly resent the sudden rise of such newcomers in their midst as Capehart and [Robert W.] Lyons," wealthy Indianapolis and Washington, D.C., attorney and chain-food-store lobbyist and an important influence in Capehart's 1944 senatorial nomination. *Indianapolis Star*, 25 May 1940; Bobbitt, tape 1, pp. 8-9; Herman O. Makey, *Wendell Willkie of Elwood* (Elwood, Ind.: National Book Co., Inc., 1940), 281; Mary Earhart Dillon, *Wendell Willkie, 1892-1944* (Philadelphia: J. B. Lippincott Co., 1952), 124, 190. See also HEC to Cyril Clemens, 8 Aug. 1940, file: Capehart, Halleck MSS, Lilly Library, Indiana University.

11. Joseph Barnes, *Willkie: The Events He Was Part Of—The Ideas He Fought For* (New York: Simon and Schuster, 1952), 194; *Indianapolis Star*, 17 July 1940; *Indianapolis News*, 19 Aug. 1940; Dillon, *Wendell Willkie, 1892-1944*, 190-92.

12. Makey, *Wendell Willkie of Elwood*, 281; HEC, interview with author, 25 Apr. 1972.

13. *Indianapolis Star*, 18 Aug. 1940; Donald Bruce Johnson, *The Republican Party and Wendell Willkie* (Urbana: University of Illinois Press, 1960), 121; HEC, tape 10, p. 251.

14. *Indianapolis Times*, 17, 19 Aug. 1940. Noninterventionist sentiment was strong throughout the Midwest, and only a few weeks later House Republicans would ignore Willkie and vote 112 to 51 against the president's Selective Service bill. Warren Moscow, *Roosevelt and Willkie* (Englewood Cliffs, N.J.: Prentice-Hall, 1968), 31; Johnson, *Republican Party and Willkie*, 123; Henry O. Evjen, "The Willkie Campaign: An Unfortunate Chapter in Republican Leadership," *Journal of Politics* 14 (May 1952): 248.

15. *Indianapolis Star*, 18 Aug. 1940; *Indianapolis Times*, 17 Aug. 1940. An article written to commemorate the thirtieth anniversary of the affair said the notification ceremony was "the largest political gathering anywhere in the world of which there is any record." *Indianapolis Star*, 16 Aug. 1970; *Indianapolis Times*, 19 Aug. 1940; HEC, interview with author, 25 Apr. 1972.

16. John D. Barnhart and Donald F. Carmony, *Indiana: From Frontier to Industrial Commonwealth*, 4 vols. (New York: Lewis Historical Publishing Co., Inc., 1954), 2:487.

17. William E. Simmons, letters to author, 19 Aug., 2 Sept. 1969; HEC, tape 9, pp. 215, 223; Pla-Mor Trade Mark Certificate Number 394, 550, 14 Apr. 1942, HECP; Minutes of the Packard Directors, 14 June 1941, ibid.; HEC, Indiana Annual Individual Gross Income Tax Return, 1941, ibid.

18. HEC, "From Music to Guns," Capehart speech, 4 Jan. 1944, Box 154, folder 6, CMSS; George E. Gill, "A Brief History of the Packard Manufacturing Corporation" (unpublished manuscript, 1944), 78-79, 81-82, HECP; HEC, interview with author, 25 Apr. 1972; *Indianapolis Star*, 10, 11

Sept. 1941; Application for Necessity Certificate, 4 Mar. 1942, Packard Certificate of Necessity File, HECP.

19. Minutes of the Packard Directors, 31 Dec. 1941; 23 Jan., 29 June, 15 Aug., 10 Nov., 1942; 2 Aug., 4 Oct. 1943; Application for Necessity Certificate, 4 Mar. 1942; Gill, "Brief History of Packard," 81-82; HEC, "From Music to Guns"; HEC, Indiana Annual Individual Gross Income Tax Return, 1942, HECP.

20. "What's Become of Homer Capehart," *Hoosier Republican*, 23 May 1941, p. 3; *Indianapolis Star*, 28, 29 Aug. 1941; 13 May 1942; Ralph Gates, interview with author, 27 Mar. 1975.

21. *Indianapolis Star*, 28, 29 Aug. 1941.

22. *Indianapolis Star*, 13 May 1942; HEC, tape 9, p. 244; Claude Billings, IUOHP, tape 1, p. 4.

23. HEC, tape 9, pp. 221-22; Barnhart and Carmony, *Indiana: From Frontier to Industrial Commonwealth*, 2:497-98.

24. *Indianapolis Star*, 23 Nov. 1943; HEC, "From Music to Guns"; Certificate of Incorporation, Packard Pla-Mor Club, Inc., 6 July 1944, Office of the Indiana Secretary of State, Indianapolis, microfilm; *Indianapolis Times*, 10 Mar. 1943; *Homer E. Capehart's Salute to Packard Mfg. Corp. Employees* 1 (Apr. 1943), microfilm, CMSS.

25. HEC, "From Music to Guns"; HEC, speech schedule for "From Music to Guns," Box 154, folder 6, CMSS; HEC, interview with author, 26 Apr. 1972. Merging business with politics and patriotism, Capehart was himself a member of the Scottish Rite, Rotary, Elks, Eagles, Moose, American Legion, State Chamber of Commerce, Athletic Club, Columbia Club, Press Club, Army & Navy Club, the Meridian Hills Country Club, the Indiana Society and Union League in Chicago, the Sons of Indiana, and the National Republican Club in New York. Recipient of a service medal from the Veterans of Foreign Wars, he also had served as chairman of the Navy Day parade and chairman of the county war savings drive in Indianapolis. When reporters asked him where he found the time, he offered them his three-point formula for getting things done: decide what you want to do in advance, delegate authority and responsibility, and never worry about things over which you have no control. *Indianapolis Times*, 23 Oct. 1943; *Who's Who and What's What in Indiana Politics* (Indianapolis: James E. Perry, 1944), 770.

26. Claude Billings, IUOHP, tape 1, p. 15; Claude Billings, interview with author, 28 July 1972. Unofficially Capehart's campaign was under way. In December Indianapolis newspapers reported that the Republican state organization would favor James M. Tucker instead of Capehart for the senatorial nomination. Capehart's response was to challenge Tucker. He sent ten thousand copies of a letter to party officials asking for the nomination, saying he would fight for the interests of party and country and would announce his candidacy the second week in January 1944. Anticipating a difficult fight for the nomination, and, if nominated, another for election, he asked his advisers—Paul Bausman, Arch Bobbitt, and Republican newsman and political writer, Horace Coats—to outline strategy. They decided that the announcement should occur in Daviess County at a chicken dinner for the seventh district county chairmen.

27. *Indianapolis Star*, 15 July 1943; *New York Times*, 5 Jan. 1944.
28. *New York Times*, 5 Jan. 1944; CMM, 42-43.
29. *Indianapolis Star*, 31 Mar. 1944.

Chapter 6

1. Frank J. Munger, "Two-Party Politics in the State of Indiana" (Ph.D. diss., Harvard University, 1955), 151, 278-79, 292.

2. James M. Tucker, IUOHP, tape 1, p. 9; *Indianapolis Star*, 17 June 1942; 31 Mar. 1944.

3. HEC, Announcement Speech, with an introduction by John S. Hastings, 14 Jan. 1944, Washington, Indiana, Box 142, folder 2, CMSS; *Indianapolis Star*, 15 Jan. 1944.

4. HEC, Announcement Speech.

5. HEC, interviews with author, 26 Apr., 22 July 1972; Campaign Scrapbook, 1944, Capehart Farms, Daviess County, Indiana. Especially important was support from the powerful GOP veterans organization, which endorsed Capehart in February. *Indianapolis News*, 7 Feb. 1944; Ralph Gates, interview with author, 28 July 1972.

6. *Indianapolis Star*, 12 May 1944; HEC, interview with author, 26 Apr. 1972. There were reports that Capehart donated some $1,450 to the "regulars." *Indianapolis Times*, 23 May 1944. Capehart's attitude toward money in politics appeared in his "From Music to Guns" speech: "I would like to recommend at this point that each of you men, when you go home tonight, look up the precinct committeeman . . . in your own precinct and shake hands with them and offer them your services, and likewise offer them a little of your money." HEC, "From Music to Guns," Capehart speech, 4 Jan. 1944, Box 154, folder 6, CMSS.

7. HEC, interview with author, 26 Apr. 1972. Robert W. Lyons was an attorney for chain stores and shipping companies. Active in the American Legion, he had been in Indiana politics during the 1920s and recently had become active again in Marion County politics. Newspapers revealed, however, that he had been the state treasurer of the Ku Klux Klan. *Louisville Courier-Journal*, 2 June 1944; *Indianapolis Star*, 26, 27 May, 3 June 1944.

8. *Indianapolis Star*, 21 May 1940; 10 May 1944. For Jenner see Michael Paul Poder, "The Senatorial Career of William E. Jenner" (Ph.D. diss., University of Notre Dame, 1976). Jenner was born in Marengo in Crawford County. He held a law degree from Indiana University and had opened a law practice in Shoals, Indiana. In 1934 he was elected to the state senate and by 1939 had risen to the position of president *pro tempore*. A notable orator, Jenner was elected in November 1944 to serve out the unexpired term of the deceased Sen. Frederick Van Nuys until Capehart, who was elected for the full term, could take office the following January. *Biographical Directory of the United States Congress, 1774-1989* (Washington, D.C.: U.S. Government Printing Office, 1989), 1260.

9. Campaign Scrapbook; Voting Record of the Republican State Convention, 1944, Box 142, folder 2, CMSS.

10. More than anyone else Joseph Daniels controlled the Marion County delegation, and he informed Gates that he would support Capehart. Ralph Gates, letter to the author, 21 Mar. 1973; Arch Bobbitt, IUOHP, tape 1, p. 5; Bobbitt, interview with author, 27 July 1972; Gates, interview with author, 28 July 1972. Capehart also benefited from Robert Lyons's effort on the convention floor. *Indianapolis Star*, 3 June 1944.

11. *Indianapolis Star*, 19, 21, 25 June 1944; *Louisville Courier-Journal*, 23 May 1944. Capehart's total reported income from his farm and from Packard was $168,239 for 1944. HEC, Indiana Annual Individual Gross Income Tax Return, 1944, HECP. James M. Tucker said Jim Bradford told him that Capehart promised $30,000 to the Marion County organization. Tucker, tape 1, p. 10.

12. *Indianapolis News*, 22 Nov. 1944; *Indianapolis Star*, 18 June, 7 Dec. 1944; HEC, interview with author, 22 July 1972. Love of people tempered his driving decisiveness. As one reporter put it, "I don't know whether he dislikes his own company or whether he has a loneliness, but he prefers to have someone with him all the time." Benjamin R. Cole, IUOHP, tape 1, p. 1; William F. Merchant, interview with author, 11 Dec. 1970; William E. Simmons, letter to author, 19 Aug. 1969; Ray Donaldson, IUOHP, tape 1, p. 14.

13. John D. Barnhart and Donald F. Carmony, *Indiana: From Frontier to Industrial Commonwealth*, 4 vols. (New York: Lewis Historical Publishing Co., 1954), 4:509; Charles F. Fleming, *The White Hat: Henry Frederick Schricker, A Political Biography* (n.p., 1966), 59.

14. HEC, Address at Wabash, Indiana, "Campaign Addresses of Homer E. Capehart, 1944," HECP, sec. 8, p. 37.

15. He also advocated extension of social security on an equal basis to farmers, domestic help, and office workers. Periods of depression, he claimed, were inevitable and asked for government aid in ameliorating their effects by seeking markets for American products and even "pre-planning" long-term and short-term public works projects. Ibid., sec. 18, p. 33.

16. Ibid. Capehart was assisted by his advisers and writers Paul Bausman, Arch Bobbitt, Horace Coats, Claude Billings, and James W. Carr, secretary of the James Whitcomb Riley Memorial Association. HEC, IUOHP, tape 7, pp. 199-200; Claude Billings, IUOHP, tape 1, p. 22. The nature and origins of the anticommunist issue in Indiana appear in Dale Sorenson, "The Anticommunist Consensus in Indiana, 1945-1958" (Ph.D. diss., Indiana University, 1980), 36-89 and James Truett Selcraig, *The Red Scare in the Midwest, 1945-1955: A State and Local Study* (Ann Arbor, Mich.: UMI Research Press, 1982), 38-44.

17. HEC, Address before Eighth District GOP Veterans, Evansville, 24 Sept. 1944, "Campaign Addresses, 1944," sec. 4, p. 24; HEC, Radio Address, WHAS, Louisville, Kentucky, ibid., sec. 3, p. 12.

18. *Indianapolis Star*, 5 Nov. 1944. The politics of fear, of course, also had certain practical advantages. Accusing his conservative Democratic opponent of Communist sympathies enabled Capehart and his fellow GOP candidates to distinguish their program from that of the New Deal without rejecting many of its features. By declaring that "the communists headed by the Browders, by Harry Bridges, and all the other deep-dyed reds and parlor-

pinks" have stolen the Democratic party, he was saying trust me and the all-American GOP. HEC, Remarks at Cadle Tabernacle, Indianapolis, "Campaign Addresses, 1944," sec. 16, p. 9.

19. HEC, Radio Address, WHAS, Louisville, Kentucky, "Campaign Addresses, 1944," sec. 3, p. 24; HEC, Radio Address, WLW, Batesville, Indiana, ibid., sec. 24, p. 23. Ignoring Soviet strength following the succession of victories after the Battle of Stalingrad, he called for the president to "tell the people" what happened at the summit conference with Stalin at Tehran. *Indianapolis Star* reporter Benjamin R. Cole said Capehart drove "sophisticated politicians . . . frantic" because they were never able to simplify things to the degree he was. Benjamin R. Cole, tape 1, p. 7. The politics of anticommunism appear in David W. Reinhard, *The Republican Right since 1945* (Lexington: University Press of Kentucky, 1983).

20. *Indianapolis Times*, 30 Oct. 1944; William E. Simmons, letter to author, 2 Sept. 1969; HEC, interview with author, 26 Apr. 1972.

21. Fleming, *The White Hat*, 48; *Indianapolis News*, 4 Nov. 1944.

22. Fred F. Bays to Edward J. Flynn, 17 Feb. 1942, Democratic National Committee MSS, Box 1124, file: Fred Bays, Franklin D. Roosevelt Library, Hyde Park, N.Y.

23. *Indianapolis Star*, 18 Nov. 1944. Indiana Republicans won nine of eleven congressional seats. Robert J. Pitchell, *Indiana Votes* (Bloomington: Bureau of Government Research, Indiana University, 1960), 90-91. William E. Jenner, nominated to serve out Van Nuys's Senate term from the November election to January, made his appearance in mid-October with a searing attack on the anti-American—"even anti-God," Communist supporters "of the man who wants to be President for sixteen years." *Indianapolis News*, 21 Oct. 1944. He led Indiana Republicans with a plurality of 81,833 over Cornelius O'Brien. In February 1945 Jenner replaced John Lauer as Republican state chairman and became perhaps the most powerful man in the party. *Indianapolis Times*, 7 Dec. 1944; *Indianapolis Star*, 9, 13 Feb. 1945. Charges of voting irregularities in Marion County placed Capehart's election in jeopardy until an investigation cleared him. His reported expenses were $10,000 in the contest with Henry F. Schricker, who reported $4,500. Patronage gave the governor considerable influence, but Republican expenditures were overwhelming. The GOP spent $505,000, compared to a mere $113,501 for the Democrats. *Report of the Special Committee to Investigate Presidential, Vice Presidential, and Senatorial Campaign Expenditures in 1944*, No. 101 (Washington, D.C.: U.S. Government Printing Office, 1945), 64.

24. *Indianapolis Star*, 31 Dec. 1944; *Indianapolis News*, 10 Nov. 1944; Pitchell, *Indiana Votes*, 90-91. Of the eleven counties that gave Capehart 60 percent or more of their votes all were rural, and eight were from the northern plains of the state. In these areas particularly Capehart benefited from the "coattail" effect. John D. Unruh, "Urban-Rural Voting Trends in the Election of Homer E. Capehart to the United States Senate" (seminar paper, Rose-Hulman Institute of Technology, 1979). This paper was based upon an analysis of "Vote in Indiana by Counties: Performance of Homer E. Capehart in Elections of 1944, 1950," computer holdings [See Table D, Indiana University Political Science Lab]. For the shift of Indiana voters from the Democrats back to the Republicans after 1936, but especially by 1944, see

Charles S. Hyneman, C. Richard Hofstetter, and Patrick F. O'Connor, *Voting in Indiana: A Century of Persistence and Change* (Bloomington: Indiana University Press, 1979), 112, 115.

Chapter 7

1. Ray Donaldson, IUOHP, tape 2, pp. 32-33, tape 3, p. 28; Charles Egenroad, IUOHP, tape 1, p. 9.

2. HEC, IUOHP, tape 5, p. 142; Donaldson, tape 1, pp. 10-11, 27-28, tape 2, pp. 41-42; Egenroad, tape 2, p. 48.

3. Egenroad, tape 1, pp. 1-2, tape 2, p. 24; Wilma Miller, IUOHP, tape 1, p. 10; Florence Barr, interview with author, 10 Nov. 1971.

4. William Krieg, IUOHP, tape 1, pp. 22, 27; Articles of Amendment to the Articles of Incorporation, Packard Manufacturing Corporation, 15 Jan., 10 Aug. 1945, HECP; Minutes of the Packard Directors, 20 Jan. 1945, ibid.; Minutes of Special Meeting of the Packard Manufacturing Corporation Directors, 4 May 1947, ibid.

5. *Congressional Record* (hereafter referred to as *CR*), 79th Cong., 1st sess., 1945, 91, pt. 7:9117; ibid., 81st Cong., 1st sess., 1949, 95, pt. 7:8711; *Indianapolis Star*, 12 Oct. 1946.

6. *CR*, 80th Cong., 1st sess., 1947, 93, pt. 9:10966.

7. Donaldson, tape 2, p. 34, tape 4, p. 35; *Digest of Public and General Bills*, 1947, 80-1, p. 93; ibid., 1949, 81-1, p. 29; HEC, Voting Record, Box 156, CMSS; *Congress and the Nation, 1945-1964* (Washington, D.C.: Congressional Quarterly Service, 1965), 38a-39a, 44a-45a; *CR, Index*, 80th Cong., 1st sess., 1945, 91, pt. 14:104-5; ibid., *Index*, 79th Cong., 2d sess., 1946, 92, pt. 13:76; ibid., *Index*, 79th Cong., 1st sess., 1947, 91, pt. 14:93-94; ibid., *Index*, 80th Cong., 2d sess., 1948, 94, pt. 13:72-73. Capehart's successful bills were Public Laws 656, 692, 657, 363, 394, and 550.

8. HEC, interview with author, 22 July 1972; *CR*, 79th Cong., 2d sess., 1946, 92, pt. 1:714, 814; ibid., 81st Cong., 1st sess., 1949, 95, pt. 4:4791; *Congressional Quarterly Almanac*, 44 vols. to date (Washington, D.C.: Congressional Quarterly, Inc., 1945-), 2:82-83.

9. HEC to Franklin D. Roosevelt, 8 Mar. 1945, William D. Hassett Papers, Roosevelt Library, Hyde Park, N.Y.; *Indianapolis Star*, 11 Oct. 1945; Position paper, 30 Mar. 1945, file: "Miscellaneous," CMSS.

10. *CR*, 79th Cong., 2d sess., 1946, 92, pt. 5:5615; *New York Times*, 23, 24 May 1946.

11. HEC to E. L. Olcott, 26 May 1949, Box 109, folder 9, CMSS; HEC to Frances Ahrbecker, 10 May 1949, CMSS; *Congressional Quarterly Almanac*, 3:576; *CR*, 81st Cong., 1st sess., 1949, 95, pt. 3:3011.

12. John L. Ingoldsby, IUOHP, tape 2, p. 40.

13. His committee memberships included the Republican Committee on Committees, Interstate and Foreign Commerce, Manufactures, Patents, Post Offices and Post Roads, and Privileges and Elections, and his work on them revealed his desire to serve businessmen. When Sen. John Thomas of Idaho died in 1946, Capehart gave up Post Offices and Post Roads and joined Banking and Currency, where he served on the Agricultural Finance, Home

Loan Bank, and Coinage subcommittees. In addition to membership on the Special Committee to Study and Survey the Problems of Small Business, he served on the Temporary Congressional Aviation Policy Board. *Congressional Quarterly Almanac*, 2:139, 159; *Congressional Directory*, July 1946, pp. 179-89; *CR*, 80th Cong., 1st sess., 1947, 93, pt. 1:115, 127; *New York Times*, 31 Dec. 1946; 18 Feb., 5 Mar. 1947; *Newsprint Supply and Distribution: Interim Report of the Special Committee to Study Problems of American Small Business May 5, 1947* (Washington, D.C.: U.S. Government Printing Office, 1947), iii, 1, 2, 7-8.

14. Fritz Machlup, *The Basing-Point System: An Economic Analysis of a Controversial Pricing Practice* (Philadelphia: Blakiston, 1949), 37, 55; *Study of Pricing Methods: Hearings before a Subcommittee of the Committee on Interstate and Foreign Commerce, Nov. 9-12, 16-19, 29-30, Dec. 6-8, 1948* (Washington, D.C.: U.S. Government Printing Office, 1948), 3-4. Statements by William Simon, the man he retained as general counsel of the subcommittee, William Simon, IUOHP, tape 1.

15. *New York Times*, 18-19 Nov. 1948; *Congress and the Nation*, 1696.

16. *New York Times*, 25 Jan. 1949.

17. *Digest of Public and General Bills*, 1948, xvi; *U.S. Statutes at Large*, 80th Cong., 2d sess., vol. 62, pt. 1, p. 470. He also introduced bills to start a program to install radar and radio-beam instruments at airports and to establish a cabinet level secretary of transportation. "It is only logical," Capehart remarked, "that government, the biggest business of them all, follow the pattern of other large businesses and set up a single transportation head or traffic manager." *Indianapolis Star*, 1 Dec. 1947; 25 Nov. 1948.

18. George E. Mowry, *The Urban Nation, 1920-1960* (New York: Hill and Wang, 1965), 247-48.

19. *CR*, 81st Cong., 1st sess., 1949, 95, pt. 9:12148. The other six senators "least likely to cooperate" were John Williams of Delaware, William Jenner of Indiana, James P. Kem of Missouri, Zales Ecton of Montana, Kenneth Wherry of Nebraska, and John Bricker of Ohio. HEC's ranking by the White House is in Memos to and from the President, 17 Feb. 1949, Box 14, Charles Murphy Papers, Harry S Truman Library, Independence, Mo.; Samuel Lubell, *The Future of American Politics* (New York: Harper and Row, 1965), 218-19.

20. Claude Billings, IUOHP, tape 1, p. 26; Robert Griffith, *The Politics of Fear: Joseph R. McCarthy and the Senate* (Lexington: University Press of Kentucky, 1970), 144. During his second senate term Jenner told his friend Robert Webb that Washington was a "God Damn hell hole." Robert Webb, IUOHP, tape 2, p. 41; William Jenner, interview with author, 20 Sept. 1971; Richard O. Ristine, interview with author, 13 Sept. 1978.

21. HEC, tape 13, pp. 73, 80-81; Paul H. Douglas, IUOHP, tape 1, p. 18. HEC recalled that Jenner never listened to him. "Jenner," he said, "was a pretty independent individual." HEC, tape 12, p. 54; Griffith, *Politics of Fear*, 316.

22. Jenner, interview with author, 20 Sept. 1971. A comparison of Capehart's and Jenner's voting records appears in *Indianapolis Star*, 1 Nov. 1949.

23. *Indianapolis Star*, 6 Oct. 1946; John D. Barnhart and Donald F. Carmony, *Indiana: From Frontier to Industrial Commonwealth*, 4 vols. (New York: Lewis Historical Publishing Co., 1954), 2:503.

24. *Indianapolis News*, 7 Jan. 1948; Capehart-for-President Club, Application for Registration of Name by Unincorporated Association, 9 Feb. 1948, Indiana Commission on Public Records, State Archives Division; *Indianapolis Star*, 13 July 1947; 31 Oct. 1948.

25. When Capehart attempted to promote a 1948 edition of the Cornfield Conference, Gov. Ralph Gates would not attend a planning meeting, and the new state chairman, Clark Springer, refused to "get the party's official organization tied up in the promotion." Finally, Thomas E. Dewey canceled a scheduled campaign stop in Indiana. *Indianapolis Times*, 22 July 1948; HEC, tape 13, p. 68; *Indianapolis Star*, 30 Apr., 1 May 1948; Claude Billings interview with David Tudor, IUOHP, tape 2, pp. 37-38.

26. HEC, tape 12, p. 57; Jules Abels, *Out of the Jaws of Victory* (New York: Holt, 1949), 256. Henry F. Schricker was elected governor again by a plurality of 135,000. Barnhart and Carmony, *Indiana: From Frontier to Industrial Commonwealth*, 2:504.

Chapter 8

1. HEC's speech of 18 Apr. 1945, Personal File, Box 499, file: 1112 (Homer Capehart), Papers of Harry S Truman, Harry S Truman Library, Independence, Mo.

2. HEC, radio address, 9 July 1945, Box 154, folder 6, CMSS. HEC recalled asking Winston Churchill whether Great Britain could live with having sold out Poland to the Russians and that the former prime minister replied, "It will not be easy." HEC, interview with author, 22 July 1972.

3. *Indianapolis Star*, 1 Aug. 1945; *New York Times*, 10 May 1946.

4. *Indianapolis Star*, 21 June 1945; HEC, Voting Record, Box 156, CMSS.

5. *Indianapolis Star*, 31 July 1945; *CR*, 79th Cong., 1st sess., 1945, 91, pt. 6:7690.

6. HEC's statement in debate on the subject "Should We Internationalize the Atomic Bomb?" on the radio program entitled "American Forum of the Air," 16 Oct. 1945, CMSS.

7. *Indianapolis Star*, 4 Oct. 1947; *CR*, 80th Cong., 2d sess., 1948, 94, pt. 6:7556-57.

8. *CR*, 80th Cong., 1st sess., 1947, 93, pt. 3:33727.

9. *Indianapolis News*, 24 Apr. 1948. It was as a spokesman for the conservative opponents of the European Recovery Plan that William E. Jenner gave his maiden Senate speech, calling the Marshall Plan a plot by Stalin to get the United States to send aid to Western Europe. Ibid., 4 Feb. 1948.

10. HEC to J. E. Dotterer, 2 Aug. 1949, Box 103, folder 5, CMSS; *Indianapolis News*, 22 July 1949.

11. *CR*, 81st Cong., 1st sess., 1949, 95, pt. 3:3185; *Congressional Quarterly Almanac*, 44 vols. to date (Washington, D.C.: Congressional Quarterly, Inc., 1945-), 4:178. What Capehart did not know was that the Soviets had been working on their own atomic bomb since 1942 and would break the American atomic monopoly in September 1949. Adam B. Ulam, *Expansion and Coexistence: The History of Soviet Foreign Policy, 1917-67* (New York:

Praeger, 1968), 414-15; Adam B. Ulam, *Stalin: The Man and His Era* (New York: Viking, 1973), 625.

12. John Lewis Gaddis, "Harry S. Truman and the Origins of Containment," in Frank J. Merli and Theodore A. Wilson, eds., *Makers of American Diplomacy: From Benjamin Franklin to Henry Kissinger* (New York: Scribner, 1974), 208-9; Richard M. Freeland, *The Truman Doctrine and the Origins of McCarthyism: Foreign Policy, Domestic Politics, and Internal Security, 1946-1948* (New York: Knopf, 1972), 141; Bradford Westerfield, *Foreign Policy and Party Politics: Pearl Harbor to Korea* (New Haven: Yale University Press, 1955), 225.

13. HEC, mimeographed statement, 18 Jan. 1949, microfilm, CMSS; Richard A. Loss, "Secretary of State Dean Acheson: The Political Dimension" (Ph.D. diss., Cornell University, 1971), 83-87; HEC, interview with author, 27 Aug. 1972; *CR*, 81st Cong., 1st sess., 1949, 95, pt. 12:468.

14. *Washington Times-Herald*, 28 Jan. 1949, quoted in *CR*, *Appendix*, 81st Cong., 1st sess., 1949, 95, pt.12:A632. For HEC's reaction to Dewey's defeat see *Indianapolis News*, 19 Nov. 1948; Ronald J. Caridi, *The Korean War and American Politics: The Republican Party as a Case Study* (Philadelphia: University of Pennsylvania Press, 1968), 3.

15. See ch. 6, notes 16-19, 23. For the Dies Committee as a popularizer of anticommunism in American politics see Robert Griffith, *The Politics of Fear: Joseph R. McCarthy and the Senate* (Lexington: University Press of Kentucky, 1970), 32; Westerfield, *Foreign Policy and Party Politics*, 189-90, 195-96. For HEC and anticommunism in GOP politics see chs. 4 and 5. *Indianapolis Star*, 6 Oct. 1946.

16. *Indianapolis Star*, 16 Mar. 1947; Susan M. Hartmann, *Truman and the 80th Congress* (Columbia: University of Missouri Press, 1971), 31-35, 46; *CR*, 80th Cong., 1st sess., 1947, 93, pt. 3:3054.

17. Freeland, *Truman Doctrine*, 202; Athan G. Theoharis, *Seeds of Repression: Harry S. Truman and the Origins of McCarthyism* (Chicago: Quadrangle Books, 1971), 115. As fate would have it, Sen. Arthur H. Vandenberg, the leader of bipartisan foreign policy, went to the hospital in 1949 with terminal cancer. Arthur H. Vandenberg, Jr., ed., *The Private Papers of Senator Vandenberg* (Boston: Houghton Mifflin, 1952), 551-52.

18. *CR*, 81st Cong., 2d sess., 1950, 96, pt. 1:755-57, 895; *New York Times*, 24 Jan. 1950; HEC, mimeographed statement, 18 Jan. 1949, microfilm, CMSS. For HEC's part in creating the political atmosphere for McCarthy see David M. Oshinsky, *A Conspiracy So Immense: The World of Joe McCarthy* (New York: Free Press, 1983), 104, 106.

19. *CR*, 81st Cong., 2d sess., 1950, 96, pt. 2:1560, 1563-64; Richard H. Rovere, *Senator Joe McCarthy* (New York: Harcourt, Brace, 1959), 124. Capehart called for a Senate investigation of "malfeasance, misfeasance, neglect or incompetency" in the Justice Department's handling of the *Amerasia* case—a 1945 lawsuit in which federal prosecutors had failed to jail six left-wing journalists for illegal possession of State Department documents. A grand jury found no wrongdoing in the prosecution, and the Senate did not support Capehart's motion. *New York Times*, 10, 14, 16 June 1950; Earl Latham, *The Communist Controversy in Washington: From the New Deal to McCarthy* (Cambridge: Harvard University Press, 1966), 203-16.

20. *CR, Appendix*, 81st Cong., 2d sess., 1950, 96, pt. 16:A4938; *Indianapolis Star*, 1 Mar. 1949; 6 Nov. 1950. For anticommunism as an issue in Indiana see Dale R. Sorenson, "The Anticommunist Consensus in Indiana, 1945-1958" (Ph.D. diss., Indiana University, 1980).

21. *CR, Appendix*, 81st Cong., 2d sess., 1950, 96, pt. 16:A4936, 10153, 10170; *New York Times*, 15 July 1950; Sen. Ralph Flanders letter, 18 Aug. 1950, Official File, B125, file 20-5, Truman Papers; Griffith, *Politics of Fear*, 122; Caridi, *Korean War and American Politics*, 40.

22. *New York Times*, 28 June 1950; John D. Barnhart and Donald F. Carmony, *Indiana: From Frontier to Industrial Commonwealth*, 4 vols. (New York: Lewis Historical Publishing Co., 1954), 3:10-11.

23. *Indianapolis Star*, 9, 29 Apr., 14 Oct. 1949; *Indianapolis News*, 21 July, 21, 31 Oct. 1949; Taft to HEC, 2 Oct. 1950, Box 819, file: "Political Republican, 1950," Taft MSS, Library of Congress; *CR, Appendix*, 81st Cong., 2d sess., 1950, 96, pt. 16:A783; HEC, IUOHP, tape 13, pp. 75-76; Claude Billings, IUOHP, tape 1, p. 15.

24. He always insisted that the family be "very punctual" when they went places together, his daughter recalled. "It was hard on my mother during the Senate years," she recalled, "because he was gone a lot or he couldn't come home for dinner. And, oh, we would spend a lot of time, it seems like, meeting planes or trains or rushing to the station all the time, because he was constantly going back and forth." Patricia Capehart Pearson, IUOHP, tape 1, p. 14; H. Earl Capehart, Jr., interview with author, 29 Nov. 1974; *Indianapolis Star*, 15 Aug. 1946; Ray Donaldson, tape 3, pp. 16-17. On one occasion during his first term on a lonely road some thirty miles north of Indianapolis, Capehart experienced a brush with death. Capehart had gone by car from Indianapolis to Fort Wayne with William Merchant, his longtime friend and business associate, to give a speech. On the return trip a car driven by a drunken soldier smashed head-on into Capehart's Packard sedan. Merchant, who was driving, received the most serious injuries: a broken wrist, collarbone, and four cracked ribs. Capehart, asleep on the back seat, was thrown forward, his head shattering the windshield. Fortunately, his skull withstood the blow. His most serious injuries were a severely lacerated tongue and a broken ankle. After an unwelcome ten-day rest in the hospital, Capehart returned to Washington on crutches, and, until his tongue healed, spoke haltingly. *New York Times*, 31 Oct. 1945; William Merchant, IUOHP, tape 1, p. 23.

25. *Indianapolis News*, 8 Nov. 1950; *Indianapolis Times*, 11 Aug. 1950; *New York Times*, 31 Oct. 1950; William Krieg, IUOHP, tape 1, p. 15.

26. Edward H. Ziegner, "Indiana in National Politics," in Donald F. Carmony, ed., *Indiana: A Self-Appraisal* (Bloomington: Indiana University Press, 1966), 41; Robert Pitchell, *Indiana Votes* (Bloomington: Bureau of Government Research, Indiana University, 1960), 97; Homer E. Capehart, 1944-1950, Indiana University Political Science Lab Computer Voting Analysis; *Indianapolis News*, 8 Nov. 1950; *New York Times*, 8 Nov. 1950. A conference of GOP midwestern state chairmen had started programs in October 1949 to encourage the forty-five million Americans who had not voted in 1948 to do so. By election day the Korean War, Communist subversion, and corruption in government—the elements that formed the

Republican presidential platform two years later—were in place. William A. Glaser, "Hindsight and Significance," in William N. McPhee and William A. Glaser, eds., *Public Opinion and Congressional Elections* (New York: Free Press of Glencoe, 1962), 274, 281-82; Griffith, *Politics of Fear*, 31; Allan Nevins, *Herbert H. Lehman and His Era* (New York: Charles Scribner's Sons, 1963), 333-34. According to historian Allan Nevins, Capehart helped to create the political mood. "Even before McCarthy spoke Senator Homer Capehart had tried to arouse panic in Congress: 'Fuchs and Acheson and Hiss and hydrogen bombs threatening outside and New Dealism eating away the vitals of the Nation! In the name of Heaven, is this the best America can do?'" Although no hydrogen bombs yet existed, a debate was going on in the highest levels of government about the possibility of developing one. This was characteristic of Capehart's dismay with administration policies and the kind of statements he was making at the time. Nevins admitted, however, "in this instance real grounds for uneasiness existed."

27. For the effects of the Chinese intervention in Korea see *Indianapolis Star*, 6 Nov. 1950. For effects of inflation see *Indianapolis News*, 1 Aug. 1950; *Congress and the Nation, 1945-1964* (Washington, D.C.: Congressional Quarterly Service, 1965), 10, 357. Like the congressional election of 1938, that of 1950 strengthened the conservatives. Democrats retained their majority in the House, 235 to 199, and in the Senate, 49 to 47, but lost 28 seats in the House, 5 in the Senate. Republican conservatives won in Ohio, Illinois, Pennsylvania, Colorado, and California. Senate majority leader Scott W. Lucas of Illinois, assistant majority leader Francis Myers of Pennsylvania, and the chairman of the Armed Services Committee, Millard E. Tydings of Maryland, all went down to defeat. *New York Times*, 8 Nov. 1950.

Chapter 9

1. HEC's successful bills were Public Laws 416, 309, and 214; his voting record on key votes appears in *Congress and the Nation, 1945-1964* (Washington, D.C.: Congressional Quarterly Service, 1965), 56a, 57a. Hoosier Democratic boss, Frank McHale, later called HEC "the greatest man for business in the United States Senate in my lifetime." Frank McHale, interview with author, 2 Aug. 1972. The *New Republic* scale of progressivism, based on fifteen Senate votes, had ranked Capehart in 1948 higher than Harlan Bushfield of South Dakota and Zales Ecton of Montana—both of whom had no "progressive" votes. With only one vote in the progressive column, he tied with Joseph R. McCarthy, John Bricker of Ohio, Hugh Butler of Nebraska, Edward Martin of Pennsylvania, and C. Douglass Buck and John J. Williams, both of Delaware, for second most reactionary senator. *New Republic*, 27 Sept. 1948, pp. 28, 30.

2. HEC, interview with John Taylor, tape 2, p. 53, in possession of the interviewer, Indianapolis; Harry S Truman to HEC, 31 Aug. 1951, Official File, Box 1011, file 327 (1951), Papers of Harry S Truman, Harry S Truman Library, Independence, Mo.; *CR*, 82nd Cong., 1st sess., 1951, 97, pt. 5:7034; ibid., 97, pt. 7:9028.

3. *CR*, 81st Cong., 2d sess., 1950, 96, pt. 4:4468.

4. HEC, press release, 11 Apr. 1951, Box 104, folder 8, CMSS; Henry Z. Scheele, *Charlie Halleck: A Political Biography* (New York: Exposition Press, 1966), 131-32.

5. Allan Nevins, *Herbert H. Lehman and His Era* (New York: Charles Scribner's Sons, 1963), 402-3; HEC, interview with author, 17 Oct. 1970; *Indianapolis Star*, 21 Apr. 1951. Capehart's violent reaction to what he termed an insult (he later asserted that Hubert H. Humphrey called him a "son-of-a-bitch") would recur in 1962 during a debate with his opponent, Birch Bayh, during his ill-fated 1962 campaign for a fourth term.

6. HEC to Sen. Robert C. Hendrickson, 28 May 1952, Hendrickson Papers, George Arents Research Library, Syracuse University, Syracuse, N.Y.; *Indianapolis Times*, 28 Aug. 1952.

7. Robert Pitchell, *Indiana Votes* (Bloomington: Indiana University, 1960), 59, 99. Evidence that William E. Jenner needed and received the support of Dwight D. Eisenhower is in Eugene C. Pulliam to Frank Carlson, 4 Aug. 1952, and Carlson to Pulliam, 9 Aug. 1952, preinaugural files, Box 5, file: Geog. Indiana, Pulliam, Eisenhower Library, Abilene, Kans.

8. Gary W. Reichard, *The Reaffirmation of Republicanism: Eisenhower and the Eighty-third Congress* (Knoxville: University of Tennessee Press, 1975), 4, 8, 10, 192, 197, 204, 272.

9. Dwight D. Eisenhower to Arthur Burns, 2 Feb. 1954, Box 3, file: Feb. 1954, Dwight D. Eisenhower Diary, Eisenhower Library; Dwight D. Eisenhower Memo: Subj. Sen. Taft, 1 June 1953, Box 5, file: copies of DDE personal (2), Dwight D. Eisenhower Diary, ibid.

10. Dwight D. Eisenhower to Gov. George N. Craig, 26 Mar. 1954, Box 3, file: Mar. 1954, ibid.

11. Robert H. Ferrell, ed., *The Diary of James C. Hagerty: Eisenhower in Mid-Course, 1954-1955* (Bloomington: Indiana University Press, 1983), 131; William Bragg Ewald, Jr., *Eisenhower the President: Crucial Days, 1951-1960* (Englewood Cliffs, N.J.: Prentice-Hall, Inc., 1981), 123; John G. Adams, *Without Precedent: The Story of the Death of McCarthyism* (New York: W. W. Norton & Co., 1983), 141, 204-6.

12. HEC to Dwight D. Eisenhower, 3 Feb. 1953, PPF 20-F-Pro-C Box 619, file: State of Union message, Eisenhower Library; Dwight D. Eisenhower to HEC, 11 Nov. 1952, Box 45, folder 2, CMSS; *Indianapolis Star*, 7 Mar. 1953; *Indianapolis Times*, 16, 17 Mar. 1953; Reichard, *Reaffirmation of Republicanism*, 123.

13. Reichard, *Reaffirmation of Republicanism*, 9-13.

14. HEC, interview with John Taylor, tape 3; David M. Oshinsky, *A Conspiracy So Immense: The World of Joe McCarthy* (New York: Free Press, 1983), 475. HEC said that Jenner never turned against McCarthy. HEC, IUOHP, tape 1, p. 5.

15. As Ray Donaldson, Capehart's administrative assistant, recalls, "It [Foreign Relations] was the glamour committee. It got all the publicity, and for those who counted, it was *the* committee." Donaldson, IUOHP, tape 2, p. 39. Milton S. Eisenhower, "Report to the President," 18 Nov. 1953, Whitman Name Series, Box 13, file: Eisenhower, Milton, Report, 1953 (2), Eisenhower Library; Milton S. Eisenhower, *The Wine Is Bitter: The United States and Latin America* (Garden City, N.Y.: Doubleday & Co., Inc., 1963).

16. HEC, press release, 27 July 1953, Box 8, folder 3, CMSS.

17. William Simon to Herman S. Dorf, 17 Feb. 1954, file: Misc. Corresp., CMSS; Letter of transmittal and *Report of the Citizens Advisory Committee to Study the Financial Aspects of Expansion of International Trade*, Dec. 1954, Box 8, folder 3, CMSS.

18. HEC's speech to the American Club and the American Chamber of Commerce, Buenos Aires, 18 Nov. 1953, Box 106, folder 1, CMSS; HEC, interview with author, 4 Dec. 1970; *Study of Latin American Countries, Interim Report of the Senate Committee on Banking and Currency, A Study of the Operations in Latin American Countries of the Export-Import Bank and the International Bank and Their Relationship to the Expansion of International Trade, 16 Mar. 1954* (Washington, D.C.: U.S. Government Printing Office, 1954), v, 641-43, 647-48. Capehart was for lending money to European countries because they had the potential to repay. Charles Egenroad, IUOHP, tape 3, p. 47.

19. *Report of the Citizens Advisory Committee*, 7-8, 12, 17. White House praise appeared in Clarence B. Randall to HEC, 23 Mar. 1954, Box 94, folder 1, CMSS; HEC's file and HEC to Dwight D. Eisenhower, telephone conversation, 30 Mar. 1954, Box 3, file: Phone calls Jan.-May 1954, Dwight D. Eisenhower Diary, Eisenhower Library.

20. *Indianapolis Star*, 30 May 1955; Charles Egenroad to HEC, memo, 25 Feb. 1954, CMSS; HEC's guest list for the 500-mile race, 1955, HECP, author's files; *Indianapolis Times*, 20 July 1955; *Indianapolis News*, 20 July 1955.

21. *New Republic*, 11 Oct. 1954, pp. 19-20 and 15 Oct. 1956, pp. 19-21; *Congress and the Nation*, 62a, 63a, 68a, 69a. The eighteen bills, amendments, or resolutions sponsored by Capehart which became laws in the period 1953-56 were the result of 125 public policy proposals and dozens of private or commemorative legislative requests. In the Eighty-third Congress they included bills relating to military and government disbursing officers (S. 2844, P.L. 442, and S. 1307, P.O. 61); an amendment to allow branch banks to own the property where they are located (S. 3481, P.L. 460); a bill to extend the Securities Act of 1933 (S. 2846, P.O. 577); an amendment allowing the Federal Reserve to participate in loans to the Small Business Administration (S. 3480, P.L. 520); a bill to incorporate a board for fundamental education (S. 1796, P.L. 507); an amendment on the purchase of metal for minor coins of currency (S. 2845, P.L. 455); a bill continuing the authorization for regulation of exports (S. 1739, P.L. 62); an amendment to the Defense Production Act of 1953 (S. 1081, P.L. 95); a bill providing for independent management of the Export-Import Bank (S. 3589, P.L. 570); a bill to authorize American participation in the International Finance Corporation (S. 1894, P.L. 350); and the oil and gas conservation pact bill (S.J. Res. 38, P.L. 185). *CR, Index*, 83rd Cong., 1st sess., 1953, 99, pt. 13:84-86; ibid., 83rd Cong., 2d sess., 1954, 100, pt. 13:81-82.

22. *Congress and the Nation*, 1728; William Simon, IUOHP, tape 1, pp. 14-16; HEC to Sen. Irving Ives, 20 Apr., 23 Aug. 1954, Ives Papers, Cornell University; "Beware of Home Improvement Racketeers," reprint from Consumer Report, with Top Secret White House memo "Conclusions on FHA," 15 Mar. 1957, Central File (confidential), Box 23, file: FHA, Eisenhower Library.

23. *Indianapolis News*, 22 Sept. 1954. For results of the FHA investigation see Dwight D. Eisenhower to HEC, 23 Oct. 1954, Whitman Name Series, Box 4, file: Capehart (FHA), Eisenhower Library; HEC to Dwight D. Eisenhower, 10 Oct. 1954, Box 113, folder 9, CMSS; *Congress and the Nation*, 1729.

24. His support of Eisenhower was based in part upon a continuing suspicion of liberals. During the Banking and Currency Committee investigation of the stock market in early 1955 Sen. J. William Fulbright, chairman, called Harvard economist John Kenneth Galbraith, who had just published a book on the Wall Street debacle of 1929, to testify about the possibility that the nation was experiencing similar conditions. Galbraith, who had served as economic adviser in the Adlai Stevenson campaign of 1952, had praised the Soviet regime for its "sincerity" in attempting to overcome "old social grievances." Capehart therefore accused him of sympathizing with the Communist system. In response to Galbraith's testimony Capehart circulated a draft minority report attributing the rising stock market to a healthy economy caused by the faith of the American people in Eisenhower. HEC's action identified him as a staunch supporter of the Eisenhower administration, but it also reminded people of his earlier association with McCarthy. Galbraith recounted the episode in the introduction of the paperback edition of his book, *The Great Crash, 1929* (Boston: Houghton Mifflin, 1955), xv–xix. Oscar T. Barck, Jr., *A History of the United States since 1945* (New York: Dell Publishing Co., 1965), 256; *U.S. News and World Report*, 1 Apr. 1955, p. 16; HEC to Sen. Irving Ives, 24 May 1955 with enclosure: "Minority Report on the Stock Market Investigation," Ives Papers.

25. *Congressional Quarterly Almanac*, 44 vols. to date (Washington, D.C.: Congressional Quarterly, Inc., 1945–), 18:428; Sen. Lester Hunt to John Bricker, 14 June 1954 and Bricker to Hunt, 16 June 1954, Box 99, file: B & C Comm., Bricker Papers, Ohio Historical Society, Columbus. Another area of cooperation was the administration's slum clearance and urban renewal program, the Housing Act of 1954. The Democrats wanted as many as 135,000 new housing units per year for two years. The House version, on the other hand, to Eisenhower's dismay, deleted public housing altogether, so Capehart's compromise of 35,000 units was about what the president wanted. Barck, *United States since 1945*, 256. Capehart was not close to Eisenhower personally, and the president did not often seek advice from him. Nevertheless, he felt friendly toward the senator, and, of course, sought his support. At the end of the Eighty-third Congress, Eisenhower complimented Capehart's "legislative skill, forceful leadership, and rich experience," which aided passage of the housing legislation. Dwight D. Eisenhower to HEC, 23 Aug. 1954, Box 45, folder 2, CMSS; HEC to Dwight D. Eisenhower, 1 Sept. 1954, ibid.

26. *Congress and the Nation*, 62a, 63a, 68a, 69a; *Congressional Quarterly Almanac*, 11:582–83; Norman A. Graebner, *The New Isolationism: A Study in Politics and Foreign Policy since 1950* (New York: Ronald Press, 1956), 220.

27. *Indianapolis Times*, 28 Nov. 1956. His support for the president was politically astute, and his activities received favorable notice of White House

assistants Gabriel Hauge and Nelson Rockefeller. The president told his trusted Secretary of the Treasury George M. Humphrey that Capehart had better ideas "than a lot of other people on the hill." Dwight D. Eisenhower to George Humphrey, telephone conversation, 29 Mar. 1954, Box 3, file: phone calls, Jan.-May 1954, Dwight D. Eisenhower Diary, Eisenhower Library; Nelson Rockefeller to HEC, 7 Mar. 1955, GF 122-f, 1955, Box 864, file: 122-G, ibid.; Gabriel Hauge to HEC, 1 Apr. 1954, OF 114, Econ, 1952-1953, Box 558, file: 114, 1954 (2), ibid. See also Dwight D. Eisenhower to HEC, 9 Dec. 1953, Box 145, folder 2, CMSS.

Chapter 10

1. Performance of Homer E. Capehart in the senatorial elections of 1944, 1950, 1956, and 1962, Indiana University Political Science Lab. He received 54.2 percent of the urban vote and 56.2 percent of the rural. John D. Unruh, "Urban-Rural Voting Trends in the Election of Homer E. Capehart to the United States Senate" (seminar paper, Rose-Hulman Institute of Technology, 1979), 4. One newspaper said "Capehart identified his campaign with the national campaign in every speech." His support for the president on roll call votes in 1956 reached 64.7 percent. Vice President Richard M. Nixon campaigned in Indiana, and a presidential telegram to a Gary Republican banquet in February saluted Capehart for "devoted service to the nation." *Michigan City News-Dispatch*, 7 Nov. 1956; Dwight D. Eisenhower to Leo Fox, 29 Feb. 1956, PPF 1088 Box 968, file: 1105 Capehart, H., Eisenhower Library, Abilene, Kans.

2. *Indianapolis Times*, 20 Mar., 16 Sept. 1956. In his congratulatory telegram to Capehart, Eisenhower said he looked "forward to continuing our close cooperation in advancing the well-being and happiness of all our people." Dwight D. Eisenhower to HEC, 9 Nov. 1956, Central Files OF 138-A-5 (5), Box 703, file: 138-A-5-A C, Eisenhower Library. HEC's support for administration bills increased from 64.7 percent in 1956 to 88 percent in 1957. William E. Jenner's dropped from 85.2 percent to 38 percent. Memo: "Senate Support, 85th Congress, 1st Session, 18 Oct. 1957," Box 10, file: 85th Cong., Admin. series, ibid.

3. *Wabash* (Ind.) *Times Star*, 5 Nov. 1956; *Evansville* (Ind.) *Courier*, 5 Nov. 1956; Dean Albertson, *Roosevelt's Farmer: Claude R. Wickard in the New Deal* (New York: Columbia University Press, 1961), 37.

4. Richard Austin Smith, "Five Hot Senate Races," *Fortune* 54 (Oct. 1956): 280-82; *Indianapolis Times*, 25 Mar. 1956.

5. *Indianapolis Times*, 5 Jan., 25 Mar. 1956; HEC to Sherman Adams, 8 June 1956, GF 166-F, Box 1261, file: 166-G, Commission on Increased Industrial Use of Farm Products, Eisenhower Library. He received support from the presidents of the Indiana Farm Bureau and the Indiana Farmers Union and persuaded the Republican National Convention to place his proposal in the platform. *Huntington* (Ind.) *News*, 17 Sept. 1956; *The Indiana Farmers' Guide*, 15 Oct. 1956.

6. Fortunately, Capehart was too strong to be denied the nomination. Party bickering, however, did not end until the state convention in June

when the forces of William E. Jenner triumphed, with Harold Handley receiving the gubernatorial nomination on the second ballot. With Handley's victory in November (against Terre Haute mayor Ralph Tucker), Jenner, Ralph Gates, and 11th district chairman H. Dale Brown were ascendant in the Hoosier GOP. *Indianapolis Times*, 15 Dec. 1955; 18 Jan., 26 Mar., 16 Apr. 1956. HEC recommended Jenner to appointment as chairman of the GOP Senatorial Campaign Committee, but Jenner asked not to be considered. HEC to Sen. Ralph Flanders, 4 Jan. 1955, Flanders Papers, Box 113, file: Corresp., George Arents Research Library, Syracuse University, Syracuse, N.Y.; William E. Jenner to Flanders, Flanders Papers, Box 113, file: Corresp., ibid.; *Indianapolis Star*, 30 June 1956; *Indianapolis Times*, 16 Sept. 1956.

7. Smith, "Five Hot Senate Races," 282, 284; William Kreig, IUOHP, tape 1, p. 13; *Michigan City News-Dispatch*, 7 Nov. 1956; *Indianapolis News*, 21 Sept. 1956; *Indianapolis Times*, 16 Sept., 15, 20 Oct., 2, 30 Nov. 1956; *Gary Post-Tribune*, 1 Nov. 1956; "Voting Record of Senator Capehart on Labor, 1952-1955," Labor's Political Education Committee flyer, in author's file. *Congressional Quarterly Almanac*, 44 vols. to date (Washington, D.C.: Congressional Quarterly, Inc., 1945-), 13:267.

8. *Congressional Directory*, Jan. 1958, p. 319.

9. *Indianapolis Times*, 5 Dec. 1956; 22 Apr., 30 Nov., 1959; 20, 22 Jan. 1960; 3, 28 Jan., 6 Apr. 1961. The aircraft carrying Tom and Nancy and thirty-five other passengers crashed during its landing approach for a fueling stop. *Indianapolis Times*, 21 Jan. 1960. In an attempt to raise HEC's spirits President Eisenhower sent the following remarkable birthday message to the Hoosier senator on 3 June 1960: "The sixth of June is a significant day for you and for me. In my memory, I think of it as the Normandy D-Day. To me it stands for the courage and ability of a great liberating force united in the attainment of a most difficult objective. The members of this force took severe casualties but they pushed forward to victory. The birth of a man, I believe, is a kind of D-Day. Life is a continual battle with great objectives along the way. Against these you have steadily advanced over the years. Your courage and ability inspire the respect of us all. On your birthday I am delighted to send my congratulations and best wishes. With warm regard. Sincerely, Dwight D. Eisenhower." Dwight D. Eisenhower to HEC, 3 June 1960, PPF 1088, Box 968, file: 1105 Capehart, H., Eisenhower Library.

10. During this time, however, Capehart did change his senatorial offices, a symbol of increased influence. In January 1959 he moved his sixteen-person staff from its quarters on the third floor of the Old Senate Office Building to a new seven-room corner office, Suite 5054, in the thirty-million-dollar New Senate Office Building. Even though he preferred the high-ceilinged rooms in the old building to the modern decor and "cubicles" of the new, he was, nevertheless, delighted with the additional private room, G 48, in the Capitol itself, which he received as recognition of his seniority in the upper house. About twenty by thirty feet, it contained a huge table with twelve leather-covered chairs, a large green carpet, and was accessible only by a semiprivate elevator. Colleagues and his staff called it "Homer's Hideaway." *Indianapolis Times*, 6 Feb., 24 Apr. 1959; 1 June 1960.

11. HEC's five-point economic program is in Sherman Adams to Raymond J. Saulnier, 31 July 1957 (with enclosed memo from HEC),

Administrative series, Box 10, file: Capehart's Economic Program, Eisenhower Library; Robert B. Anderson to Dwight D. Eisenhower, memo, 9 Aug. 1957, ibid.; Saulnier to Dwight D. Eisenhower, memo, 9 July 1957, ibid.; *Indianapolis Times*, 19 Jan. 1958; 20 Jan. 1960; *Nation's Business*, 46 (Aug. 1958): 36-37, 59. HEC remained extremely busy. Besides membership on Banking and Currency and Foreign Relations, he filled the vacancy left by Joseph R. McCarthy's death on the Senate Government Operations Committee and was a member of the committees on Aeronautical and Space Sciences and Rackets. *Indianapolis Times*, 22 May 1957; 24, 29 Jan. 1959. During his last six years in the Senate, however, only ten bills dealing with substantive national policy that he either sponsored or cosponsored and only three in behalf of Hoosier interests became law. The national legislation included three bills affecting the Export-Import Bank (P.L. 85-340, 15 Mar. 1958; P.L. 85-424, 22 May 1958; and P.L. 87-311, 26 Sept. 1961), two bills affecting housing (P.L. 85-442, 4 June 1958 and P.L. 86-119, 31 July 1959), two affecting international trade (P.L. 85-21, 20 Apr. 1957 and P.L. 85-466, 25 June 1958), two affecting banking (P.L. 86-463, 13 May 1960 and P.L. 86-114, 28 July 1959), and one concerning retired government employees (P.L. 86-724, 8 Sept. 1960). The Indiana legislation concerned Jackson School Township (P.L. 85-29, 4 Sept. 1957), Rochambeau Memorial Bridge (P.L. 85-76, 1 July 1957), and Vincennes University (P.L. 85-100, 11 July 1957).

12. *Indianapolis Times*, 24 June 1958. HEC's own farm, of course, also benefited from federal programs. In fact in 1955 his farm received the second largest subsidy in the state: $21,742.08 for 9,536 bushels of wheat placed in storage. He collected government subsidies in 1956, 1957, and 1958 totaling $146,679. *Indianapolis Times*, 7 Sept. 1956; 7 May 1959; 27 Dec. 1960.

13. *Indianapolis Times*, 26 July, 14 Aug. 1959; HEC to Bryce Harlow, 5 Sept. 1959, Bryce N. Harlow, Highway, Box 11, file: Housing, Eisenhower Library. HEC was praised by the National Association of Real Estate Boards and received a distinguished service award for his voting record from the Americans for Constitutional Action on 1 June 1961. See *Indianapolis Times*, 30 Sept. 1961; Certificate from ACA, HECP.

14. *Indianapolis Times*, 25 July 1957; 9 Apr. 1960. HEC's correspondence from his constituents ran heavily against civil rights legislation. See HEC to Mr. Hancock, 9 July 1957, HEC to D.W. Turner, 13 Aug. 1957, Box 136, folder 17, CMSS; quote on freedom rides, *Indianapolis Times*, 29 May 1961; and *Congress and the Nation, 1945-1964* (Washington, D.C.: Congressional Quarterly Service, 1965), 81a, 87a. Capehart's unsympathetic attitude toward the civil rights movement brought him criticism from Rufus Kuykendall, a black Indianapolis attorney, who was a former assistant staff director of the United States Commission on Civil Rights and former member of the Indiana Advisory Committee on Civil Rights. *Indianapolis Times*, 24 Mar. 1960. One observer described Capehart's view on civil rights as follows: "The real name of this game, what it is all about, is jobs and more income. All these other things are just so much frosting on the cake, but the real cake is jobs and income." John L. Ingoldsby, IUOHP, tape 2, p. 35.

15. *Indianapolis Times*, 26 Apr. 1959; 2 Nov. 1960; 16 Jan. 1962; *Congress and the Nation*, 75a, 80a, 81a, 86a.

16. *Indianapolis Times*, 10 Feb., 9 Mar., 15 Apr. 1959; *New York Times*, 11 Feb. 1959; Robert F. Kennedy, *The Enemy Within* (New York: Harper and Brothers, 1960), 302; Charles Egenroad, IUOHP, tape 2 and 3, pp. 41-42.

17. *Indianapolis Times*, 1 Apr. 1961; 11 Sept. 1962; *Congress and the Nation*, 86a, 87a.

18. William S. White, "The Senate's Eyes on World Affairs," *New York Times Magazine*, 3 Mar. 1957, p. 12; HEC to Gabriel Hauge, 27 Aug. 1957, G.F. 1-0-1, Box 40, file: Revisions in barter prog., Eisenhower Library; HEC to Hauge, 11 July 1957, OF 149-B-2, Box 798, file: telegram, ibid.; *Indianapolis Times*, 28 Nov. 1956; 26, 27 Aug., 13 Nov. 1957. Only five pieces of legislation concerning foreign affairs that Capehart sponsored became law during his last term. In each case the bill sought a continued international role for the United States in the realm of foreign trade. They included the Anglo-American Financial Agreement (S.J. Res. 72, P.L. 85-21); the extension of the Export Control Act of 1949 (S. 3903, P.L. 85-46b); and three bills affecting the Export-Import Bank: (S. 3149, P.L. 85-424) increasing its lending authority, (S. 961, P.L. 85-340) extending the period for loans, and (S. 2325, P.L. 87-311) amending and extending the Export-Import Bank Act of 1945. He also acted in favor of statehood for Alaska and Hawaii; against requiring Congressional approval of a presidential veto of Tariff Commission findings; to support the Foreign Relations Committee's provision for financing the Development Loan Fund by Treasury borrowing of $1 billion a year; against increasing army procurement funds by $230 million; and for a treaty ensuring the permanent use of Antarctica for peaceful purposes. *Congress and the Nation*, 74a, 75a, 80a, 81a.

19. *Indianapolis Times*, 5 Mar., 5 Aug., 16 Oct. 1957; 20 July 1958; 23 Feb., 5 Apr. 1959; Sherman Adams to HEC, 17 July 1958, GF 122-EE (4), Box 884, file: 122-EE (4), Eisenhower Library; Bryce Harlow to HEC, 23 July 1958, ibid. For Hoosier support see Samuel Lubell to Adams, 22 July 1958, ibid.; Adams to Lubell, 25 July 1958, ibid. HEC's efforts in behalf of the administration continued as late as June 1960. Homer Gruenther to Harlow, 29 June 1960, Staff Files Gruenther, Box 4, file: Reporting-1960, ibid.

20. *CR*, 85th Cong., 2d sess., 1959, 104, pt. 14:17574, 17575, 17602, 17606; Wilton B. Persons to HEC, 18 Aug. 1958, GF 3-A-5, Box 61, file: Prog. Cong., Eisenhower Library. For the correctness of Capehart's position on the "missle gap" see Michael R. Beschloss, *MAYDAY: Eisenhower, Khrushchev, and the U-2 Affair* (New York: Harper and Row, 1986), 366-67.

21. *Indianapolis Times*, 15 June 1960; Dwight D. Eisenhower to HEC, 19 Aug. 1958, OF 99-V, Box 368, file: 99-V (5), Eisenhower Library.

22. *Indianapolis Times*, 3 Aug. 1959. HEC refused to attend a Foreign Relations Committee reception for Khrushchev. *Indianapolis Times*, 13 Sept. 1959; 10 May, 28 June 1960.

23. A year before Castro's takeover in Cuba in January 1959, Capehart had expressed fear of Soviet "progress" in Latin America. Castro's rebels in July 1958 kidnapped a Hoosier, A. F. Sparks, from the United Fruit Company's sugar and agriculture school in Guaro. Capehart called it an outrage. *Indianapolis Times*, 2 July 1958; 15 Jan., 1 Dec. 1959; HEC to Sherman Adams, 8 Mar. 1958, GF 122-F, 1955, Box 864, file: 122-6, 1958, Eisenhower Library; Harlow to HEC, 25 Mar. 1958, ibid. See also *Indianapolis Times*, 19

Jan., 17 Aug. 1959; 30 Nov. 1960. On 8 Aug. 1960, the Organization of American States in San José, Costa Rica, condemned Soviet involvement in Cuba. By early 1961, Sen. Kenneth Keating (Republican, N.Y.) was calling for a complete embargo against all Cuban goods. Capehart and Keating soon were joined by other senators including Strom Thurmond (Democrat, S.C.), Barry Goldwater (Republican, Ariz.), John Tower (Republican, Tex.), Karl Mundt (Republican, N. Dak.), Thomas E. Dodd (Democrat, Conn.), George Smathers (Democrat, Fla.), Gordon Allott (Republican, Colo.), and Carl Curtis (Republican, Nebr.). David L. Larson, ed., *The "Cuban Crisis" of 1962* (Boston: Houghton Mifflin, 1963), 300; *CR*, 86th Cong., 2d sess., 1960, 106, pt. 11:14177; ibid., 87th Cong., 1st sess., 1961, 107, pt. 4:5191; Dwight Dively, "Capehart, Keating, and Kennedy: Three Policies on Cuba" (seminar paper, Rose-Hulman Institute of Technology, 1979), 3-4.

24. *Indianapolis Times*, 6 June, 4 July, 5, 17, 23, 30 Aug., 10 Dec. 1961.

25. HEC, news release, 14, 21, 29 Apr., 6, 19 May 1961, Box 151, folder 7, CMSS.

26. HEC to John F. Kennedy, telegram, 23 May 1961, Box 107, file 10, CMSS; HEC, press release, 29 May 1961, Box 151, file 10, ibid. HEC, news releases, 10 June 1961, Box 107, file 8, 23 June 1961, Box 104, file 7, ibid. The magazine article appeared in the same file as Larry O'Brien to Ken O'Donnell, 26 May 1961, CO 55 (Executive), White House Central Files, John F. Kennedy Library, Boston, Mass.

Chapter 11

1. John H. Fenton, *Midwest Politics* (New York: Holt, Rinehart and Winston, 1966), 165-66; Fletcher Knebel, "'Highway Robbery' in Indiana," *Look*, 10 Dec. 1957, pp. 34-35; *Indianapolis Times*, 12, 17 Dec. 1957.

2. William E. Jenner had won in 1952 by 109,436 votes. *Congressional Directory*, Feb. 1954, p. 288; HEC, IUOHP, tape 13, pp. 72-73; H. Earl Capehart, Jr., IUOHP, tape 2, p. 36.

3. *Time*, 27 Feb. 1956, p. 27; *Indianapolis Star*, 15 Oct. 1957; Paul R. Squires to Gov. Sherman Adams, 17 Oct. 1957, GF 109-A-2, Indiana, Box 502, file: 109-A-2 Ind. (5), Eisenhower Library, Abilene, Kans.

4. *Indianapolis Times*, 20 May, 22 Nov., 3 Dec. 1957; Bryce Harlow to HEC, 23 May 1957, GF 109-A-2, Indiana, Box 502, file: 109-A-2, Ind. (4), Eisenhower Library; Rodney J. Ross, "Senator William E. Jenner: A Study in Cold War Isolationism" (Ed.D. diss., Pennsylvania State University, 1973), 14-15; Claude Billings, interview with David Tudor, IUOHP, tape 2, pp. 42-44.

5. *Time*, 30 Dec. 1957, p. 62; *Indianapolis Times*, 17 Dec. 1957; Charles Halleck to Dwight D. Eisenhower, 29 Sept. 1954, OF 99-V McCarthy, Box 368, file: 99-V (1), Congressional Letters, Eisenhower Library.

6. *Indianapolis Times*, 11 Nov. 1958; 17 June, 4, 10 Nov. 1959; 23 Apr. 1961.

7. *Indianapolis Times*, 20 Jan., 20 June, 21 Oct. 1958; HEC, interview with John Taylor, tape 3, in possession of the interviewer, Indianapolis. Election statistics appear in *Congressional Directory*, Mar. 1959, p. 325 and Edward H.

Ziegner, "Indiana in National Politics," in Donald F. Carmony, ed., *Indiana: A Self-Appraisal* (Bloomington: Indiana University Press, 1966), 41-43.

8. Lee W. Huebner, "The Republican Party, 1952-1972," in Arthur M. Schlesinger, Jr., ed., *History of U.S. Political Parties*, 4 vols. (New York: Chelsea House, 1973), 4:2998, 3003; *Louisville Courier-Journal*, 8, 9 Nov. 1963; Matthew E. Welsh, *View from the State House: Recollections and Reflections, 1961-1965* (Indianapolis: Indiana Historical Bureau, 1981), 14-16, 43-63; Paul Kleppner, "Searching for the Indiana Voter: A Review Essay," *Indiana Magazine of History* 76 (Dec. 1980): 362-66.

9. Larry Conrad, IUOHP, tape 1, p. 15; Richard O. Ristine, interview with author, 13 Sept. 1978. For the conservative trends in the election of 1962 see *Louisville Courier-Journal*, 10 Aug. 1962 and *Indianapolis Star*, 8, 10 Nov. 1962. Capehart supported Nelson Rockefeller for the GOP nomination in 1960 but Indiana voted for Richard Nixon and Hoosier conservatives stopped contributing to HEC's campaign. Cale Holder, interview with John Taylor, tape 1.

10. Capehart's wealth seemed to have turned against him. Cale Holder recalled that "Homer could raise money that Bill [Jenner] could not touch [figuratively]." Cale Holder, interview with John Taylor, tape 1. By 1962, however, Capehart felt the Hoosier Republican party often depended upon him too much. "Too often," he said "they say don't worry. Capehart can pay for it himself." HEC, interview with author, 4 Dec. 1970; *Louisville Courier-Journal*, 8 Nov. 1962.

11. *Biographical Directory of the United States Congress, 1774-1989* (Washington, D.C.: U.S. Government Printing Office, 1989), 592.

12. *Indianapolis Times*, 30 Mar. 1961. To rally the faithful, Capehart predicted the GOP would "have an uphill fight on its hands." He then launched his campaign with a replay of the Cornfield Conference of 1938 for some three thousand Republicans, who joined him on his farm for an old-fashioned rally on 24 September. He criticized John Kennedy at every opportunity—for having lunch with Khrushchev's son-in-law, for proposing a joint U.S.-Soviet cooperation in space, and for "building a dynasty to compel Americans to bow and ask for favors." "The worst of the Tribe," he declared, was Attorney General Robert Kennedy. Ibid., 25 Sept., 26 Oct. 1961; 12 June 1962.

13. *Indianapolis Times*, 24 June 1962.

14. Theodore C. Sorensen, *Kennedy* (New York: Harper and Row, 1965), 2, 672, 674; Graham Allison, *The Essence of Decision: Explaining the Cuban Missile Crisis* (Boston: Little, Brown, 1971), 189; Conrad, tape 1, p. 8; *Indianapolis Times*, 24, 26 Oct. 1962.

15. Conrad, tape 1, p. 5; *Congressional Quarterly Almanac*, 44 vols. to date (Washington, D.C.: Congressional Quarterly, Inc., 1945-), 18:1030; George H. Gallup, *The Gallup Poll: Public Opinion, 1935-1971*, 3 vols. (New York: Random House, 1972), 3:1787; Charles A. Halleck, interview with Stephen Hess, 22 Mar. 1965, pp. 23-24, John F. Kennedy Library Oral History Project, Kennedy Library, Boston, Mass.

16. *Indianapolis Times*, 20 Sept., 8 Oct. 1962; "The Pugilists," *Time*, 28 Sept. 1962, p. 18.

17. *Indianapolis Times*, 6 Dec. 1961; 29 Aug., 3, 6 Sept., 2, 28 Oct. 1962.

18. *Indianapolis Times*, 7 Dec. 1961; 25, 29 Oct., 5 Nov. 1962; *Louisville Courier-Journal*, 8 Nov. 1962. Bayh did not seem to sense the importance of Cuba, until too late in the campaign. In the words of Bayh's campaign manager, "It started out . . . as just sort of a voice in the distance. Homer was talking about Cuba, Cuba, Cuba . . . and nobody was listening because the majority of the people were the other way . . . I think he just happened to land on Cuba because it was close to us." Conrad, tape 1, p. 5.

19. The lyrics of Birch Bayh's campaign song were composed by Mrs. Larry Conrad to music from the Broadway musical *Wildcat*. Conrad, tape 1, pp. 13-14.

20. Ristine, interview with author, 13 Sept. 1978.

21. Numbers of registered voters, urban and rural vote by county, and percentages of vote which Capehart received are available at the Indiana University Political Science Lab.

22. *New York Times*, 8, 11 Nov. 1962; *Indianapolis Star*, 10 Nov. 1962; Charles O. Hendricks, *General Election Report of the Secretary of State of the State of Indiana, 1962: General Election Statistics* (Indianapolis, 1962).

23. Homer Capehart, said his administrative assistant, Charles Egenroad, was the "proudest man in the world that he came from the son of a poor tenant farmer to the United States Senate and served longer than any other Indiana senator. . . . He was so damn proud of that accomplishment that he suffered badly when it ended. There's nothing else, nothing could match [that] as far as he was concerned." Charles Egenroad, IUOHP, tape 2, pp. 30-31.

Chapter 12

1. HEC considered his wife "exceptionally good to her children and trained them well" although he admitted that he "was always more optimistic and enthusiastic about my projects than she was." Ray Donaldson, IUOHP, tape 1, pp. 17, 18; HEC, IUOHP, tape 7, p. 181; Irma Capehart, interview with author, 25 July 1969.

2. H. Earl Capehart, Jr., IUOHP, tape 1, pp. 9, 14.

3. *Indianapolis Times*, 8, 10 Nov. 1962; HEC, IUOHP, tape 7, pp. 203-5; HEC to William Simmons, 17 Sept. 1965 and 26 Apr. 1966, HECP; HEC, interview with author, 14 Aug. 1978.

4. HEC, interview with author, 4 July 1971.

5. Ibid.

6. Margaret Chase Smith, interview with author, 15 Oct. 1974.

7. HEC told interested students that a United States senator must, above all, have the following qualities: perseverance, the capacity to identify and reconcile a variety of conflicting interests, willingness to compromise, the ability to endure the frustration of not being listened to, and an interest in working long hours on legislation, knowing all the time that it might get "knocked down" by the president or the House. He, nevertheless, considered the system to be the best there is for arriving at the laws necessary for running the country. HEC, interviews with author, 13 Nov. 1970 and 4 July

1971. He received an honorary doctor of laws degree from Butler University in 1955. *Indianapolis Star*, 8 Feb. 1955; *Indianapolis News*, 7 June 1978.

8. *Indianapolis Star*, 4, 7 Sept. 1979. Eulogies appeared in the *Indianapolis Star*, 5 Sept. 1979; the *Indianapolis Times*, 8 Nov. 1962; and the *Martinsville* (Ind.) *Daily Reporter*, 9 Nov. 1962.

9. HEC, interview with author, 17 Oct. 1970.

Bibliographical Essay

General and Interpretive

Materials which revealed Homer E. Capehart's activities and attitudes included the interviews by the author with support from the Indiana University Oral History Project (IUOHP); the former senator's personal papers (HECP) in the possession of his son H. Earl Capehart, Jr.; his Senate papers (CMSS) at the Indiana Division, Indiana State Library; and conversations with the author during the period 1968 to 1979. The sources relating to Capehart's public life were the *Indianapolis Times* (especially the clipping files in that now defunct newspaper's morgue at the Indiana University Department of Political Science), the *Indianapolis Star*, the *Indianapolis News*, and the *New York Times*. Other information came from his son, H. Earl Capehart, Jr.; the former senator's late wife, Irma; and his late daughter, Patricia Pearson. An abundance of material on his ancestry and life through his first Senate term was in the *Washington* (Ind.) *Herald*, 3 July 1950 (special Capehart campaign edition).

Theories useful in explaining the sources of ambition in men such as Capehart were in Erick Erickson, *Childhood and Society*, second edition (New York: Norton, 1978); Abraham H. Maslow, *Motivation and Personality*, second edition (New York: Harper and Row, 1970); Lucien W. Pye, "Personal Identity and Political Ideology" in Bruce Mazlish (ed.), *Psychoanalysis and History*, revised edition (New York: Grosset and Dunlap, 1971); and Harold D. Lasswell, *Power and Personality* (New York: Norton, 1948).

Helpful for interpreting Capehart's business career were Thomas C. Cochran, *The Inner Revolution: Essays on the Social Sciences in History* (New York: Harper and Row, 1964); John A. Garraty, *The Nature of Biography* (New York: Knopf, 1957); Irvin G. Wyllie, *The Self-Made Man in America: The Myth of Rags to Riches* (Brunswick, N.J.: Rutgers University Press, 1954); and, in small part, Robert Coles, *Migrants, Sharecroppers, Mountaineers*, vol. 2, *His Children of Crisis* (Boston: Little, Brown, 1971) and Moses Rischin (ed.), *The American Gospel of Success: Individualism and Beyond* (Chicago: Quadrangle Books, 1965).

Early Life and Business Career

Capehart's genealogy was available in his personal papers, the Pike County auditor's office and family grave sites in Pike and Daviess counties, the memory of his nephew Jack B. Haskins, and the genealogy divisions of the Indiana State Library and the Library of Congress. The most useful published sources were the following: John Bennett Boddie, *Southside Virginia Families*, 2 vols. (Redwood City, Calif.: Pacific Coast Publishers, 1955-56); Calvin I. Kephart, "A Danish Royal-Skioldung Lineage," *National Genealogical Society Quarterly* 31 (June 1943); Eva DeBruler, *A Historical, Biographical and Genealogical Account of Certain Branches of the DeBruler and Hargrave Families* (Bloomington, Ind.: Feltus Printing Co., 1938); Agnes L. Kendall, "Some Pike County, Indiana, Families" (unpublished manuscript, Genealogy Division, Indiana State Library); and Marie Arrington Davidson (comp.), *Andrew Foster Kelso: History and Descendants* (Twin Falls, Idaho: n.p., 1957). Capehart's North Carolina origins appeared in C. F.

W. Coker's letter to the author from the North Carolina Department of Archives and History, 9 November 1971.

The best accounts of Capehart's childhood were Beulah Gray, "Half of Capehart's Life Spent in Near-Poverty," *Washington Herald*, 3 July 1950; Capehart manuscript memoir entitled "A Little Sound Ignorance" (unpublished campaign biography, 1943) in Capehart's personal papers; and interviews with John S. Hastings, Marion C. Borders, Paul Capehart, Bessie Haskins, and Adeline Lehman in the Indiana University Oral History Project. Interviews with Mrs. John Selman, Mrs. Clem Brown, Gladys Hubbs, and Robert Hyatt in Washington, Indiana, and with Annabelle McGrath and Robert Bellows in Polo, Illinois, were also useful. The registrar's office of the high school he attended retained his grade cards, and activities of Capehart's father were recorded in the auditor's office in Pike and Daviess counties and Ogle County, Illinois. Photographs of the young Capehart were in his high school yearbook, *The Washingtonian*, in the Washington Public Library. His certificate of army service was in the Indiana Commission on Public Records, State Archives Division, his honorable discharge was in his personal papers, and *The Twelfth U.S. Infantry, 1789-1919: Its Story—By Its Men* (New York: Knickerbocker Press, 1919) in the military history division of the National Archives revealed regimental activity during Capehart's years.

The most complete accounts of his career as a salesman, entrepreneur, and jukebox executive were the following: Capehart, "A Little Sound Ignorance" (unpublished manuscript, 1943); George E. Gill, "A Brief History of the Packard Manufacturing Corporation" (unpublished manuscript, 1944) in the Capehart personal papers; "The Capehart," *Fortune* 23 (February 1941); and John Krivine, *Juke Box Saturday Night* (London: New English Library, 1977), which summarized and identified Capehart's contribution. Such information appeared especially in taped interviews with William F. Merchant, William R. Deaton, and Kenneth F. Valentine in the Indiana University Oral History Project. William E. Simmons and Gerald C. Crary also sent useful information. Farny R. Wurlitzer consented to an interview and allowed access to certain Wurlitzer Company correspondence files at North Tonawanda, N.Y. The director of public relations at Wurlitzer, A. D. Palmer, Jr., provided interesting background on the Wurlitzer-Capehart years, especially that contained in the famous Capehart to Farny Wurlitzer letter of 3 April 1933 (see pp. 30-31). Useful company histories were Lloyd Graham, "The Story of the Rudolph Wurlitzer Family and Business" (North Tonawanda, N.Y., 1956, unpublished manuscript) and the Wurlitzer Company, *Wurlitzer at One Hundred* (pamphlet, North Tonawanda, N.Y., 1956).

Capehart's background as a salesman-promoter appeared in Frank Hoke, "Two Heads Are Better: The Story of Holcomb & Hoke Manufacturing Company" (Indianapolis, 1958, unpublished manuscript); James Irving Holcomb, *Salesology of the Butter-Kist Popcorn and Peanut Machines* (Indianapolis: Holcomb and Hoke Manufacturing Co., 1923); Homer E. Capehart, *Creative Selling* (Fort Wayne, Ind.: The Capehart Automatic Phonograph Corporation, 1929); and the interview with Frank Hoke, 1 October 1971. The rise and fall of Capehart's phonograph operation was recorded at the Indiana Commission on Public Records, State Archives Division, in the articles of incorporation of his various corporations and the annual reports to the secretary of state. Oliver Read and Walter L. Welch, *From Tin Foil to Stereo: Evolution of the Phonograph* (Indianapolis: H. W. Sams, 1959) and Roland Gelatt, *The Fabulous Phonograph: From Edison to Stereo* (New York: Appleton-Century, 1966) identified the Capehart phonograph in the history of the American phonograph industry. An account of Capehart's activities at Wurlitzer also was available in *The Billboard* and *The Talking Machine Journal*. The jukebox industry was discussed by Geoffrey Parsons and Robert Yoder in "A Nickel a Tune," *Reader's Digest*, February 1941, and by T. Murray in "You Pay before You Play: Coin Operated Phonograph," *Nation's Business*, June 1940. Numerous clippings, pamphlets, and brochures depicting the growth of the Capehart line in Huntington and Fort Wayne, Indiana, were on microfilm, Indiana Division, Indiana State Library. See especially the *Fort Wayne Journal-Gazette* and *News-Sentinel*. Capehart advertisements appeared in the *Saturday Evening Post* and *House and Garden*. See also *Printer's Ink*, 1 March 1928; *The Talking Machine Journal*, April 1928; *Radio Broadcast*, December 1929; Capehart Corporation Records, Bureau of Foreign and Domestic Commerce, National Archives, and brochures entitled *The Capehart Orchestrope*, "The Capehart '400,'" and "Pride of Possession."

Documents from Capehart's business career were in the Capehart manuscripts on microfilm. An interview with Irma's brother Carlton Mueller in the Indiana University Oral History Project provided information about Capehart's career in Green Bay, Wisconsin. The origin and progress of the Packard Manufacturing Corporation appeared in the minutes of the Packard directors and the Packard stock book in Capehart's personal papers. The effect of the war on Packard was in Capehart, "From Music to Guns," the speech he gave on 4 January 1944 and many times afterwards. The latter was in the Capehart manuscripts. Other material on Capehart's war manufacturing was in Indiana War History Commission, *Indiana at War: Civilian Directory* (Bloomington, Ind.: Indiana War Commission, 1951); and Bernard Friedman, *The Financial Role of Indiana in World War II* (Bloomington: Indiana University Press, 1966). See also Packard Corporation magazines in the Capehart manuscripts. Thomas C. Cochran, *The Great Depression and World War II, 1929-1945* (Glenview, Ill.: Scott, Foresman, 1968) and George Soule, *Prosperity Decade: From War to Depression, 1917-1929* (New York: Rinehart, 1947) gave

the effect of the Great Depression and war on the nation's economy. Capehart's memories of his leaving the Capehart Corporation were supported by Louis F. Niezer's letter to the author of 2 December 1971. Niezer is the son of the man who fired Capehart.

Capehart's wealth during the period 1934 through 1944 was revealed in his Indiana and U.S. Income Tax returns in his personal papers. His purchases of farmland in Daviess County appeared in the county auditor's office beginning in 1936. The financial conditions of the Wurlitzer Company before and after Capehart arrived were in John Sherman Porter (ed.), *Moody's Manual of Investments: American and Foreign: Industrial Securities* (New York: Moody's Investors Service, 1933) and *Prentice-Hall Capital Adjustments: Stock Dividends, Stock Rights, Reorganizations* (Englewood Cliffs, N.J.: Prentice-Hall, 1970). Capehart's memberships in fraternal and service organizations were in Anna Rothe (ed.), *Current Biography, 1947: Who's News and Why* (New York: H. W. Wilson, 1948); *The National Cyclopedia of American Biography*, Vol. G, 1943-46; *The Indiana Freemason*, June 1971; *Who's Who and What's What in Indiana Politics* (Indianapolis: James E. Perry, 1944); and the Indianapolis Columbia Club, *The Columbian*, January 1967.

Indiana Politics

Published analyses of Indiana politics after 1920 are not abundant. The most valuable of these included writings by two newspapermen. Edward H. Ziegner, longtime political writer and editor of the *Indianapolis News*, published an excellent article entitled "Indiana in National Politics" in Donald F. Carmony (ed.), *Indiana: A Self-Appraisal* (Bloomington: Indiana University Press, 1966). Irving Leibowitz, former managing editor of the *Indianapolis Times*, discussed political history in his book of reminiscences entitled *My Indiana* (Englewood Cliffs, N.J.: Prentice-Hall, 1964) and corresponded with the author. The best published account was John H.

Fenton's book *Midwest Politics* (New York: Holt, Rinehart and Winston, 1966). Essential background was provided by Frank J. Munger's "Two-Party Politics in the State of Indiana" (Ph.D. dissertation, Harvard University, 1955). The dissertations on Senator Jenner by Rodney J. Ross, "Senator William E. Jenner: A Study in Cold War Isolationism" (Ed.D. dissertation, Pennsylvania State University, 1973) and by Michael Paul Poder, "The Senatorial Career of William E. Jenner" (Ph.D. dissertation, Notre Dame University, 1976) were helpful. Darrell Bigham's article "The Other LaFollette: Charles Marion LaFollette and Liberal Republicanism, 1942-1951" in *Their Infinite Variety: Essays on Indiana Politicians* (Indianapolis: Indiana Historical Bureau, 1981) provided useful perspective on the conservatism of Jenner and Capehart.

For many years the standard textbook on Indiana history was John D. Barnhart and Donald F. Carmony, *Indiana: From Frontier to Industrial Commonwealth*, 4 vols. (New York: Lewis Historical Publishing Co., 1954). For Capehart see volume two. An excellent one-volume history is James H. Madison, *The Indiana Way: A State History* (Bloomington and Indianapolis: Indiana University Press and Indiana Historical Society, 1986) and the era when Capehart entered business and politics appeared in Madison's more detailed *Indiana through Tradition and Change: A History of the Hoosier State and Its People, 1920-1945* (Indianapolis: Indiana Historical Society, 1982). Also helpful were the biography of Charles A. Halleck entitled *Charlie Halleck: A Political Biography* (New York: Exposition Press, 1966) by Henry Z. Scheele and the interviews with Edward H. Ziegner and Claude Billings in the Indiana University Oral History Project. Capehart and the resurgence of the Hoosier and national GOP in 1938 appeared in William B. Pickett, "The Capehart Cornfield Conference and the Election of 1938: Homer E. Capehart's Entry into Politics," *Indiana Magazine of History* 73 (December 1977) and in Iwan Morgan, "Factional Conflict in Indiana Politics during the

Later New Deal Years, 1936-1940," ibid. 79 (March 1983). The early career of Capehart's 1956 opponent was recounted in Dean Albertson, *Roosevelt's Farmer: Claude R. Wickard in the New Deal* (New York: Columbia University Press, 1961). An excellent account of the Hoosier origins of anticommunism was Dale R. Sorenson, "The Anticommunist Consensus in Indiana, 1945-1958" (Ph.D. dissertation, Indiana University, 1980). The end of the Republican resurgence in the late 1950s and early 1960s appeared in Matthew E. Welsh, *View from the State House: Recollections and Reflections, 1961-1965* (Indianapolis: Indiana Historical Bureau, 1981). The best sources for the behavior of Hoosier voters were the Indiana University Political Science Lab, "Election Vote in Indiana by Counties" (computerized voting statistics for major national and state offices beginning in 1920); Charles S. Hyneman, C. Richard Hofstetter, and Patrick F. O'Connor, *Voting in Indiana: A Century of Persistence and Change* (Bloomington: Indiana University Press, 1979); and Paul Kleppner, "Searching for the Indiana Voter: A Review Essay," *Indiana Magazine of History* 76 (December 1980). The performance of Homer E. Capehart versus his opponents in 1944, 1950, 1956, and 1962 was tabulated by John D. Unruh, "Urban-Rural Voting Trends in the Election of Homer E. Capehart to the United States Senate" (seminar paper, Rose-Hulman Institute of Technology, 1979), using statistics collected by the Indiana University Political Science Lab, Computer Voting Analysis, "Vote in Indiana by Counties: Performance of Homer E. Capehart in Elections of 1944, 1950." Finally, extremely helpful political reporting appeared in the three Indianapolis newspapers and the *Louisville Courier-Journal*.

A number of oral history interviews augmented these sources. They include Arch N. Bobbitt, James Tucker, Ralph F. Gates, William Krieg, Felix McWhirter, Robert Webb, Alvin Cast, Larry Conrad, and Charles Halleck in the Indiana University Oral History Project; Sherman Adams in the Oral

History Division of the Dwight D. Eisenhower Library; and the untaped interviews with William E. Jenner, Frank McHale, Richard O. Ristine, Cecil Harden, and Clarence Jackson in the author's files. John Raymond Taylor, Carmel, Indiana high school teacher, is author of "Homer E. Capehart: United States Senator, 1944-1962" (Ed.D. dissertation, Ball State University, 1977). Particularly helpful were Taylor's taped interviews in his personal papers with Capehart (five), Ralph Gates, Cale Holder, and H. Dale Brown.

The most valuable manuscripts on recent Indiana history generally were those of Charles Halleck and Wendell Willkie in the Lilly Library, Indiana University; Raymond Willis in the Indiana Division, Indiana State Library; Democratic National Committee Files in the Franklin D. Roosevelt Library; Herbert Hoover in the Hoover Library; and Eisenhower Pre-Inaugural Files, Central Files, and Leonard Hall Files, Eisenhower Library.

A considerable body of scholarship on national trends is available. The best of these were James Truett Selcraig, *The Red Scare in the Midwest, 1945-1955: A State and Local Study* (Ann Arbor, Mich.: UMI Research Press, 1982); Malcom Moos, *The Republicans: A History of Their Party* (New York: Random House, 1956); George H. Mayer, *The Republican Party, 1854-1964* (New York: Oxford University Press, 1967); the two-volume biography of Franklin D. Roosevelt entitled *Roosevelt: The Lion and the Fox* (New York: Harcourt, Brace, 1956) and *Roosevelt: The Soldier of Freedom* (New York: Harcourt Brace Jovanovich, 1970); *Deadlock of Democracy: Four-Party Politics in America* (Englewood Cliffs, N.J.: Prentice-Hall, 1967) by James MacGregor Burns; Samuel Lubell's book *The Future of American Politics* (New York: Harper and Row, 1965); Milton Plesur's article "The Republican Congressional Comeback of 1938," *Review of Politics* 24 (October 1962); two books by James T. Patterson, *Congressional Conservatism and the New Deal: The Growth of the Conservative*

Coalition in Congress, 1933-1939 (Lexington: University of Kentucky Press, 1967) and *The New Deal and the States: Federalism in Transition* (Princeton, N.J.: Princeton University Press, 1969); and the article entitled "The Republican Party: Up from the Grave" in *Fortune* 20 (August 1939).

Useful analyses of the Willkie phenomenon were Henry O. Evjen's article "The Willkie Campaign: An Unfortunate Chapter in Republican Leadership," *Journal of Politics* 14 (May 1952); Donald Bruce Johnson, *The Republican Party and Wendell Willkie* (Urbana: University of Illinois Press, 1960); "Fortune Survey: GOP Elephant Boy," *Fortune* 19 (February 1939); and Joseph Barnes, *Willkie: The Events He Was Part Of—The Ideas He Fought For* (New York: Simon and Schuster, 1952). Also very useful were Mary Earhart Dillon, *Wendell Willkie, 1892-1944* (Philadelphia: J. B. Lippincott, 1952); Herbert S. Parmet and Marie B. Hecht, *Never Again: A President Runs for a Third Term* (New York: Macmillan, 1968); and the fine sketch of Willkie by Justin H. Libby in Ralph D. Gray (ed.), *Gentlemen from Indiana: National Party Candidates, 1836-1940* (Indianapolis: Indiana Historical Bureau, 1977).

The national elections beginning in 1944 were analyzed in Leon Friedman, "Election of 1944" in Vol. 4, Arthur M. Schlesinger, Jr., and Fred L. Israel (eds.), *History of American Presidential Elections, 1789-1968* (New York: Chelsea House, 1971); Richard S. Kirkendall, "Election of 1948," ibid.; Malcom Moos, "Election of 1956," ibid. See also William A. Glaser, "Hindsight and Significance" in William N. McPhee and William A. Glaser (eds.), *Public Opinion and Congressional Elections* (New York: Free Press of Glencoe, 1962); Richard Austin Smith, "Five Hot Senate Races," *Fortune* 54 (October 1956); Lee W. Huebner, "The Republican Party, 1952-1972" in Vol. 4, Arthur M. Schlesinger, Jr. (ed.), *History of U.S. Political Parties* (New York: Chelsea House, 1973).

Other books concerning Indiana politics were the following: Robert J. McNeill, *Democratic Campaign Financing in In-*

diana, 1964 (Bloomington: Institute of Public Administration, Indiana University, 1966); Herbert C. Hoover, *Addresses upon the American Road, 1933-1938* (New York: C. Scribner's Sons, 1938) and *Further Addresses upon the American Road, 1938-1940* (New York: C. Scribner's Sons, 1940); *Biographical Directory of the United States Congress, 1774-1989* (Washington, D.C.: U.S. Government Printing Office, 1989); Charles Francis Fleming, *The White Hat: Henry Frederick Schricker, A Political Biography* (Indianapolis: n.p., 1966); Hilton U. Brown, *A Book of Memories* (Indianapolis: Butler University Press, 1951); James Eli Watson, *As I Knew Them* (Indianapolis: Bobbs-Merrill Co., 1936); Joe Martin, *My First Fifty Years in Politics* (New York: McGraw-Hill, 1960); Warren Moscow, *Roosevelt and Willkie* (Englewood Cliffs, N.J.: Prentice-Hall, 1968); and Herman O. Makey, *Wendell Willkie of Elwood* (Elwood, Ind.: National Book Co., Inc., 1940).

Additional miscellaneous materials were Homer E. Capehart, scrapbooks at the Capehart Farms (subsequently destroyed by fire) and "Campaign Addresses, 1944" in the Capehart personal papers; transcripts of the Capehart-Jacobs debate of 1949, speeches entitled "Dealing with the Relief Problem" and "Lincoln Ideals Brought Up-to-Date" in the Capehart manuscripts; Robert J. Pitchell, *Indiana Votes* (Bloomington: Bureau of Government Research, Indiana University, 1960); U.S. Congress, Senate, *Report of the Special Committee to Investigate Presidential, Vice Presidential and Senatorial Campaign Expenditures in 1944*, 78th Congress, 2d Sess. (Washington, D.C.: U.S. Government Printing Office, 1945); Kan Ori, "Basic Ideas in Federal-State Relations: The Indiana 'Revolt of 1951'" (Ph.D. dissertation, Indiana University, 1961); *The Indiana Farmers' Guide*, 15 October 1956; Labor Political Education Committee, flyer entitled "Voting Record of Senator Capehart on Labor, 1952-1955," Capehart manuscripts; *General Election Report of the Secretary of State of the State of Indiana, 1962: General Election Statistics*, Indianapolis;

U.S. Congress, House, *Hearings before a Special Committee on Un-American Activities 76th Cong. 1st Sess., May 18, 1939*; U.S. Department of Commerce, Bureau of Census, *Sixteenth Census of the United States: 1940, Population*, Vol. 1.

Senate

The most important sources for Capehart as senator were the oral history interviews with his first two administrative assistants, Ray Donaldson and Charles Egenroad; the attorney who assisted him with all his major committee projects, William Simon; his friend, another Washington, D.C., attorney, John L. Ingoldsby; and *Indianapolis Star* Washington, D.C., correspondent Benjamin R. Cole—all in the Indiana University Oral History Project. The most valuable written sources locating and summarizing Capehart's Senate activities were the Congressional Quarterly Service publications, including the *Congressional Quarterly Almanac* published yearly in Washington, D.C., by Congressional Quarterly, Inc., and *Congress and the Nation, 1945-1962* (Washington, D.C.: Congressional Quarterly Service, 1965), and the dissertation by John R. Taylor mentioned above. Also useful are interviews with former senators Margaret Chase Smith, Gordon Allott, John Bricker (in the author's file), and Paul Douglas (IUOHP); Gen. William C. Lewis (in the author's file); and Capehart's staff members Wilma Miller (IUOHP) and Florence Barr and Lois Elliott (author's file).

Much documentary evidence was of course in the *Congressional Record*, the Dwight D. Eisenhower Library, and the Harry S Truman Library. Information also was located in the Ohio Historical Society (Bricker papers); the George Arents Library, Syracuse University (Flanders and Hendrickson papers); the Library of Congress (Taft papers); and the Collection of Regional History and University Archives, Cornell University (Ives papers).

The best treatments of the Senate during the Capehart years were Donald R. Matthews, *U.S. Senators and Their World* (Chapel Hill: University of North Carolina Press, 1960); William S. White, *The Citadel: The Story of the U.S. Senate* (New York: Harper, 1957); and the excellent biography of Taft by James T. Patterson entitled *Mr. Republican: A Biography of Robert A. Taft* (Boston: Houghton Mifflin, 1972). See also Randall B. Ripley, *Power in the Senate* (New York: St. Martin's Press, 1969).

Three series published in Washington, D.C., by the U.S. Government Printing Office were essential to this part of the research. The *Digest of Public and General Bills* summarized specific legislation; the *Congressional Directory* told the membership of the various committees and subcommittees; and *U.S. Statutes at Large* contained the bills passed into law in each Congress.

Domestic Affairs

Domestic policy was the main concern of a number of excellent general histories, including: Henry Bamford Parkes and Vincent P. Carosso, *Recent America: A History*, book two (New York: Crowell, 1963); Oscar T. Barck, Jr., *A History of the United States since 1945* (New York: Dell Publishing Co., 1965); William E. Leuchtenburg, "Consumer Culture and Cold War: American Society, 1945-1960" in William E. Leuchtenburg (ed.), *The Unfinished Century: America since 1900* (Boston: Little, Brown, 1973); James T. Patterson, *America in the Twentieth Century*, Part Two, *A History since 1939* (New York: Harcourt Brace Jovanovich, 1976); George E. Mowry, *The Urban Nation, 1920-1960* (New York: Hill and Wang, 1965); Willard Hurst, *The Legitimacy of the Business Corporation in the Law of the United States, 1780-1970* (Charlottesville: University Press of Virginia, 1970); Seymour Harris, *The Economics of the Political Parties, with Special Attention to Presidents*

Eisenhower and Kennedy (New York: Macmillan, 1962); and the summaries of legislative activity which appear at the end of each Congress in the *New Republic.*

More specialized accounts dealing with the period in national politics were the following: David W. Reinhard, *The Republican Right since 1945* (Lexington: University Press of Kentucky, 1983); Cabell Phillips, *The Truman Presidency: The History of a Triumphant Succession* (New York: Macmillan, 1966); Susan M. Hartmann, *Truman and the 80th Congress* (Columbia: University of Missouri Press, 1971); Jules Abels, *Out of the Jaws of Victory* (New York: Holt, 1949); David M. Oshinsky, *A Conspiracy So Immense: The World of Joe McCarthy* (New York: Free Press, 1983); Robert Griffith, *The Politics of Fear: Joseph R. McCarthy and the Senate* (Lexington: University Press of Kentucky, 1970); Richard H. Rovere, *Senator Joe McCarthy* (New York: Harcourt, Brace, 1959); Richard Hofstadter, "The Pseudo-Conservative Revolt (1954)," in Richard Hofstadter (ed.), *The Paranoid Style in American Politics and Other Essays* (New York: Vintage, 1965); Allan Nevins, *Herbert H. Lehman and His Era* (New York: Charles Scribner's Sons, 1963); Ronald J. Caridi, *The Korean War and American Politics: The Republican Party as a Case Study* (Philadelphia: University of Pennsylvania Press, 1968); Athan G. Theoharis, *Seeds of Repression: Harry S. Truman and the Origins of McCarthyism* (Chicago: Quadrangle Books, 1971); Richard M. Freeland, *The Truman Doctrine and Origins of McCarthyism: Foreign Policy, Domestic Politics, and Internal Security, 1946-1948* (New York: Knopf, 1972); Fritz Machlup, *The Basing-Point System: An Economic Anlaysis of a Controversial Pricing Practice* (Philadelphia: Blakiston Co., 1949); Earl Latham, *The Group Basis of Politics: A Study of Basing-Point Legislation* (Ithaca, N.Y.: Cornell University Press, 1952); Robert L. Branyan, "Anti-Monopoly Activities during the Truman Administration" (Ph.D. dissertation, University of Oklahoma, 1961); William Simon, *Geographic Pricing Practices: Basing-Point Selling* (Chicago: Callaghan, 1950); Walter Adams (ed.), *The Structure of American Industry*, fourth edition (New York: Macmillan, 1971); Peter Asch, *Economic Theory and the Antitrust Dilemma* (New York: Wiley, 1970); U.S. Congress, Senate, *Newsprint Supply and Distribution: Interim Report of the Special Committee to Study Problems of American Small Business, May 1, 1947* (Washington, D.C.: U.S. Government Printing Office, 1947); U.S. Congress, Senate, *Hearings before the Special Committee to Study the Problems of American Small Business, Newsprint Supply and Distribution, May 5, 1947* (Washington, D.C.: U.S. Government Printing Office, 1947); U.S. Congress, Senate, *Study of Pricing Methods: Hearings before a Subcommittee of the Committee on Interstate and Foreign Commerce, Nov. 9-12, 16-19, 29-30, Dec. 6-8, 1948* (Washington, D.C.: U.S. Government Printing Office, 1948); U.S. Congress, Senate, *Hearings before the Special Committee to Investigate Organized Crime in Interstate Commerce, February 8 and 9, 1951* (Washington, D.C.: U.S. Government Printing Office, 1951). See also Sen. Hugh Butler papers, Nebraska State Historical Society, and the Charles Murphy papers in the Harry S Truman Library.

The best general accounts of the Eisenhower administration were Stephen E. Ambrose, *Eisenhower: The President* (New York: Simon and Schuster, 1984) and *Nixon*, vol. 1, *The Education of a Politician, 1913-1962* (New York: Simon and Schuster, 1987); Herbert S. Parmet, *Eisenhower and the American Crusades* (New York: Macmillan, 1972); Peter Lyon, *Eisenhower: Portrait of the Hero* (Boston: Little, Brown, 1974); and Emmet John Hughes, *The Ordeal of Power: A Political Memoir of the Eisenhower Years* (New York: Atheneum, 1963).

The Eisenhower Library contained material about Capehart and the issues in which he was interested in the following sets of papers: Eisenhower diary, Whitman Name Series, Hagerty papers, Harlow papers, PPF-20-F, Official Files, Administrative Series, Morgan Files, Central Files, White House photographs.

On other topics the following were helpful: Richard Neustadt, "The Presidency at Midcentury," *Law and Contemporary Problems* 21 (August 1956); Gary W. Reichard, *The Reaffirmation of Republicanism: Eisenhower and the Eighty-third Congress* (Knoxville: University of Tennessee Press, 1975); and Margaret L. Coit, *Mr. Baruch* (Boston: Houghton Mifflin, 1957). Robert F. Kennedy, *The Enemy Within* (New York: Harper and Brothers, 1960) and U.S. Congress, Senate, *Hearings before the Select Committee on Improper Activities in the Labor and Management Field, February 10, 1959*, documented the unsuccessful efforts of the Democrats to associate Capehart with organized crime in the jukebox industry. Also useful were the Prescott Bush interview in the Columbia University Oral History Research Office; the Banking and Currency Committee, Correspondence file, in the Congressional Division, National Archives; and John Kenneth Galbraith's memories of Capehart in the preface of his book entitled *The Great Crash, 1929* (Boston: Houghton Mifflin, 1955). Magazine articles about Capehart and Jenner appeared in *Commonwealth*, *Nation's Business*, *U.S. News and World Report*, and *Reporter*. The Kennedy period is covered in Arthur M. Schlesinger, Jr., *A Thousand Days: John F. Kennedy in the White House* (Boston: Houghton Mifflin, 1965) and *Robert F. Kennedy and His Times* (Boston: Houghton Mifflin, 1978); and especially in Herbert S. Parmet, *JFK, the Presidency of John F. Kennedy* (New York: Dial Press, 1983) and Theodore H. White, *The Making of the President, 1964* (New York: Atheneum, 1965).

Foreign Affairs

Excellent accounts of American foreign policy generally and foreign policy and the Senate during the Capehart years were the following: Robert H. Ferrell, *American Diplomacy: Twentieth Century* (New York: Norton, 1988); John Lewis Gaddis, *The Long Peace: Inquiries into the History of the Cold War* (New York: Oxford University Press, 1987); Robert A. Divine, *Since 1945: Politics and Diplomacy in Recent American History* (New York: Wiley, 1975); Malcolm E. Jewell, *Senatorial Politics and Foreign Policy* (Lexington: University of Kentucky Press, 1962); Stephen E. Ambrose, *Rise to Globalism: American Foreign Policy since 1938*, fourth revised edition (New York: Penguin Books, 1985); John Gary Clifford, "Change and Continuity in American Foreign Policy since 1930" in James T. Patterson (ed.), *Paths to the Present: Interpretative Essays on American History since 1930* (Minneapolis: Burgess Publishing Co., 1975).

The best history of Soviet foreign policy during the period was Adam B. Ulam, *Expansion and Coexistence: Soviet Foreign Policy, 1917-73* (New York: Praeger, 1974).

Franklin D. Roosevelt's foreign policy and the end of World War II appeared in the biography of Roosevelt by James MacGregor Burns and in Roland Young, *Congressional Politics in the Second World War* (New York: Columbia University Press, 1956); John Toland, *The Rising Sun: The Decline and Fall of the Japanese Empire, 1936-1945* (New York: Random House, 1970) and *Adolph Hitler* (Garden City, N.Y.: Doubleday & Co., Inc., 1976); Robert E. Sherwood, *Roosevelt and Hopkins: An Intimate Story* (New York: Harper, 1950); Brian L. Villa, "The U.S. Army, Unconditional Surrender, and the Potsdam Proclamation," *Journal of American History* 62 (June 1976); and Burton K. Wheeler, *Yankee from the West: The Candid, Turbulent Life Story of the Yankee-Born U.S. Senator from Montana* (Garden City, N.Y.: Doubleday & Co., Inc., 1962).

The most useful books on Truman's foreign policy and the outbreak of the cold war were the following: John Lewis Gaddis, *The United States and the Origins of the Cold War, 1941-1947* (New York: Columbia University Press, 1972) and "Harry S. Truman and the Origins of Containment," in Frank J. Merli and Theodore A. Wilson (eds.), *Makers of American Diplomacy: From Benjamin Franklin to Henry Kissinger* (New York: Scribner, 1974); Robert A. Pollard, *Economic Se-*

curity and the Origins of the Cold War, 1945-1950 (New York: Columbia University Press, 1985); George F. Kennan, *Memoirs, 1925-1950* (Boston: Little, Brown, 1967); Robert H. Ferrell, *Harry S. Truman and the Modern American Presidency* (Boston: Little, Brown, 1983); Daniel Yergin, *Shattered Peace: The Origins of the Cold War and National Security State* (Boston: Houghton Mifflin, 1977); Joyce and Gabriel Kolko, *The Limits of Power: The World and United States Foreign Policy, 1945-1954* (New York: Harper and Row, 1972); Ernest R. May, *"Lessons" of the Past: The Use and Misuse of History in American Foreign Policy* (New York: Oxford University Press, 1973); Bradford Westerfield, *Foreign Policy and Party Politics: Pearl Harbor to Korea* (New Haven: Yale University Press, 1955); Louis J. Halle, *The Cold War as History* (New York: Harper and Row, 1967); and Norman A. Graebner, *The New Isolationism: A Study in Politics and Foreign Policy since 1950* (New York: Ronald Press, 1956). Probable Soviet intentions appear in Adam B. Ulam, *Stalin: The Man and His Era* (New York: Viking, 1973).

The following also were useful: Arthur M. Schlesinger, Jr., "The New Isolationism," *Atlantic* 189 (May 1952); Arthur H. Vandenberg, Jr. (ed.), *The Private Papers of Senator Vandenberg* (Boston: Houghton Mifflin, 1952); Walter Millis (ed.), *The Forrestal Diaries* (New York: Viking Press, 1945); and Richard A. Loss, "Secretary of State Dean Acheson: The Political Dimension" (Ph.D. dissertation, Cornell University, 1971).

The best analyses of Eisenhower's foreign policy were in Herbert S. Parmet, "Power and Reality: John Foster Dulles and Political Diplomacy," in Frank J. Merli and Theodore A. Wilson (eds.), *Makers of American Diplomacy; From Benjamin Franklin to Henry Kissinger* (New York: Scribner, 1974), Vol. 2; John Lewis Gaddis, *Strategies of Containment: A Critical Appraisal of Postwar American National Security Policy* (New York: Oxford University Press, 1982) and *The Long Peace: Inquiries into the History of the Cold War* (New York: Oxford University Press, 1987); and Michael R. Beschloss, *MAYDAY: Eisen-*

hower, Khrushchev, and the U-2 Affair (New York: Harper and Row, 1986). Valuable references were H. W. Brands, Jr., *Cold Warriors: Eisenhower's Generation and American Foreign Policy* (New York: Columbia University Press, 1988); Townsend Hoopes, *The Devil and John Foster Dulles* (Boston: Little, Brown, 1973); Robert A. Divine, *Eisenhower and the Cold War* (New York: Oxford University Press, 1981); Milton S. Eisenhower, *The Wine Is Bitter: The United States and Latin America* (Garden City, N.Y.: Doubleday & Co., Inc., 1963); William S. White, "The Senate's Eyes on World Affairs," *New York Times Magazine*, 3 March 1957, and George H. Gallup, *The Gallup Poll: Public Opinion, 1935-1971*, Vol. 3 (New York: Random House, 1972).

Capehart's activities in Latin America appeared in U.S. Congress, Senate, *Report of the Citizens Advisory Committee to Study the Financial Aspects of International Trade, Dec. 1954* (Washington, D.C.: U.S. Government Printing Office, 1954); and U.S. Congress, Senate, *Study of Latin American Countries, Interim Report of the Senate Committee on Banking and Currency, A Study of the Operations in Latin American Countries of the Export-Import Bank and the International Bank and Their Relationship to the Expansion of International Trade, March 16, 1954* (Washington, D.C.: U.S. Government Printing Office, 1954).

The best analyses of the Cuban missile crisis were Arthur M. Schlesinger, Jr., *Robert Kennedy and His Times* (Boston: Houghton Mifflin, 1978); Graham T. Allison, *The Essence of Decision: Explaining the Cuban Missile Crisis* (Boston: Little, Brown, 1971); and Thomas G. Patterson and William J. Brophy, "October Missiles and November Elections: The Cuban Missile Crisis and American Politics, 1962," *Journal of American History* 73 (June 1986). Also valuable were Theodore Sorensen, *Kennedy* (New York: Harper and Row, 1965); David L. Larson (ed.), *The "Cuban Crisis" of 1962* (Boston: Houghton Mifflin, 1963); Herbert S. Dinerstein, *The Making of a Missile Crisis* (Baltimore: Johns Hopkins Press, 1976); and the books critical of Kennedy by Robert A. Divine (ed.), *The Cuban Missile Crisis* (Chicago: Quadrangle Books, 1971); Richard J. Walton, *Cold War and Counterrevolution: The Foreign Policy of John F. Kennedy* (Baltimore: Penguin Books, 1972); and Louise FitzSimons, *The Kennedy Doctrine* (New York: Random House, 1972). One memo from Larry O'Brien to Ken O'Donnell, 26 May 1961, in the Kennedy Library revealed Capehart's adamant opposition to JFK's proposal to trade tractors for captured Bay-of-Pigs invaders. The effect of Capehart's use of Cuba as his main campaign issue appeared in Charles A. Halleck, Recorded Interview, 22 March 1965, John F. Kennedy Library Oral History Project. Finally, two students at Rose-Hulman wrote seminar papers which elaborated Capehart's role in the events surrounding the missile crisis: Dwight Dively, "Capehart, Keating, and Kennedy: Three Policies on Cuba" (seminar paper, Rose-Hulman Institute of Technology, 1979) and Kevin Barrer, "Capehart and the American Attitude Toward Cuba" (seminar paper, Rose-Hulman Institute of Technology, 1979).

Index

Designer: Tony Woodward

Typeface: Bembo

Typographer: Weimer Typesetting Co., Inc., Indianapolis, Indiana

Paper: 70-pound Cougar Opaque Natural, Smooth

Printer: Evangel Press, Nappanee, Indiana